*...with*

# COMPASSIONATE
# UNDERSTANDING

Other books by Rosemary and Steve Weissman include:

*Der Weg der Achtsamkeit,* Hugendubel-Irisiana, Germany, 1994
*Meditation, Compassion & Lovingkindness,* Samuel Weiser, Inc., USA, 1996
*Méditation Vipassana,* Médicis-Entrelacs, France, 1996

# *...with* COMPASSIONATE UNDERSTANDING

A Meditation Retreat

by

Rosemary and Steve Weissman

PARAGON HOUSE
St. Paul, Minnesota

Published in the United States of America by

Paragon House
2700 University Avenue West
St. Paul, Minnesota 55114

The drawing on the cover shows a view of Wat Kow Tahm International Meditation Center, Koh Pah-ngan (Island), Surat Tani, Thailand.

Library of Congress Catalog-in-Publication Data

Weissman, Rosemary.
    — with compassionate understanding : a meditation retreat  / by Rosemary and Steve Weissman.
      p.   cm.
    Updated edition of: With compassionate understanding / by Steve and Rosemary Weissman, 1990.
    ISBN 1-55778-769-7
    1. Spiritual life—Buddhism. 2. Retreats—Buddhism.
I. Weissman, Rosemary, 1952-   . II. Weissman, Steve, 1949-   With compassionate understanding.   1990.
BQ5612.W45   1999
294.3'4435—dc21                   98-41221
                                                CIP

*To our parents, our teachers,*
*and all who have preserved the Buddha's teachings,*
*so we could benefit and be able to help others.*

# CONTENTS

# FOREWORD

This book contains most of the talks given in 1997 during the 10-day meditation retreats led by Steve and Rosemary Weissman at Wat Kow Tahm International Meditation Center, Koh Pah-ngan, Thailand.

In 1987, the head nun at Wat Kow Tahm requested that we begin teaching the many Western travelers who come to Koh Pah-ngan and find their way to this monastery seeking meditation instruction. As the numbers of visitors increased, and as we saw the potential for offering more formal teaching, we initiated in May, 1988, the current format of intensive 10-day retreats.

These retreats have been designed as a basic introduction to many of the methods found within Theravadin Buddhist teachings for training the mind in order to find deep, inner Peace and Wisdom.

The emphasis of the retreats is the development of beneficial qualities such as Compassion, Lovingkindness, Equanimity, Joy, Patience, Perseverance, Endurance, Energy, Understanding and Wisdom, and the lessening of unbeneficial qualities such as greed, hatred, anger, jealousy, fear, worry, grief and ignorance.

An important part of this type of mental training is to develop keen Awareness of our actions, speech and thoughts. This Awareness, also referred to as Mindfulness, is essential in order to develop clarity and strength in the mind. With this clarity and strength we are then able to see which actions, speech and thoughts lead to stress and difficulties, and which lead to Peace and Harmony in ourselves and in others.

Developing this Understanding enables us to learn how to let go of the stress and difficulties that come from our attachment to greed, aversion and ignorance.

We have found in our own practice that the development of Mindfulness and the letting go of difficulties have been aided greatly by the development of a Compassionate Intention behind, and a Compassionate Attitude toward our actions, speech and thoughts. A Compassionate Attitude encourages us not to cause harm or difficulty for ourselves or others. The more we develop Compassion within, the more we see that Mindfulness is an extremely valuable way to develop our Understanding of Life in all aspects. Then, with this Understanding, we can work toward increasing beneficial qualities and lessening unbeneficial qualities. This will create the causes and conditions that will produce more Peace, Contentment and deeper Happiness.

In the beginning there were overwhelming requests from people who completed our retreats to have copies of the talks in written form. This led us to typing the talks and instructions so that photocopies could be made. These proved to be extremely popular and of great benefit to retreatants. They had something they could take with them to refer to and refresh their memory at a later date.

For this reason, in 1990, we first published "...with Compassionate Understanding: A Meditation Retreat," up-to-date at that time of all retreat talks. This became more convenient for retreatants and also helped others who were interested in Meditation. Although not presented in a standard form for a beginner's Introduction to Meditation, it has been seen that many new meditators have been able to use these talks to help begin their practice. The talks have stayed fairly similar but as there have been some significant additions we now present this updated edition.

It was decided to leave the talks in retreat style, and to have extra information included which pertained only to the retreat setup. This was done in order to help convey the retreat atmosphere to the reader. This has benefitted many new and experienced meditators.

It may also be helpful for the reader to know that the general instructions and teachings presented in this book were not the full teachings that each retreatant received. There were also private interviews with the teachers where more personal instruction was given.

As well, supplementing the formal meditation training were special stretching exercises which greatly aided many people to develop more awareness and flexibility of the body. This helped them in the physical aspects of the various postures, especially in sitting meditation.

Please note: As the English language does not have a gender-neutral term for the third-person singular, we have chosen at times to use the word "they," rather than "he" or "she."

We would like to express our deepest appreciation for the hospitality, encouragement and support that we have received at Wat Kow Tahm by the Head Nun, Mae Chee Ah Mohn Pahn, and the other nuns and monks of the monastery during our years of teaching here.

A special thank-you to Ruth Weissman and Peter Sudworth for their time and efforts in helping to edit the text of the first edition of this book, and to Abby Karp, Kay Zumwinkel, Patrick Wolf, Margot Sangster, Josie Miller, Christine Lem, Marianne Vandale, and Sandy McNaughton for helping to edit and type this expanded second edition of the book. Our apologies if we missed anyone.

We hope this book will aid many to find more Peace and Contentment and to lessen difficulties and problems, with Patience, Lovingkindness, Equanimity, Joy, Acceptance, Wisdom and
...with Compassionate Understanding.

Steve and Rosemary Weissman
Wat Kow Tahm
Koh Pah-ngan
Thailand
January 22, 1998

# DAILY SCHEDULE

| | |
|---|---|
| 4:00 am | Wake up |
| 4:45 | Sitting |
| 5:30 | Exercises with Mindfulness |
| 6:35 | Sitting |
| 7:05 | Breakfast |
| 8:15 | Working Meditation |
| 9:00 | Walking |
| 9:30 | A talk given by the teachers and Sitting |
| 10:15 | Sitting or Standing |
| 10:25 | A talk |
| 10:30 | Walking |
| 11:00 | Lunch |
| 1:00 pm | Walking |
| 1:45 | Standing or Sitting |
| 2:45 | Walking |
| 3:30 | Sitting |
| 4:15 | Sitting or Standing |
| 4:30 | Walking |
| 5:15 | Light Dinner |
| 6:15 | Sitting |
| 6:45 | Standing or Walking |
| 7:15 | A talk |
| afterward | Optional Meditation or Sleep |

# INTRODUCTION AND SITTING INSTRUCTION

Welcome to Wat Kow Tahm and welcome to a 10-day Meditation Retreat. Our names are Steve and Rosemary. We will be teaching the retreat. The purpose of this 10-day Meditation Retreat is to try to develop some basic meditation practices that can help each one of us throughout our life.

The words Mental Development will be used often during this retreat. As used here, Mental Development means to develop beneficial mental qualities and to lessen unbeneficial mental qualities. The meditation methods that we will be teaching are all concerned with Mental Development. We could say that we are teaching Meditation and we could also say that we are teaching Mental Development. As we will be using these words, they are basically the same.

Let us consider why anyone wants to learn about Meditation or Mental Development.

For all of us, there occur experiences in life which are not totally satisfying. Whether it be something physically minor, like headaches or small cuts, to something major like cancer or death. Whether it be something mentally minor, like annoyance that the bus is late, to something major, like the grief that comes from the death of loved ones. Whether physical or mental, we are continually confronted from time to time with circumstances in life that are not totally satisfying.

One way to deal with the unsatisfactoriness of life is to ignore it. But this is only a temporary method. Another way is to escape from it. Whether it be alcohol, drugs, work or whatever, once again this is only a temporary method. These methods may give us some relief from our difficulties for a short time, but they are not sufficient to deal totally with life.

The roots of our problems are not eliminated. But, if we can learn how to deal with the constant changes in life's situations and our reactions to them, then we can experience a peace of mind that is not dependent on external supports. Mental Development is concerned with learning how to deal with life in all situations.

During this Meditation Retreat, we will be teaching methods that can be used by all types of people in all types of living conditions. A person of any religion, any country, any race. Whether man or woman, old or young, healthy or sick, rich or poor. The methods that you will learn here can basically work for anyone, anywhere.

All of us experience some difficulties, problems and obstacles in life. We were born and we will die. If we live long enough, from time to time we will get sick, our bodies will get old, and normally weak and feeble.

Often we are separated from what we like. Often we have to be with what we do not like. And often we simply do not get what we want. These things are facts of life. They are frequently unpleasant and difficult to deal with.

When a person breaks an arm, this is obviously unpleasant and can be very painful. The arm then needs to be treated by a doctor, put in a cast and allowed to heal. This is one type of difficulty, a physical problem which can be fixed by certain standard practices. For many people with a broken arm there is another problem which comes from their reaction in the mind towards the broken arm. Sometimes the reaction is: "Oh! My arm! My arm! What will I do now? How can I do anything! Oh! Oh!" and on and on. Sometimes with a lot of agitation and worry, and sometimes with only a little agitation and worry.

This extra problem comes from thoughts *about* an actual physical difficulty. These mental problems are extra, we do not need to have them. This is a place where Mental Development can help. It can reduce or eliminate the extra problems that we cause for ourselves and that we cause for others; the extra problems that we often cause in our *reactions* to life's experiences.

There may be many reasons why all of you are here. Among them will be the wish to learn methods and techniques of Mental Development in order to deal successfully with the various difficulties and problems that you have in life. This wish to reduce difficulties or to remove the cause of the difficulty is what we will be referring to when we use the word Compassion.

Compassion is a basis of Mental Development and Meditation practice. Without seeing difficulties and having Compassion towards the difficulties, then there may exist no desire to solve the difficulties and possibly no desire to practice Mental Development and Meditation.

Another reason why you are here could be that you wish to find more Happiness, more Contentment, more Peace in your life. The wishing for Peace and Happiness is what we will be referring to when we use the word Lovingkindness. This word is used within this practice to mean a type of kindness that is deeper than normal kindness, and a type of love which is different from how we normally use the word "Love."

Compassion and Lovingkindness are closely connected. Together they are a combined wish for the welfare of whomever they are wished for. Compassion is the wish to solve or remove the cause of difficulties and unhappiness. Lovingkindness is the wish for Peace and Happiness. As this retreat is designed to help us solve our difficulties and problems, much will be said about developing Compassion and Lovingkindness.

Compassion and Lovingkindness are thoughts in the mind. So how do we put these thoughts into action? In order to solve any problem, it is important to understand the problem. To see when it exists; to see where it comes from; to see how it can pass away; and, most important, to see how the problem will not arise again in the future.

Here it is important to use what we call Mindfulness or Awareness. To become aware of our thoughts, speech and actions. Mindful of what we think, say and do. As we become more mindful and aware, we will make fewer mistakes, we will cause fewer difficulties for ourselves and fewer difficulties for others.

With Mindfulness we can get closer to life's experiences and build Understanding. With this building of Understanding, we can apply the Compassion and Lovingkindness that we feel and can work toward solving problems and removing their causes, thus providing a foundation for the growth of Peace and Happiness.

Here is an example of how Mindfulness can work to help solve difficulties:

Most of us find that similar problems recur over and over. Let us say that we have a type of aversion. Perhaps we do not like a type of situation or person and we react with anger or irritation. This occurs again and again and in reacting, we often cause problems for ourselves as well as problems for others.

Then one day after a similar situation has happened and we have reacted in the usual way, causing more difficulties, we decide that we would rather not have reacted in such a way. This is a first step in Mindfulness and the developing of Understanding. To see a problem *after* it occurs and wish that it had not happened. This wish can be a combination of Compassion and Lovingkindness: wishing to solve the problem and wishing for a more peaceful and contented future. With these wishes and the understanding that there exists a problem, we try to increase our Mindfulness to further understand the problem.

We may see the problem after it occurs many times until there comes a time when our Mindfulness is stronger and we actually realize that the problem has come again while we are reacting. That is, rather than after the situation, the Mindfulness has arisen *during* the situation. With our past Understanding about similar problems, we may be in a position to change the ending of the situation to be better than previously.

As our Mindfulness gets stronger, at some stage we will become aware that we are in a similar situation as it is *beginning* to happen. Then we will be in a much better position to change the situation and avoid many of the difficulties that might otherwise have followed.

When our Mindfulness is strong enough, we will actually be able to understand the causes and conditions that *bring about* the problems. With this Understanding, we will be able to see when a similar situation may occur in the future and be able to avoid it entirely.

So these five aspects of the Meditation practice can work together in the following way: First, we realize that a difficulty exists. Then Compassion arises toward the difficulty and those involved. Lovingkindness can also arise. With these thoughts, we then practice Mindfulness of our actions, speech and thoughts. By using Mindfulness, we develop Understanding. With this Understanding, we can then solve our problems.

In this same way of working with our problems or unbeneficial qualities, we can also work with our beneficial and positive qualities. We can try to use Mindfulness to develop the Understanding of how we can maintain and strengthen them, so that every aspect of our life can benefit in this way. With our unbeneficial qualities, we learn how to decrease them. And with our beneficial qualities, we learn how to increase them.

From this you can see how valuable it is to be mindful and aware of our thoughts, speech and actions. During this retreat, we will be explaining many techniques to help develop Mindfulness and Awareness, so that we can understand more about ourselves. The Meditation practice of developing Mindfulness and Awareness and trying to understand who and what we are—that is, the true reality of who and what we are and not just who and what we think we are—is often referred to as Vipassana or Insight Meditation. It is helpful to make a point here that when I use the term "Vipassana Meditation," this does not mean a specific technique. Rather it means the resulting wisdom or insight which comes from using skillful techniques. There are many different techniques taught to help develop this wisdom. This is helpful to know because Buddhism is very new in relative time periods in the West, and there does exist some confusion regarding this word "Vipassana." Trying to understand and develop Insight into reality.

As I mentioned with the broken arm, many of the extra problems that we cause for ourselves or for others come from our reactions. If we can learn how to deal with our reactions to life's situations, we will be well on our way toward solving any difficulty, and creating more Peace, Contentment and Happiness.

From every experience that we have, there follows one of three types of feeling. A pleasant feeling may occur. An unpleasant feeling may occur. Or a neutral feeling, which is neither pleasant nor unpleasant, may occur. From these feelings comes a reaction.

If our reaction is wise and considerate, with Compassionate Understanding, then extra problems usually will not develop. But if we lack wisdom, proper consideration and Compassionate Understanding, then our reactions often can cause more difficulties.

Developing Mindfulness and Understanding of our reactions is a major part of mental development. It is important to realize that our reactions are due to our past conditioning. We are who we are because of the past. We are conditioned people. We have conditioned minds. We have conditioned reactions, conditioned likes and conditioned dislikes. What we are is due to the many different ways in which we have grown up and developed.

A person from one country grows up in a certain way, different in some way from those in other countries. Within each country, people grow up in different ways: different religions, different school systems, different climates, different foods. Many, many different causes and conditions have occurred to produce who and what we are.

We think certain ways due to our past conditioning. We react certain ways due to our past conditioning. Some of our reactions are wise, some are not wise. Some are proper, some are not proper. Some arise with Compassion and Love, some with anger and hatred. Some lead to Peace and Happiness, others to problems and difficulties.

All of us would like to have more Peace and Happiness. All of us would like to have fewer problems and difficulties. Developing Mindfulness of our thoughts, our speech, our actions and our reactions is a major step in the process of mental development. This is not easy. It takes time. As we have been conditioned to be who we are over many, many years, we cannot change things overnight. We have to respect that our habits and thought patterns have become strong over so many years, and that it takes time to change. Patience is needed. Compassion is needed. Perseverance is needed. Equanimity is needed. Different beneficial mental qualities need to be developed and strengthened.

Keep in mind that practicing and developing Meditation is much like learning something new in everyday life. Let us take the example of someone who wants to learn to swim:

On the first day of swimming lessons, can this person expect to be able to swim across the swimming pool? Not usually. It takes time. There are certain techniques and methods that must be learned, practiced and developed. And there are certain stages of development, a certain basic order of progression. A beginning swimmer is not taught how to do racing starts or racing turns. These things are important for later if the swimmer wants to swim in races, but they cannot be taught first. As well, fine details about arm movement and kicking cannot be taught until the swimmer has learned the basic swimming techniques.

If a new swimmer, who cannot yet swim across a pool is taught racing starts, turns, or fine details, then there will be no ability to understand or utilize the instructions of these advanced techniques. This would normally cause confusion and problems, and probably slow down the swimmer's development.

Some swimmers will learn quickly, some will learn slowly. If all new swimmers who are physically able persevere with patience and endurance, continually trying, learning and practicing, then these new swimmers will be able to learn to swim.

The same things are true for learning Meditation. It takes time. There are certain techniques and methods that must be learned, practiced and developed. There are certain stages of development. A new meditator needs to work with learning the basic techniques. Getting too involved with what might happen later in meditation training, before learning basic practices, may cause confusion and problems. And, possibly, it may slow down meditation development.

Some will learn quickly. Some will learn slowly. If there is Perseverance, Patience and Endurance, continual trying, learning and practicing, then Meditation can be developed.

For some of you, this is something new. During this retreat, we will be giving many basic meditation instructions. Try your best to do as instructed. Much of the instruction is simple to explain but each of us must work to achieve beneficial results. The rewards of this work are very worthwhile, extremely valuable.

This is a rare and precious opportunity that you have given to yourself. The willingness to try some of these methods and techniques that can help you throughout your life is such a *wonderful, precious opportunity.* Take advantage of this gift that you have given to yourself. Work as well as you can with the techniques that we are explaining. Try to understand them and then they will be of benefit to you.

It is very important to keep an *open* mind. Some of what we say might be very clear and most of you will understand what is meant. There also may be parts that are not very clear and some of you might not understand. That is OK. Try not to worry about it. There will be a lot of information given during these 10 days and it may not be possible to understand everything. Take whatever you do understand and try your best to work with that. Leave whatever you do not understand for now. It might be of help at a later date.

There are many different aspects of Mental Development and it is basically impossible to work on all of them at the same time. Due to our different personalities and conditioning, each of us will tend to work on different aspects of the practice at different times.

Staying open is especially important in your relationship with me, with Rosemary, and with what we will be trying to teach. There is a saying that goes like this:

> You can please some of the people all of the time.
> And you can please all of the people some of the time.
> But you cannot please all of the people all of the time.

Rosemary and I do not expect to be able to please all of you with every part of this retreat. And we would like to advise you not to expect to be pleased with every part of this retreat. Basically this is just not possible. But if you find any parts of this retreat to be upsetting, unpleasant, things that you do not like, try to be open, try to be honest with yourself. Occasionally there can be the impulse to run away from things that we do not like. But often things that we do not like are just things that we do not understand. If you have any problem in understanding anything during the retreat, then there will be opportunities for you to discuss these things with Rosemary or myself. Try to be open, try to be honest with yourself, and with this retreat.

Being open can mean the willingness to change and adapt. This includes the willingness to admit that we might be wrong in our views and opinions. I am sure all of us have had the experience of thinking that we knew something and then later finding out that we were wrong. This is very normal. As we are not perfect yet, we often will make these types of mistakes.

With this in mind, it is beneficial to consider that what we see in life appears to be changing constantly in some way. Wherever we look there is change. As human beings, each of us is constantly changing in some way. Our bodies change, our thoughts change, our views and opinions change.

Many of the difficulties that we experience in life come from holding onto our views and opinions about life, and not accepting the changes of life. We often become fixed in our ideas about things and this can block our Understanding and Peace. If we can try to let go of our views and opinions about things and try to be open to each experience, we will be able to build a better understanding of life. Trying to *learn about* life instead of thinking that we *already know* everything. This is another important part of our personal growth and of creating the conditions for Peace and Happiness to develop.

The expression "Letting go" is another term that will be used often during this retreat. In this usage, the development of Peace and Happiness and the lessening of problems and difficulties is not so much of a going and getting something. Instead it is a letting go of the various obstacles that are blocking this process from naturally happening.

We all have the seeds within us for the growth of Peace and Happiness and the lessening of problems and difficulties. If we apply proper methods, these seeds will grow. Letting go of parts of our past conditioning which block this growth can be difficult. But with Compassion, Lovingkindness and Mindfulness, we can develop the Understanding necessary to gradually change our conditioning little-by-little, bit-by-bit. Mental Development is a gradual process.

Our habits and tendencies have energies that are very strong at times, and to try to stop these energies often can create more difficulties. Instead of trying to get rid of any unbeneficial habit or tendency all at once, we can use the energy present and gently bend the direction of this energy. With Compassionate Understanding of why we are doing, saying or thinking things in certain ways, we can bend unwise energies into wise energies.

With the different techniques and methods that will be explained here, each of us can work toward creating new and beneficial causes and conditions for our future. We are who we are due to what we did in the past. We can change who we will be by what we do in the present. The more we work toward increasing beneficial mental qualities and decreasing unbeneficial mental qualities, the more we will gain Peace and Happiness and lessen problems and difficulties.

Much of Mental Development is to learn who and what we are. In understanding who and what we are, we will learn how to accept ourselves and accept others, how to forgive ourselves and forgive others, how to have Compassion and Lovingkindness toward ourselves and toward others. We will learn about our interrelationships with others and with the environment. We will learn how we have been conditioned. We will learn about our qualities that are beneficial and about our qualities that are unbeneficial. As we understand these things, we will be better able to apply remedies and solutions to any problem that we encounter.

This is basic: If we want to change our thoughts, habits or patterns of living in beneficial ways, we first must start to understand ourselves.

As I said, this is just like other things in life. Doctors who perform heart surgery must study the heart and all the areas of the body which are related to such an operation. Before performing such an operation, much practice and study must be done. They will probably learn basic medicine treatments first and after much time they will develop the ability to perform such an operation.

Meditation is similar. We have to study and work on our minds. Understand them, learn about them. See which parts of our minds are beneficial and which parts are unbeneficial. We are trying to discover who and what we are, and then trying to work *with* who we are, not *against* who we are.

It is important to try to work with basic practices and with smaller problems before working with larger ones. We frequently cause extra difficulties for ourselves because we want to accomplish something that is beyond our limits. There is often a big difference between what we *can* do and what we think we *should* be able to do. This is a difference between Reality and Idealism.

The reality of a situation is what we can work with, objectively seeing who and what we are and starting from there. Too many people want to start with who and what they think they are or think they should be, having some ideal about themselves or about their capabilities. Frequently this causes aversion, pain, grief, despair and frustration. When we think we should be a certain way, but in reality we are not, then a lot of self-hatred and doubt can arise.

Often we have been told, "You should do this, you should not do that." But we have not always been told how to do this, how not to do that. This difference between what one thinks one *should* be able to do and what one actually *is* able to do is a common problem for many meditators.

We prefer, as much as possible, not to use the word "should." Instead we will try to say, "Try to do this, try not to do that." And, we also will try to show how to do this, how not to do that.

Problems and difficulties can be lessened if we start with who and what we are, learn some techniques and methods of *how* to do things, and try to apply these techniques and methods to ourselves.

So we will be spending quite a bit of time and quite a bit of effort trying to explain to you some valuable techniques and methods of how to work with Mental Development. And, hopefully, you will be spending quite a bit of time and quite a bit of effort trying to learn these valuable techniques and methods for yourself.

What I have talked about is just a basic outline of much of the practice. We will be talking about most of this again and again in more detail throughout this 10-day Meditation Retreat.

We hope that you will find this practice of Meditation and Mental Development very rewarding and helpful while you are here, and very rewarding and helpful for the rest of your life.

### Now, formal sitting meditation. How and what to do.

When we sit in meditation, we will be dealing with what is called a primary concentration object. The primary concentration object that we will start with tonight is the breath; to be aware of our breathing.

This is a universal object. Everyone breathes. It is something that is with us every moment of our life until we die. The breath simply is. Breathing in. Breathing out. The breath is normally a neutral object in regard to our feelings and emotions; that is, it normally does not excite us or upset us. This makes it a very good primary object of meditation.

Even better than these, the breath can help us to learn about ourselves, our mind, our body. The breath is often a link between thoughts and bodily reactions. When we observe our breathing, we will find that changes in breathing, whether fast or slow, coarse or fine, rough or smooth, will often indicate various mental states. Other parts of our body are indicators also. A clear example of this is when a person gets very angry. This emotional state of mind causes the person to breathe very fast and rough, and causes tightness and tension throughout the body.

Often it is difficult to see our emotional states clearly and for this reason, if we can build awareness of our breathing and bodily reactions, then we can use this awareness to see more clearly our emotions and thoughts.

The basic practice to start with is this; sit and be aware of your breathing, each breath, coming in and going out. Let it be natural, no forcing. If it seems long, just realize that it seems long. If short, short. If it seems rough, just realize that it seems rough. If smooth, smooth. Whatever it is, fine, no problem. Our work is just to observe it and start to understand it as it is. We will try to use every breath. Here we do not consider one breath to be better than another. Every breath can be part of our meditation practice.

This is a very basic practice but it is not easy. Our minds are not used to concentrating on just one single object. Our minds are used to thinking about this, that and everything. We may watch our breathing for two seconds and then "off," the mind starts its thought process, sometimes thinking of the past, sometimes the future, and sometimes the present. We may get lost in a daydream for 5-10 minutes. This will happen many times while we are sitting in meditation. As soon as you become aware that your mind has wandered away from the breathing, then the practice is just to gently realize that the mind has wandered and then return to watching the breathing.

This noticing of our wandering thoughts is actually a very important part of our meditation practice. This is where we start to learn who and what we are. Our thought patterns are due to our past conditioning. The wandering is a normal part of this conditioning. Much of the practice is to understand who and what we are and then use this Understanding.

Our thoughts about the past, the future, whatever; our angry thoughts, our loving thoughts, our lonely thoughts, our frightened thoughts; any thought is part of our meditation. But the object is not to just think about anything. The object in the beginning is to try to be aware of our breathing. And, each time that we catch our mind wandering, just to note that it is wandering and then return to the breath.

There need not be any judgment of, aversion to, or indulgence in the thoughts. No need to figure out anything about the thoughts or why we had them. It is all due to past conditioning. We try to see them each time and just realize that they are there. Then gently let go of the thought and return to the breath. There is no need to get upset when you discover that your mind cannot stay on the breathing for very long before off it goes on another thought pattern. This is normal.

Bit-by-bit, little-by-little with perseverance, patience and endurance, your concentration and mindfulness will grow. Each time that you notice your wandering mind is actually a moment of mindfulness and a moment of growth, and your practice will develop.

It will be normal sometimes to get upset at the wandering mind. And thoughts such as "Oh, I cannot be aware of the breathing even for one full second." But actually to be aware that you are not able to concentrate *is* a moment of mindfulness. It is a growth in Understanding to know when you can not concentrate. And it is a valuable part of the practice.

This is a process of continually coming back again and again to the awareness of breathing. Seeing that our mind is off thinking, realizing it and starting again with the breathing. Breathing in and breathing out.

To observe the breathing, there are two main areas of the body to choose from, to focus your attention upon. The first is at the nose area where the air comes in and goes out. Breathing through the mouth is not normally used. There is an actual physical sensation present at the nostrils, or tip of the nose, or upper lip where the air touches. The second is the stomach-chest area. The expanding and contracting or rising-falling movement that takes place during the breathing.

You are advised to choose one of these two areas and keep your attention focused there. Try not to jump back and forth between these two. This will only cause confusion and difficulty.

The actual physical sensation of the breath touching the nose area or the stomach-chest area rising-falling, is to be the primary object of concentration. This is not easy, concentrating on one single object. But we have a method that can help you to develop this concentration. When you are breathing in and out, what we recommend is that you make soft mental notes of the actual process.

If you are observing the breathing at the nose area, you can use the words "Breathing in, breathing out" as the air comes in and goes out. Or if you prefer just "In, out." If you are focusing on the stomach-chest area, you can use the words "Rising, falling." "In, out" describes part of the actual physical process occurring at the nose area. "Rising, falling" describes part of the actual physical process occurring at the stomach-chest area. This method can help you to develop stronger concentration and awareness.

OK, we sit in meditation observing the breathing and softly noting "in, out," "breathing in, breathing out," or "rising, falling." Then off goes our mind wandering. When we realize that our mind is wandering, we can use this same type of method. As soon as we catch ourselves wandering, we can softly note to ourselves "wandering, wandering" or "thinking, thinking." Then we gently try to let go of the thoughts and start again on the breathing. If noises distract our attention, we can gently note "hearing, hearing" and then try to return to the breathing. Before mealtime it is possible that the odors from the food will distract our attention. If they do, we can try to note "smelling, smelling." Any time that we find that our attention is not on the breathing, we can try to note what is happening and then return to the breathing.

There are a few different ways to sit in meditation. I will show you some of them. Some people use pillows and some do not. There is regular crossed; the semi-half lotus; the half lotus; the full lotus, if your body is flexible enough, not many people can do this. Then there is just legs parallel in front; or one leg can be back on the side. Even sitting like this, with your knees up and arms resting on your legs, is OK for a short rest and then try to go back to a more proper posture. There is also the Japanese style, sometimes with a little bench, and sometimes with pillows under our buttocks. Some people with physical problems can meditate sitting in a chair as well.

A very important part of the sitting posture is to be comfortable and relaxed. Also to keep the back straight. Straight but not tense. As this is like a new physical sport, it will take time to train the body.

Many meditators have to relax the back often. Try your best. During the meditation period, try to stay still for the entire time but if you have too much difficulty, then it is quite OK to change your legs around. When you do have to move, try to do this quietly so that you do not disturb the other meditators. And, as you move, try to be mindful of the action of moving the body.

The hands can be in the lap, on the knees, up, down, whatever. Again, comfortable and relaxed. Normally we close the eyes but not tight. Softly, gently. If you feel, at any time, a bit sleepy, then we advise you to open your eyes and look down about four or five feet in front of you.

The mouth is an important area to be aware of. Closed lips but not tight. Perhaps the teeth not quite touching, and the tongue touch-

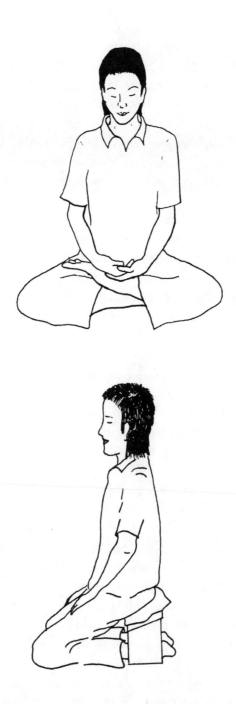

ing the back of the top teeth. The head is slightly tilted forward.

We will now do a group sitting meditation. Please settle yourself in a sitting posture. Relaxed, not stiff. It is good to first check over your body and try to relax. Check your legs to see that they are settled comfortably. Then you may like to lean forward enough to raise your buttocks off your sitting mat or pillows. Using the muscles of your lower back, gently push your buttocks backward and then sit down again. This action can help with any problems of the lower back.

Next check over the rest of your back and stomach-chest area. Check the hands now, and the rest of your arms up to your shoulders. Trying to relax your body as best you can. Now the neck and your head. The face muscles relaxed, eyes softly closed. The mouth relaxed, not tense, softly, gently closed. Try to relax and sit comfortably. Back straight but not rigid or tense.

It may also help to relax by taking a couple of big breaths to start with and then focus your attention on the breathing, either at the nose or stomach-chest area. Noting "in, out," "breathing in, breathing out," or "rising, falling." Allow the breathing to be as it will. If it is short, then it is short. If it is long, then it is long. If rough, rough; smooth, smooth; or whatever. Just allowing it to be whatever it is. Starting to get to know the breath and all of its aspects. Breath coming in, breath going out.

When you find that your mind has wandered, gently realize that it was wandering and then return to the breathing, noting "wandering, wandering" or "thinking, thinking." Occasionally during this sit I will say a few words to help you develop this method.

(6 minutes)   If you find your mind wandering, gently realize that it is wandering and return to the breath. At the nose or stomach-chest area.

(12 minutes)   The thoughts go to the past and they go to the future. After you realize that your thoughts are here and there, gently return to the breath. The air coming in and out or the stomach-chest area rising and falling.

(18 minutes)    If sound distracts your attention, try to just note "hearing, hearing" and gently return to the breathing.

(24 minutes)    The mind is used to wandering. As you catch it, realize that it was wandering, note, "wandering, wandering" and then gently return to the breath. In, out. Rising, falling.

(30 minutes)    Slowly, gently, relax the body, open the eyes and come out of meditation.

# STANDING AND WALKING INSTRUCTION

Throughout our day, we find ourselves in four main postures; sitting, standing, walking and lying down. Steve has already instructed you in the basic sitting meditation. We are also going to teach you formal standing and walking meditation. During the exercise periods there will also be instruction on forms of lying down meditation. Most of the day, however, we will be practicing sitting, standing and walking meditation. The lying down posture is generally only recommended if you are ill or injured, or just before going to sleep, because it is just simply too easy to fall asleep in that posture, and then it becomes sleeping and dreaming instead of meditating.

**Why do we learn standing meditation?**

What we are trying to build is Mindfulness, Awareness. By learning how to practice mindfulness in the various postures, we can make mindfulness stronger and stronger, becoming more and more aware. If we are to find out who and what we are, we have to be able to look closely, to try to make our mindfulness as continuous as possible. Learning standing meditation enables one to continue the mindfulness from the sitting into the standing posture.

During our everyday life we stand a lot of the time. For example; as travelers you may find yourself standing in a bus; standing in line for tickets at the train or bus station; standing in line to get your passport checked at the border or the airport; standing waiting to change money at the bank; standing at the food store; standing while talking to fellow travelers.

While you are here, you will be standing in line for the food and for washing your dishes. Many times during these instances, if we are not mindful, we can be building boredom, impatience, frustration, aversion or desire, which only increase our difficulties and our lack of mental peace.

By practicing standing meditation we can often prevent these difficulties from arising. If we do find ourselves lost in unwise reactions, the "mind spin," we can remember to bring ourselves back to the moment by "grounding" our awareness in the body, often simply by feeling the touch of the feet on the ground.

In this way the formal practice of standing acts as a sharpening stone for the mind, developing a sharpened awareness. This sharpened awareness can be applied to our everyday life. It helps to prevent difficulties from arising or helps to let go of them when they have already arisen. By learning how to meditate in the various postures, we can then use the various postures as opportunities to develop the mind, finding more Peace and Balance in our life.

With the formal standing meditation, we're just going to try to be aware, try to stand as a normal person would, without creating anything special. Standing normally, we are not creating any "special" posture. This allows us to do standing meditation anywhere, relaxed, without drawing attention to ourselves. If you have done any other types of standing meditation in any other traditions, especially in Martial Arts, please do not confuse that standing meditation with what we will be teaching here. If you do confuse another type of standing meditation with what we are teaching here, you could cause yourself a fair bit of extra difficulties. So please be open, and practice what we are explaining here.

With standing meditation we try to be aware not only of the main object of awareness, which will be the breath, but also of our posture: standing. This is because it is a little more dangerous than sitting. If we get sleepy and drowsy, it is possible that we might fall down and hurt ourselves.

Start out with the feet slightly apart to keep the balance. Try not to arch the back so that the hips go too far forward, as this will place strain on the back. Bring the stomach and hips in line with the shoulders so that the body is supported by the lower back. The body not tense; relaxed.

The hands can be together, elbows bent, palms toward the body, in the area from the abdomen up to the chest. The fingers can be loosely interlocked, or you can have one hand with palm resting against the body, and the second hand with palm resting on the back of the first hand. Or the arms can be hanging loosely beside you. Many people find that if they put their hands behind their back, this tends to push the shoulders forward, creating strain on the back and the neck, so we do not advise this.

The head is in line with the body or slightly tilted forward. The face area is the same as for sitting. The eyes are gently closed. If you feel sleepy, then open your eyes and look downward in front of you. Try to relax the jaw area.

With standing meditation we can begin by being generally aware of the posture. That is, we bring attention to the body standing there; the whole body. Then we can bring our attention to the head. Starting from the head we can go through the body slowly. Checking the eyes, the face, the head, the shoulders. Relaxing and going through the body. The hands either placed in front in the area from the stomach up to the chest or hanging loosely at the sides, relaxed. Continue down the body, checking to see that the hips are not tilted too far forward, but in line. Going through the legs, until we feel the feet firmly on the ground.

You may find that keeping your attention on the feet for a little while helps to ground and stabilize the body. So keep the attention on the feet, feel the sensation of the touch of the feet on the ground.

Now bring your attention again to the whole body standing there. Take a few deeper breaths and then become aware of the breathing, either at the nose area or the chest-stomach area. Allow the breath to become natural, breathing in, breathing out, rising, falling. Use the mental noting if you find that it helps you.

If you find that there is a gap, a pause, between the out-breath and the in-breath, the rising and the falling, try to be aware of the standing posture or the feeling of the feet touching the ground during the pause. Let the breath come again in its own time. Just as with the sitting meditation, if the mind wanders, gently note that it is wandering, thinking, and try to return to the breathing gently.

**Now I would like to instruct you in walking meditation.**

During the course of our everyday life, we normally find ourselves walking a lot. We often walk hundreds of kilometers every year. For example; we are now on a small island in the Gulf of Thailand. Many of you were staying at the beach before coming to this retreat. You probably took long walks along the beach.

I wonder, while you were walking along the beach, were you really there—walking along the beach? Or were you thinking where you have been, where you are going, who you are going to meet, what you are going to eat for lunch, what you are going to do next week, or even further into the future? All the while, not really experiencing the reality of the moment—of walking along the beach.

Many times in our life we do this. We are at a particular place and we are not really there, not really experiencing the place. Instead we often only experience our thoughts about the place, or our thoughts about the future or the past.

Walking meditation helps to develop more energy in the mind. It can be used to flow the sharpened awareness developed in sitting meditation into the broader awareness necessary for moving and walking.

Most of you lead fairly active lifestyles. If you are to bring an attitude of focused awareness to your everyday life, it's very important to learn how to center the mind while the body is more engaged in the surroundings, in more active activities, or when the body is moving. So I'd like you to treat the walking meditation as carefully as you would a sitting meditation. It is not just a time to go for a walk in the surroundings and enjoy the scenery. It's a time where we can develop the focused, centered awareness, and learn how to bring our meditation practice into our everyday life. So we don't have a split between the formal meditation, which we think is sitting, and the rest of our life, over there.

The formal sessions of walking meditation are another sharpening stone, helping to sharpen the mind. We can then use this sharpened awareness and try to apply it to our everyday life. Becoming more aware, we try to watch ourselves in all aspects of life. We can then try to drop the obstacles to being aware in the present moment, trying to come back to the present moment, and experience what is actually happening. Keen awareness of the body helps us to see more clearly how we think, and our awareness starts to include more aspects of ourselves.

In walking meditation, you are going to be walking back and forth. But you are not going anywhere—to some specific destination. Try to let go of thoughts about arriving and leaving. Try instead to arrive in each moment, each footstep and the feeling of the body and legs; the experience of walking. For walking meditation you need a walking "track," preferably a flat, clear area. It is very helpful to mark each end of the track. Then you do not have to think about where you will be turning around, which could create extra thoughts and doubts in the mind. Some people like quite a long track, thirty to forty paces. Others find that this allows more opportunity for their mind to wander and they prefer a shorter track. If the track is too short, some people feel that they are turning around too often and sometimes this may create extra restlessness. Try a track about twenty paces long and experiment for yourself, to see whether you prefer a longer or shorter track.

You begin by standing at one end of the walking track. Become aware of the body standing and the posture for a few moments. The head is slightly tilted forward. The eyes looking forward but downcast, about two meters in front of you. There are two reasons for this. First, it will help add a compassionate intention to your walking. If you see that there are any ants, snails, millipedes or other creatures in front of you on the ground, you can avoid stepping on them, either harming them or yourself. The other reason is that it helps you to be less distracted by the other meditators and the surroundings. Less sense contact with the eyes helps you to bring your awareness to the body and the movements. Try your best not to gaze around.

The hands can be placed in a position similar to the standing meditation posture, either hanging loosely beside you, or placed on top of each other or interlaced in front of you. They can be at the level of the stomach or, with the elbows bent more, at the level of the chest. Run your attention through the body starting from the head, relaxing into the posture, until the attention comes to the feeling of the feet on the ground.

To begin, walk at a normal easy pace, not too fast, not too slow. Direct your attention to the feeling of the touch of each foot on the ground; the touch of the right foot, the touch of the left foot as you walk. Try to keep your awareness on the touching sensation. If you wish, you can use mental noting; "left, right, left, right" or "stepping, stepping" to aid you in keeping your awareness with the feet. If you find your mind wandering, then gently note "wandering" or "thinking." Try not to get upset at the wandering mind. The mind is used to wandering, it's not used to concentrating, it's used to thinking. So rather than getting upset at the mind, we try to note just what is happening; if the mind is thinking, we note "thinking, thinking," and then gently return to the footsteps.

When you reach the end of the walking track, we would like you to stop. The reason for this is that sometimes the mind just wanders off, the walking becomes automatic and you may not really be aware that it has wandered off. By stopping, you can check to see if the mind is actually there, giving yourself the opportunity to bring the mind back to the body.

You can stand for a few moments, feeling the feet on the ground, or being aware of the whole body. If you wish, you can note "standing, standing." Some meditators may also become aware of the breathing for a few moments. If you wish to stop for longer than a few moments, that is OK. When you want to turn around, note your intention to turn and then slowly turn around. While turning, try to feel the motion of the body and/or the movements of the legs and then stop again.

When you decide to start walking again, note your intention to walk and then bring your attention to the legs and begin again with stepping, stepping or left, right, left, right. The mental noting is used as an aid in awareness. Try not to let the noting overpower the actual experience of the feeling of the feet touching the ground. If you do use the mental noting, it is quite important to realize that it is an aid to awareness, it's not awareness in itself. Our main focus is to be aware of the feet, and to use the mental noting to aid us in knowing what is happening, describing what is happening, it's just a soft, mental word. Our main focus is not on the words. Otherwise you may find that you are saying "placing" while you are lifting, or you are saying "lifting," while you are placing.

When you find that your mindfulness, awareness is a little stronger, that you are able to concentrate and keep the attention with the touching of the feet more clearly, then you may wish to begin with the two phase walking. To practice the two phase walking, try to be aware not only of the touching of each foot on the ground, but also of the lifting of each foot off the ground. If you wish, mentally note "lifting, placing, lifting, placing." When you move into being aware of the two phase walking, it's quite important to let one foot come completely to the ground before you lift the other foot. This is so that you can transfer your awareness from the one foot, and be aware of the whole process of lifting, noting "lifting, placing, lifting, placing." Some meditators find that they naturally slow down a little at this time. In the beginning, it is probably better not to exaggerate the slowness, as the mind may feel too restricted and forced. If there is any slowing down, allow it to happen naturally.

As your awareness starts to increase, and you find that you can be with the two phase walking for some time, you may wish to move into the three phase walking. Try to be aware of each foot lifting off the ground, moving through the air, and the placing on the ground. The lifting, moving, placing of the right foot, the lifting, moving, placing of the left foot. Again, you can use mental noting to try to tie the awareness to the actual experience; "lifting, moving, placing, lifting, moving placing."

As well, try to remember that when the mind starts to think, we want to try to note this objectively. Not getting upset that we've wandered away from the footsteps, but developing the ability to note the mind objectively, noting gently "thinking, thinking," "wandering, wandering." Then, letting go of the thoughts and coming back to the footsteps, with "stepping, stepping," "lifting, placing," or "lifting, moving, placing."

# BEFORE BREAKFAST DAY TWO

# FOOD REFLECTION AND EATING INSTRUCTION

Within the Buddhist training of Mental Development and Meditation practice, Food Reflection is another technique which we can use to help develop the mind in beneficial mental qualities. It is taught that after we have our food in front of us and before eating, it is beneficial to consider certain factors that concern our food and our relationship to our food.

There are traditional methods that are found within the Buddhist scriptures and we have a variation of these which I will explain to you. As I mention the aspects of this reflection, please look at your food and try to consider and reflect upon what I will be talking about.

This reflection has three main parts. The first part is to consider to ourselves, "Why do we eat?" The basic reason why all of us eat is to keep our body alive and healthy. To alleviate dis-ease and to enable us to continue on with our inner development.

Probably most of the food that we eat tastes pleasant. Some of the food will be unpleasant. But whether the food is pleasant or unpleasant, the main basic reason for eating remains the same: to keep our body alive and healthy. If we can keep this reality in mind, then the unpleasant foods will not bother us as much as they used to. Pleasant foods are not always a problem, but for those of you who do have a problem in getting carried away with wanting pleasant foods, then this reflection can also help. To see our food as basically to keep our body alive and healthy, trying not to have unbeneficial reactions which can disturb our Peace of Mind.

The second part of our reflection is to reflect upon just how fortunate we are to have so much food at a time when many, many people around the world are starving. This, too, will help to balance any excessive overconcern as to whether, in our opinion, the food tastes pleasant or unpleasant. This is a type of reflection that many of us were told by our parents when we were children when we did not want to eat our food. As children, perhaps we could not understand what our parents were trying to tell us. But now we are adults, and we all have a deeper understanding about the rest of the world and the millions of people who are starving to death. Just to have clean, fresh, drinking water, and as much as you want. Just that in itself indicates how fortunate you are.

We can use this reflection to help us to be more peaceful, more content with whatever food we have, whether pleasant or unpleasant, knowing how very fortunate we are and that there are many in the world with far less than we have.

The third part of our reflection is to consider the difficulties in getting our food to us. Even whether or not we are a vegetarian, there are numerous beings that are dying so that we may eat. When the fields are plowed for planting rice or vegetables, many, many animals and insects are killed. The growing and producing of nearly all foods causes the deaths of other beings.

As well, to reflect upon the hardships of the farmers, transport people, store owners, and all of the people who have helped get this food to us, all the way to the people who are cooking and preparing the food for us. In this way we can see how interrelated we are with the rest of the world. We like to recommend here, in particular, some extra special reflection toward those preparing our food. For each retreat that we have had here at this Wat, special foods have been prepared for us and we can be very thankful for this kindness.

After you have done a food reflection while looking at your food, try to use mindfulness while you are eating. Try to be right there with the actual process of eating. Often when we eat our food, when it is pleasant, we may taste the first mouthful and actually know that it is pleasant. But then, many times, our mind starts to think "about" the food, and "off" it goes. And we can be eating, and we can be eating, and we may never taste any of the rest of our food. So even though the food is pleasant, we may not even be aware of the pleasantness. Trying to use mindfulness while you are eating will help you to be more present with the actual experience that is happening at that moment.

Try to observe the process of your body movements. The hand grabbing the spoon, dipping into the food, raising the spoon to your mouth, opening the mouth, placing of the food, closing the mouth, pulling the spoon out, chewing the food, tasting the flavors, swallowing the food. If you wish you can possibly aid your concentration and awareness with mental noting, such as; grabbing, dipping, raising, opening, placing, closing, pulling, chewing, tasting, swallowing. Try to be right there with the actual process of eating. If the food tastes pleasant, OK, just try to realize that it tastes pleasant. If it tastes unpleasant, OK, just try to realize that it tastes unpleasant. Try not to have unbeneficial reactions toward your food no matter how it tastes. Try to be mindful, try to be aware. Try to see if you can let go of thoughts "about" the food, as well let go of future thoughts, past thoughts, worries, fears and such. Try to find a peace and a balance which can exist just in the simple action of eating your food.

So please try to reflect about your food and your relationship towards your food each time before you eat. The reflections that I have just mentioned include considering, "Why do we eat?"; basically to keep our body alive and healthy. As well, how fortunate we are to have so much food when others in the world have so little. And thirdly, considering the difficulties in getting our food to us.

# LISTENING AND SILENCE

Whenever we give instruction or a basic talk about Mental Development and Meditation, it is very important and beneficial for you to try your best to listen and understand what is being said. Try to listen, try to focus on what is being said as best you can.

Listening is a very important part of all of our lives, but many people cannot listen very well at all. So often when people are listening to others, they are not really there; their minds go off, thinking about something totally different, or they think about what the person is saying, or they think about what they want to say, as soon as the other person stops talking.

Learning how to listen with a clear, open, awake mind is very much a part of our growth and development. For this reason, we ask all of you to sit in a meditation posture as best you can for listening to whatever Rosemary and I will be talking about. Please treat it as a sitting meditation, but instead of trying to concentrate on the breathing, turn your attention to try to concentrate on what is being said. Try to listen as best you can.

The only part of your actual sitting posture that some of you may wish to change is just your eyes. Some meditators prefer to watch the speaker and some keep their eyes closed.

If any pains develop in your body, again it is OK to shift your legs, relax your back, etc. However, this time do not worry about being strongly mindful about your actions. Try to move quietly so that you do not disturb others, yet try to keep most of your concentration on listening to whatever is being said. By sitting in a meditation posture, you will be giving yourself the best possible conditions for keeping alert and concentrated on listening.

Try to stay in a sitting posture for the entire time that the talk is being given, as well as during the normal sitting meditation periods. That is, for going to the toilet or getting a drink of water, it is best to do so during the walking periods or regular breaks. The sitting posture is a stationary posture and it is best to try to stay stationary for the entire period. So, please try not to disturb any of your sitting periods and especially try not to disturb any of the talks and instructions.

The more you can concentrate on listening, the more you will be able to understand. The more you can understand, the more benefit you will receive. The more benefit the talk has for you, the more benefit the talk will have for others also.

There is another aspect of listening that is very seldom talked about in the normal, everyday world. It is listening to quiet, silence, calm. Most of our societies are not interested in quiet...silence...calm. Most people do not understand the value and importance of quiet and silence. And many people do not understand when it is appropriate and beneficial to be quiet or silent.

For many, there is a type of fear toward silence, almost as if it were some terrible enemy. The moment that their environment becomes too quiet, they feel threatened in some way. So they turn on the TV or stereo, call someone on the phone or simply go to a busier place. These people have not yet learned the value and importance of quiet and silence and how we can learn, grow and appreciate life within the moments of silence that we can experience.

Doing a silent meditation retreat such as this can help you to discover how valuable and important quiet and silence can be. You can discover how appropriate and beneficial it can be at times to stay quiet or silent. As well, you can learn to understand just how peaceful and calm silence and quiet can be. You can learn how to be with silence without being afraid of it or feeling threatened by it.

This is a rare and wonderful opportunity in life, where we are actually allowed to be quiet and encouraged to be quiet. Often in normal life, people who are somewhat quiet are considered strange. So many times when we want to be quiet, we feel the pressure of our society and think that we must talk or else something is wrong. But it can be OK and appropriate at times to be quiet and this retreat can help you to see this value. This is not to say that keeping silent in normal, everyday life is always appropriate, because obviously at times, it is not appropriate to be silent and it is more appropriate to say something.

Much of this Mental Development practice is to learn when certain actions are proper and when they are improper. There are some actions that are proper outside but they are not proper here. Saying "Hello" to others, smiling at others, communicating in different ways can be very appropriate and healthy at times in normal life. But here this produces unbeneficial results instead.

Very important in this practice is to understand our motivation or intention behind whatever we do, and to try to develop a Compassionate Motivation behind our actions, speech and thoughts, not wishing to cause harm or difficulties.

In normal life a Compassionate Motivation often leads us to saying "Hello" to others, smiling at others, communication with others, wishing to help others. But here, if you talk to others, smile at them, communicate with them, you will actually be disturbing their practice and inward journey, as well as disturbing your practice and inward journey.

These actions, if done here, are not coming from a Compassionate Motivation. They are not appropriate here to express your caring of others, to express your friendliness, Compassion and Lovingkindness.

Here, to express your caring is to be silent, allowing each meditator to experience the retreat in the best way. This is the way that each of you can show your friendliness, Compassion and Lovingkindness. To stay silent. To help each other.

This can be more difficult between friends, due to our conditioning. But...if you are really friends, if you really care for each other, you will stay silent and do your best so that you do not cause difficulties for your friends.

And...you may find that, after the retreat ends, you will actually have a deeper, more caring, richer relationship between yourself, your friends and all others; through developing these techniques in silence.

We will now do sitting meditation. When you start your sitting meditation, be sure to try to check over your body. Checking all areas and see if they are relaxed. The legs, hips, back, stomach, chest, hands, arms, shoulders, neck, face, eyes, mouth, teeth, etc.

Each time that you observe the breathing, just try to watch the breathing as it is. Not trying to change the breathing to be in a different way. If it is long, then just know that it is long. Short, short. Fast, fast. Slow, slow. In whatever way that the breathing is, try to allow it to be that way. And try to just observe. Starting to get to know and understand the breathing.

Every time that the mind wanders and you catch the wandering, just gently note it and then try to return to the breathing. It is a natural, conditioned process for the mind to wander.

This is a continual effort of trying to come back, trying to come back, trying to be mindful, trying as best you can. Each time that you catch your wandering mind, just start again on the breathing, slowly learning about your breathing and slowly learning about your mind.

During this hour, there is normally the sound of the cuckoo clock from across the path at 10:00. Try to see if you can just note "hearing, hearing" if you hear it. Try not to get involved in what it actually is or in thoughts about the clock, which will distract your attention from the breathing.

After you have checked over your body then perhaps a couple of bigger breaths and then relax and let the breath be as it is. Watching at the nose or stomach-chest area. If you wish with mental noting, "breathing in, breathing out," "in, out," "rising, falling."

(end of period)

During the retreat, each day, we will be asking you to pay special attention to some activities that you usually do as a normal part of living here.

Today and for the rest of the retreat, we would like you to try to pay extra special attention to going in and out of doorways. For most of you this means entering and leaving the bathrooms. For some of you, your dorm rooms.

Try to be mindful of the actual process; the arm reaching for the handle, the hand grabbing, the pulling out or pushing in of the door, stepping through the entrance, turning of the body, pulling or pushing the door closed, letting go, etc. If you wish, you can use mental noting to try to help you with developing stronger awareness; reaching, grabbing, pulling/pushing, stepping, turning, pulling/pushing, etc.

To be right there. Try to let go of the past, let go of the future. Try to find the Peace that can exist right there in the moment of opening and closing a door.

## EVENING DAY TWO

# THE FIVE HINDRANCES

When we start to meditate and try to develop concentration on the breath or on the walking, we soon find that there are certain thoughts that may be giving us difficulty or problems—which draw us away from the meditation object. We find that we cannot stay with the breath or the walking meditation for more than a few moments. These obstacles to concentration also often cause the building of stress in the mind and body. Within the Buddha's teaching, these obstacles to concentration are called the Five Hindrances.

In meditation leading to Vipassana, working with these hindrances is a large part of our practice. They can be used as vehicles for the development of Insight and Understanding.

We can learn to recognize thoughts and the mind states that they produce, when they arise. We can learn to "step back" a little and observe their effect on the mind and body. We can try to observe their particular energy as it is. We try not to get lost in them or push them away. By objectively observing them, we will gradually understand their nature and learn how to let them go.

Generally, the usual response to these thoughts and emotions is to get involved with them, and we get caught in a cycle of reaction. Our contacts with everything become clouded and colored by them. They gain in power and dominate the mind.

When this happens, it is very difficult to see things in a clear way. All we see, then, is our views and opinions about things. It is like putting on tinted glasses, viewing the world through them. Everything gets stained by the color of the glasses.

We are trying to build Awareness. When we continually recognize the hindrances in the mind, then we will gain in the ability to observe them without continuing to "feed" them. We can learn to investigate their nature, see the effect that they have on the body and mind, and be able to see their unsatisfactory nature.

With the continual investigation, seeing in this way, Compassion may arise for the unsatisfactoriness, stress and difficulty in the mind and body. And we gently learn how to "let go." We will then be able to see their impermanent nature. They arise and pass away.

If you never look at them objectively, but continually become involved in them—I am angry, I want, I am agitated, I am worried; rather than, there is anger, there is desire, there is agitation, there is worry—then we will not be able to develop the ability to allow them to pass through the mind. They will then continue to cause a long chain of thought and reaction.

In the beginning, we may only be able to recognize the hindrances after we have been involved with them for some time. We may come to notice, first, the continuing struggle or stress, the inability to concentrate, or, that we are simply lost and are not really clear what we have been thinking.

With the gradual building of Mindfulness, Awareness, we can suddenly remember—"we are meditating"—that we have become lost. This moment of Mindfulness is very precious. This moment of recognition allows us to investigate and gently let go. With the strengthening of Mindfulness and Compassionate Understanding, we will gradually start to see the hindrances closer to the beginning of their arising.

Rather than viewing what arises in the mind; thoughts, emotions, as a problem, something to be annihilated or destroyed at all costs, they can become vehicles for Insight, Understanding and Compassion. Vipassana meditation seeks to develop non-attached awareness and clear understanding of the characteristics of the body and mind, seeing their impermanent, unsatisfactory, impersonal, conditioned nature.

Things are arising within the body and the mind, and passing away. The breath is coming and going, thoughts are arising in the mind and passing away, feelings arise in the body and pass away.

This is a reflection of the continual change in nature.

When a hindrance arises in the mind, we try to use mindfulness and be aware that it has arisen. We try to identify it and, if we can, let it go, seeing it pass away. If it is sticky or difficult to let go, we can investigate its nature, its energy, and we will be able to let go more easily.

Try not to have aversion to the hindrances, thinking that they should not be there. Try to recognize them when they have arisen. Try to use Compassionate Understanding, realizing that the mind is a product of conditioning. Whatever is arising in the present is the result of our past conditioning and actions: how we have reacted and thought in the past, the conditioning of society, our upbringing, beliefs, parents, friends, teachers.

Suppressing the hindrances is one extreme; indulging them is the other. If we suppress these things, then we will not get to know them and have the opportunity to let them go. If we indulge them, we will be continually under their power, sowing seeds for their continual arising in the future. We will not be able to see deeper into their nature and will be unable to get beyond their power to dominate the mind.

Habitual thinking will continue to arise in the mind, especially the untrained mind. A great deal of Patience, Perseverance, Energy and Compassionate Understanding—that gentle, caring attitude—is needed. It often feels very uncomfortable trying to resist the impulse to flow with the habitual energy and, instead, to step back, to just watch, without suppressing or indulging. But that is OK. It's part of developing deep inner Peace and Balance, the ability to be in uncomfortable situations and energies, understand them, and gradually learn to transform negative energy into positive energy.

You may begin to see that the mind and mind objects are different, that the mind has the ability to be unaffected, to have Equanimity and to see the arising and passing of these energies. Necessary qualities are Persistence, Patience, Compassion and the willingness to continually start again.

Often you do not think that you are doing very much if you cannot stay with the breath, with the footsteps, with your activities for very long. Yet, just by trying, trying to continually come back, come back, recognize what is in the mind, you are building Patience, Persistence, Effort and Energy, and Compassionate Understanding of your mind and the mind of others. You are also learning to gently resist impulsive reaction to thought.

This, in turn, will allow you to let go easier and develop Equanimity. Equanimity is that evenness of mind which can be with whatever arises with Balance.

**The first hindrance to recognize is sense desire.** Sense desire is a feeling of wanting, a feeling of incompleteness and poverty in the mind. There is the desire for pleasant sights, sound, odors, tastes and feelings in the body. When these pleasant feelings have arisen there is also the wish for them not to end, and the wish for them to be continually available for us. Sense desire is a constant thirst and reaching outwards.

The particular energy of desire is a very strong one in most of us. During much of our lives, sense desire has dominated and ruled. A lot of our dissatisfaction arises because what we have in the moment is not good enough. We may continue to seek the excitement of a better sight, a better sound, the most delicious food, the best partner. We want to be admired; we want to be loved. We are continually seeking experiences that will satisfy us, so many thoughts are involved in fantasies, or dreams about obtaining the object of our desire.

It is not the object of desire that causes the difficulty—it is the feeling of lack within ourselves and the deeply held belief that if we had everything we wanted, we would be happy. Most of us have had many opportunities to fulfill our desires and wants. Most of us grew up in fairly wealthy countries, with abundant food, clothes and material things, and with many opportunities we took for granted.

Yet by having this abundance of opportunities and by continually satisfying desires, have we gained Serenity or Peace of Mind?

The problem with seeking lasting Happiness and Peace in sense experience is that it is so temporary, so fleeting, and so dependent on external things, which themselves are temporary, and impermanent. It may satisfy for a short while, but it is often followed by boredom, dissatisfaction, restlessness, and the seeking of a new experience.

It also so conditions the mind toward seeing happiness dwelling in some future moment that it becomes impossible for us to be awake and experience the present. Often dissatisfaction and emptiness cloud the moment, and the mind is continually longing for the illusory future. How many of us get lost in the very common thought pattern of "if...then."

If I had some nice land somewhere, then I'd be happy.
If I had the right partner, then I'd be happy.
If I could meet the right spiritual teacher, then I'd be happy.

This list can go on and on. "If I had this, if I had that, then I'd be happy." We continually postpone peace and happiness. We may never reflect on nor see the pain and stress of our desire, of living our life in this way. And our peace and happiness will remain dependent on something outside of ourselves.

Perhaps peace may be the fading away of the stress without having to gain anything, the absence of desire, and a feeling of flowing with the moment, whatever it contains.

So how does desire manifest while we are practicing here in the retreat? A common one for many of us is that it is getting nearer to meal time and we find that it is really hard to concentrate during the sitting or walking beforehand. The mind starts drifting off to food; "I hope there's some sweets," "I hope there's plenty of fruit and salad," "Actually, what I really want is a candy bar and yogurt—that would be great!" Many meditators find that it is very difficult to be with each step as they are walking to meal time.

We can start to daydream about music, start singing in our head. It seems *much* more exciting and creative than sitting here in silence, watching the breath. Or we can get lost in our future plans. They seem much more exciting than sitting, watching the breathing.

On a more subtle level; there is the desire for blissful feelings of concentration, bright lights, visions in the meditation. There is the desire to be concentrated for the whole sit, even desire for the next breath. And especially, the desire for the bell to ring.

Desire is a reaching for, a wanting to gain something, a feeling of lack and non-contentment, a pushing away of the moment. This is very different from the feeling of flowing into the moment with non-resistance and non-clinging, the feeling of settling back, which is a feeling of fullness.

So how do we work with the energy of desire? The first thing is to recognize it, see it for what it is. "Desire, desire." Try not to judge it for being there. The condemning quality of the mind does not carry with it the Compassionate Understanding that the mind is a process of conditioning. What is arising in the present are the fruits of what we have thought in the past, how we have reacted, how we have been conditioned.

We try not to indulge in it either. This is because we realize that if we do, we will remain under its power, claim its stress and condition the mind to continually reach out for and be dependent on external things. Thus we may never experience the Peace that comes from within. Instead, we can try to watch desire, recognize it and begin to understand its turbulence, agitation and unsatisfactoriness. By doing so, we can learn to gently let go and return to the primary object of meditation.

With this clear seeing, perseverance and non-reaction we are gently de-conditioning the mind. We are strengthening Mindfulness, Equanimity and our ability to let go. We are also increasing our understanding of the mind and seeing the nature of sense desire as stressful. Also that it arises, stays for a while and passes away—it is impermanent.

So the first hindrance is sense desire.

**The second hindrance is aversion, dislike.** This is the opposite of desire. It is a "pushing away" rather than a "reaching for." There are, for all of us, things in life that are unpleasant. This is normal. What we add to this unpleasantness is aversion, the condemning quality of the mind.

Aversion usually has a rather strong energy in the mind. Because it is a strong energy, many people find it quite stimulating. They enjoy the involvement, the absence of dullness and boredom. Anger and hatred give them a powerful sense of identity.

However, these people have not yet investigated deeply the negative effect that anger and aversion have on their own mind and body, and the effect that anger and aversion directed toward others have on other people. It is pretty easy to see the devastating effect that aversion and hatred have had, and are having, in the world.

There are many forms of aversion. There is jealousy, judgment, fear, prejudice, annoyance, irritation, hatred, anger, etc. There is aversion towards sights, sounds, odors, tastes, feelings in the body, thoughts in the mind. There is aversion towards people who are not pleasing to us; who challenge us in any way, who hold different beliefs and opinions, or maybe, who do not fulfill our expectations of them.

Aversion and annoyance can arise when desire is frustrated and remains unfulfilled. When we do not get what we want, we may start to blame the outside, judging situations and people, elevating ourselves in comparison, justifying our anger and aversion. Our usual way has been like this.

These experiences of pushing away or condemning create deep impressions in the mind. They can make the mind "simmer" about the past long after the actual event has ceased, ruining our present moment, our Peace. In meditation practice, when we try to concentrate on the breath, these deep impressions from the past often surface. If we do not have enough awareness and the ability to step back a little and recognize anger, aversion, then we may get lost in recreating these scenes from the past, feeding the cycle of thought and reaction to thought.

The stress, unpleasant feelings that arise are the characteristics of aversion, judgment, depreciating comparisons, frustrated desire, and unfulfilled expectations. The cause of the stress, the difficulties, lies within our own mind, in our reaction to experience. But for most of us, the usual way is to blame the outside—the people, the situation—rather than our own reaction to our experiences, our own expectations.

In this retreat you cannot talk to the other meditators, so if you are experiencing aversion then you cannot express it or "throw" it at the other person. So it remains with you. From this it is fairly easy to see; the others are not suffering—you are, from your attachment to aversion.

What are some common aversions that meditators experience in a retreat?

You may be sitting peacefully and *finally* you are able to keep with the breath, it is coming in, going out, or rising, falling and you are actually staying with it. Then the people near you start to move and fidget, making a lot of noise, or even get up and leave the hall. Suddenly the mind starts to "spin" with thoughts such as; "Why do they have to make so much noise? Can't they sit still? It's distracting me!" You start to judge them.

Perhaps the Thais are speaking a little bit too loud or laughing, and you get caught in judging them.... Maybe you feel that there is *too* much sitting or *too* much walking.... Somehow people can make themselves into instant experts on what a meditation retreat should be, or how it should be organized.

Some people may be taking a long time in the food line, they might be trying to take their food so very slowly and mindfully. You may become impatient and think to yourselves, "They really don't have to be so slow to be mindful."

You may be having a difficult time sitting and concentrating. The actuality of the retreat may be very different to your projected hopes of, perhaps, good times and an easy "high." So you may start to blame the schedule or the teachers, having thoughts such as; "How can they be *so* insensitive? They make us sit and walk, sit and walk, sit and walk. It's just *too* much!"

You may find in the next moment that you turn the blame onto yourself, building self-aversion. You may think, "I'm hopeless, I can't meditate!" You look around the hall: "Everyone else is sitting like little Buddhas! I can't meditate! Here I am, I can't sit still, I can't concentrate! There's really no hope for me! My mind is a hopeless mess!"

So how do we work with aversion? First we can try to prevent it from arising. When we hear a sound, we try to note "hearing, hearing" and watch the sound pass away. It is the same process with odors, sights, or feelings in the body. We can see how they arise, exist a while and pass away. This is applying mindfulness to the sense contacts. We try not to get involved in the outward things and our reactions to them.

If we miss this and find that we are lost in aversion, try to recognize it. We may have been thinking in this way for some time, that does not matter. We have *now* become aware. We can try to note objectively, "aversion, aversion," "judging, judging." Try to see its true nature without falling into more aversion or justifications. Try not to have aversion toward the aversions. This only hinders the ability to let go and continues the energy of aversion.

We can try to understand that this tendency of mind is deeply conditioned by our past habitual thinking and actions—recognizing the Law of Conditioning—yet also know that we have the opportunity to step back, stop justifying and begin to recondition the mind towards better conditioning. We can learn to let go.

Often we cannot let go of aversion solely by trying to observe it objectively, because the attachment, the justifications are deep. In this case we can investigate. What do I mean, "investigate"? We are not going to investigate the object of the anger, who or what the anger is directed towards, the story line, or why we feel justified in having the anger. We are going to investigate the characteristics of the energy of anger, aversion.

What is anger? What is aversion? How does it feel in the body, and how does it feel in the mind? Run your attention through the body. How do the eyes feel, are they closed tightly? The jaw? The hands, are they clenched? The shoulders? The breath, is it rough, is it short? See the tightness and tension in the body. Look also at the turbulence in the mind. Clearly open to the unsatisfactoriness, the stress, the suffering of aversion.

With Awareness and Wisdom, we see aversion's nature is stress. If we never open to it, become willing to investigate it, we will never see aversion clearly as stress. We may not want to let go of attachment, self-righteous justifications, or the blame we place on the outside for our own suffering.

If we open to it, Compassion may arise for the stress, honestly seeing the cause of the stress within ourselves, and we can learn to gently let go. Forgiving ourselves, letting go of the wish to manipulate others. This is bending the strong energy of aversion and transforming it into the energy of Compassionate Understanding.

Gradually with the building of Awareness, we will be able to see when aversion is present or when it arises in the mind. If we are able to watch and investigate without continuing it with more aversion, and without getting lost and indulging it by our attachment to it, then we will get to know its particular energy. And we will be able to recognize it sooner and more easily.

We also may come to understand how aversion arises and how to bring Equanimity and Compassionate Understanding to all of the unpleasant things that help to activate this feeling. Through understanding the unsatisfactory nature of its energy, we build the ability to let go, strengthened by Compassion. In this way, aversion will have less power over us.

So there are the hindrances of sense desire and aversion.

**The third hindrance is called sloth and torpor.** In common language sloth and torpor can mean laziness, inertness, dullness, sleepiness, boredom, not wanting to put forth any energy.

You may find sleepiness, tiredness a problem in the first few days of the retreat. This may be because you are doing something different. You are waking up at 4 am, trying to sit and walk many hours throughout the day. It is a lot different to what most of you are used to, and it is a lot different to lying on the beach.

Sleepiness and tiredness are very common and most meditators experience this. Try to have patience with this, understanding that as the retreat progresses, you will probably get more used to the conditions and you may find the mind becoming brighter. This has been the experience of many meditators. Try to recognize and observe the sleepy mind: dull, inert, lacking in energy, bored, making all things fuzzy and unclear.

Often the next thing that happens for us is that we bring up aversion toward the sleepiness—wanting it to go away. "I don't want to be sleepy, I don't want to feel like this." Or we may bring up aversion toward the schedule: "It's too hard!" But wanting the sloth to go away by generating aversion only makes us more tired. The attachment with it, wanting to go to bed, not wanting to put in the energy, and sinking into the pleasantness of the dullness often results in our just giving up in the sit or walk.

How do we work with sloth and torpor? When it is present, it is difficult to be with the breath. The breath is a fine, subtle object and the mind has become too dull. The breath, also, sometimes has a tranquilizing effect on many meditators. So if we stay with the breath, we may find that we get more and more sleepy.

Watching the breath while sloth is present can be compared to being lost in a forest in a fog, and trying to find our way out of the forest by trying to recognize small pebbles on the ground. This is very difficult. But, if we try to recognize a huge boulder, a familiar outline, it will be easier to find our way out of the forest. In this case the boulder is the body.

Let go of the breath and focus your attention on the body. Run your attention through the body noting the various sensations. The eyes, are they heavy? Note "heavy, heavy." The head, is it tilted? Note this, feel it without straightening it. Allow the mindfulness to arise, then straighten it. The back, is it slouched? Note this, feel it without straightening it. Allow the mindfulness to arise, then straighten it. Keep running your awareness through your body, investigating the various sensations arising and try not to being up aversion to them.

If you still find that you are having a problem, open your eyes and just sit. Feel the body sitting, note, "sitting, sitting," then focus into a smaller area such as the hands touching or the buttocks touching and note, "touching, touching." Then broaden the awareness out to the whole body sitting, note, "sitting, sitting." Keep focusing in and broadening out the awareness to keep the mind active. Perhaps after a while the sleepiness may lessen, you can close the eyes again and go back to feeling sensations in the body or to the breath.

What the investigation does is to break up the sloth and torpor with moments of Mindfulness, which has an energizing quality. We may see that sloth, tiredness and sleepiness can actually pass and be followed by a bright mind.

When we investigate this hindrance without condemning or attachment, we can come to see that its nature is impermanent. In Vipassana meditation, we try not to push anything away. Instead, we try to investigate and see things as they are, not as we think they are, or as we think they should be, or as we want them to be, but the actuality of things as they are.

If you are having difficulty with sloth and torpor, here are a few more hints which may be of benefit to you. If you are drowsy in the early morning, splash water on your face or take a cold bath. Some people find this very refreshing. If it occurs during the walking meditation, you could quicken the pace a bit to help get the energy moving, and broaden the awareness to the simple touching of the feet on the ground. You can try to prevent sloth and torpor from arising by being mindful of the amount of food that you eat. Eating too much often gives one a heavy feeling. A brisk walk after meals can also help.

You could also increase the mental noting. This can often prevent us from drifting into a dream state. It is also important to know the difference between sloth that arises from boredom and the sleepiness, physical tiredness that comes after a "long, hard day." Try not to create ideals. Try not to force the mind to excesses.

Here you have the opportunity to get an adequate amount of sleep. You also have time after the meals to relax. So a lot of the tiredness that you feel may not be due to lack of sleep. It may be that you are not used to working the mind to develop Concentration and Mindfulness, and putting forth the effort needed to do so. It may be boredom which arose from trying to watch a neutral object such as the breath or steps. It just doesn't seem "exciting" enough. It may be that you did not catch the aversion that came before the sleepiness, which depleted the energy in the mind. Or perhaps it may be you just do not want to look at something in the mind—you would rather hide from it.

Try not to give up and drift into it. Try to put forth a little effort to investigate and brighten the mind. Or try to have patience with it until it passes. Try to remember those moments of brightness within the "fog" and those may encourage you.

So there are the hindrances of sense desire, aversion and sloth and torpor.

**The fourth hindrance is restlessness and worry.** This is the opposite feeling to sloth and torpor. Restlessness often manifests with out-of-control thoughts. Frequently there is neither rhyme nor reason to them. There may be a feeling of agitation and speediness: thoughts going on and on, jumping into the future, the past, here, there and everywhere.

Jumping into the future, we create situations and worry about the outcome of what may never happen, developing fear and anxiety by thinking about two days in the future, two weeks, two years, twenty years. Jumping into the past we stir up memories, often creating guilt or grief, becoming upset. This can overwhelm the mind.

Restlessness and worry are usually strong obstacles when we begin to train and develop the mind in meditation. Much of our excitement and identity is concerned with the future or the past. Staying in the present is difficult for us.

This agitation in the mind often manifests in the body as a powerful urge to get up and go away. It is the inability to sit still even if there is no real major discomfort. It is often a pressure in the mind and body, and sometimes it gets so strong we feel that we will explode if we do not stop this sit soon or the bell does not ring.

A common worry of meditators comes from a projection into the hugeness, the enormity of the task; gazing forward, putting into the present moment all the rest of the future moments that we will have to deal with. When we do this, we can exhaust the mind.

This is a particularly common tendency in the first stages of a retreat. In the beginning, Concentration and Mindfulness are fairly weak. We seem to be constantly working with one thought, one hindrance after another, and we have not yet experienced a feeling of ease in the mind. Frustration may arise and we may begin to burden this moment with all the future moments—the next eight days...the next three sits...the 4 am wake-up bell tomorrow, "I can't possibly wake up at 4 am again! I'm exhausted now!"

Try to remind yourself that you only have to deal with the next step, the next breath, not the whole of the retreat; this day, not the whole of the rest of your life. What you are capable of doing now, do. In the future, the mind will have changed in some way. And then, again, there will just be one moment arising after another to deal with. As the mind gets stronger, its limits will expand. Try not to create limits that are static and unreal. Try to let the fear drop away whenever you catch this tendency. Feel the stress in the body and the suffering in the mind. Try to observe the characteristics of worry and fear in the body and mind. Try not to draw away from it.

If you can open to it, Compassion may arise for the stress, the difficulty, and you will want to let go. Allow yourself to feel the relief of coming back to deal with the present, only this moment, *now*. It is the letting go of worry and fear. Try to experience deeply the moment of letting go, of softening, the absence of turmoil, the spaciousness. At this time, you can experience the "fruits" of letting go immediately. This experience will help strengthen the ability to let go in the future.

By not hiding from the uncomfortable energies in the mind—restlessness, agitation, fear, worry, regret, guilt, etc.—we can recognize and learn how to deal with them. Also, we may be able to recognize them sooner and more easily in the future: "Ah...there's fear, there's worry...I know you...you're just paper tigers come to try to scare me."

Try not to react with a heavy judging mind or conceptual thoughts, such as "worry is bad," "restlessness is bad," "fear is bad." This is not clearly seeing its actual energy, and letting go through Compassionate Understanding.

Also try not to react with excessive idealism, thinking that we should not have fear, worry or restlessness. Again, try to remember the "Law of Conditioning," that the thoughts arising in the present are fruits of our past reactions, past tendencies, past living. How we deal with them *now*, however, creates conditions for our future.

With restlessness and worry, you can also encourage yourself, if you find it difficult to "open" and let go. Try to increase the concentration factor in the mind by using a few words, a small phrase; "Just one breath at a time," "Just one step at a time," "Start again, start

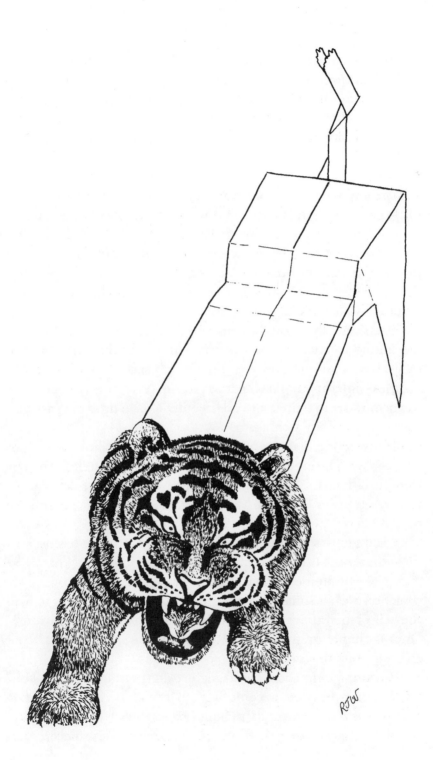

again," "Settle back into the moment," "Care for each step," "Care for each breath," or whatever words appeal to you. This often puts a brake to the projection, the out-of-control mind, with an aid to concentration. These words can help, just as "in, out" aids in staying with the breath, and they have the added power of encouragement for our mind.

What starts out simply as restlessness and lots of thinking can activate a whole chain of hindrances if we do not catch ourselves in the beginning. It often goes like this: First restlessness arises, and we start to have aversion for our restlessness and thoughts. This is followed by desire for a better experience. All this thinking can cause the mind to become exhausted, giving rise to sloth and torpor. With sloth and torpor, we cannot concentrate or see anything clearly so a lot of self-doubt and hatred arises.

This is usually called the "multiple hindrance attack." Most new meditators experience it quite often. This can be discouraging; you may feel that it is just hopeless. You need to encourage yourself during these times and not let it get you down. It is a normal experience when you start to train the mind. In order to help drop the past, you have to continually start again.

Try to realize that the mind and its various qualities are full of flux, change. During the next sit you may be able to strengthen your Concentration and Mindfulness enough to let go of the thoughts or your reactions to the thoughts for a while. You may then be quite peaceful, with Awareness very strong.

Realize the conditioning of the mind up until now has been to allow the thoughts to be dominant. This conditioning is strong. The energy of Mindfulness in the present is weak. The ability to let go is weak because it is something new that you are doing. Try not to hate yourself or the mind for what it is. Although Mindfulness sometimes is simply overpowered by past conditioning, often it is the difficult times that teach us the most.

When the hindrances are strong, we don't just give in. We keep putting forth the effort to come back, to let go. This is doing a lot. It may give us the opportunity to build the beneficial, balancing energies of the mind—Strength, Perseverance, Patience, Persistence, Equanimity and Compassionate Understanding. Even, simply, the ability to be in the constant onslaught of thoughts in a more balanced way.

We may see the thoughts coming and going with no rhyme or reason to them, like bubbles in a stream—sometimes stupid, useless or low, sometimes intelligent, lofty or sublime. Ask yourselves, "Which of these thoughts is really me?" And so, in these moments, there may be an ability to detach, to gain insight into the non-personal quality of thought.

So there are the hindrances of sense desire, aversion, sloth and torpor, and restlessness and worry.

**The fifth hindrance is doubt.** Doubt is a hesitation in the mind. Doubt has an immobilizing energy; it is a blockage, a dark fog, a not-knowing, and especially a lack of confidence.

There is doubt about yourself. You may be having difficulty sitting still, you open your eyes and everyone else may be still for that particular moment; "Everyone else can meditate, I can't!"

There is doubt about the retreat. Everyone is walking around not talking to each other. Sitting, walking back and forth, walking back and forth, walking back and forth—"Is this some type of mental hospital?!"

There is doubt about the teachers! "I come to Thailand and these people are Westerners, they look just like us! No robes, no beads, no beard, no fancy names, they aren't even monks or nuns!"

There is doubt about the teaching. "Is it really going to help me?? Is this the right path for me?? How am I going to become "enlight-ened," find answers to all my burning questions by just sitting, watch-ing my breathing??"

There is doubt about the future. "Where will I go after the re-treat? What will I do? What am I going to do with my life?"

Doubts about whether you can possibly make it through eight more days of this! Doubts about whether you are practicing cor-rectly.

Doubt is an important hindrance to recognize because the power of doubt lies in its ability to stop us, to make us run away from our challenges in life, and to dissolve the best intentions.

With doubt in the mind, there is not much practice done but instead a lot of thinking and halfhearted effort. Because it creates such a stop-start practice, results do not come quickly, if at all. Because results and understanding do not come quickly, you may start to blame the method rather than your doubt and lack of efforts.

Also it is dangerous in that if you hold onto your doubts, without asking questions in order to clear up the doubts, they can easily transform into aversion and hatred toward the person or thing doubted. With aversion in the mind, one turns away, wishes not to listen, seeking out instead reasons and justifications for doubting and not listening.

This does not mean that we accept things blindly. We weigh what we hear intelligently, trying to stay open, and if it sounds like it may be of help to us, then we try to put in the effort to practice and confirm things for ourselves by experience. Without some effort, we cannot experience for ourselves the benefit of practice; it will continue to be another person's experience.

So how do we work with doubt? As before we first have to recognize it as doubt. The hesitation in the mind gives us the clue. Also there may be lots of arguments and debates going on in the mind.

With self-doubt we can reflect that a lot of it comes from a sense of unworthiness that has been conditioned into us. Also it may come from the competitive drive that is so strong in the West. Try not to let it overpower you. You do not have to have perfect Wisdom, Equanimity and Concentration tomorrow. Continue to remind yourself of this.

Try not to compare yourself with anyone else. Just do the best you can in the present moment. You may feel inspired by others, but try not to add unworthiness and self-doubt. Often it comes from creating ideals of "how we think we should be."

In Vipassana Meditation we are investigating the actuality of things as they are, not as we want them to be or think they should be. We are trying to develop the ability to be with what is arising with Equanimity and Balance, so that our Peace does not depend on whether things are perfect, but on a coming into harmony with change and impermanence.

We are going to get lost again and again. That is OK. Simply start again. Return to the moment again and deal with only that moment.

Doubt has certain characteristics; hesitation, uncertainty, lack of confidence. Try to recognize its energy and note it clearly, "doubt, doubt." This is important because attachment "feeds" it. Watch it. Try to open to its difficult energy; see its particular kind of unsatisfactoriness and stress. Allow Compassion to arise for this unsatisfactoriness and stress, and gently learn to let go.

When we know its quality and see it often enough, it will come to have less power over us. We will be able to recognize it sooner without involvement. Try to allow the "space" in the mind—to feel comfortable with not knowing.

With doubts about the practice, try to clear them up as soon as possible. This is important. Do not waste your time here, it is very precious. Leave a note for Steve or myself if you have difficulty understanding. Some of your doubts may dissolve the more we explain things as the retreat goes on.

When it arises in meditation try to recognize it. Note it; "doubt, doubt"—even if you have to do it many times. And if you can, try to let go of the doubt. It may be helpful to agree with yourself to test these methods *fully* for these 10 days so that doubts do not prevent you from working as best you can and receiving the most benefit from these days. Try to come back to the moment, to be content with one step at a time, one breath at a time, not what may happen in meditation in the future. Try to treat these days as a "Journey of Discovery."

So there are the hindrances of sense desire, aversion, sloth and torpor, restlessness and worry, and doubt.

These are the five major hindrances that pull the mind off balance and create problems for us until we recognize them, understand their energies and see how to let go of them. Try to investigate with Compassionate Understanding: the hindrances are arising due to conditioning, how we have thought and reacted in the past. Try to investigate without suppressing or indulging the hindrances. Try to develop non-attached awareness of things as they are.

Mindfulness gives us the capability of realizing when the hindrances are present. Then we can try to investigate, to learn how these particular energies affect the mind and body. Investigating and opening in this way, we may come to see their unsatisfactory nature, and how attachment to and involvement with these energies create difficulties and stress for ourselves. Compassion may then arise for the difficulty and we gently learn to let go.

As Mindfulness increases, we may recognize these energies earlier and more often, understand them, and be able to allow them to pass away more easily. In this way, the dominance they once held in the mind gradually decreases. We also may come closer to realizing the causes for their arising and may be able to see how they will not arise in the future. We can use these hindrances as vehicles for developing Insight and Compassion.

Vipassana meditation is the awareness of and understanding the characteristics of the body and mind: the breath, the sensations in the body, the feelings, the thoughts. All is arising, staying for awhile and passing away.

We can begin to see the impermanent nature of things and try to come into harmony with this impermanent nature. We can begin to see the unsatisfactoriness, the stress and the suffering of attachment to self-images based on impermanent things. The developing of this Compassionate Understanding strengthens our wish and our ability to gently let go.

# FURTHER BASIC INSTRUCTIONS

I would like to compliment you on the effort you are making. It is not easy. Transforming the mind and our inner reactions to experience is not a small task. But it can be done, little by little, bit by bit.

Continue to make the effort to come to all of the sits and all of the walks. It is OK if you have to move during the sits, relax for a short while and then begin again. Just by coming, making the effort, you are building Patience, Endurance, and you are helping to strengthen the mind.

For many, beginning this practice seems a bit like starting out to train your body so that you can run in a marathon. It is hard going but after a while, after a bit of training, your body becomes fit and running long distances becomes easier and easier.

I would like to explain a little more about being mindful of your breathing. Try to pay attention to the energy of your concentration. Try to make it a "light" awareness, not a forced or strained awareness. If you focus in too much, then you may be forcing your breath rather than watching it, just as it is. This can build tension.

If you find this is happening, try to relax a little, "settle-back," and watch the breath as it is. This may mean a constant adjusting of the fineness of the awareness, as the breath goes through many changes.

An image that may be of help to you is that of a seashore. You are standing at the seashore watching the waves come in and go out. You are standing with your feet near the edge, watching the waves lap in and recede. Some flow in farther than others and take longer to recede. Some do not quite make it to your feet and then recede quickly.

You are simply watching—seeing the waves come in and go out.

The same applies to the breath: some breaths are short, some are long, some are deep, some are shallow. Try to watch them just as they are. Try to be aware of the whole of the in-breath, the rising, from the beginning to the end. The whole of the out-breath, the falling, from the beginning to the end.

Some meditators may be more aware of the in-breath/rising and tend to wander, let their awareness slip, during the out-breath/falling. Often this is because the in-breath is more predominant and their out-breath is more fine and subtle. These meditators often build tension through strong awareness of the in-breath, with subtle holding of the breath, and then little or no awareness of the out-breath. If you tend to do this, try to make an extra effort with the awareness of the out-breath. Try to flow the tension out with the out-breath.

If there seems to be a pause between the out-breath and the in-breath, or vice versa, just try to wait. Don't worry, it will come again in its own time. At those times, you can try to be aware of sitting until the breath comes again. If you are focusing on the rising/falling, you could add the feeling of the buttocks on the pillow or mat during the pause. With the in/out, you could rest the awareness in the area of the upper lip or feel the whole body sitting.

A little more instruction concerning walking meditation which may be of help to you.

First; concerning the posture in the walking. Try not to have the head bent down too far forward. This may cause tension in the neck. If you find a lot of tension coming in the neck and shoulders, this may be the reason for it. You may be trying to watch the feet, rather than bringing the awareness down through the body and feeling the legs and feet. Try to have the head just slightly tilted forward and the eyes focused about two meters in front of you.

Another reason tension may come in the shoulders of some people is if you clasp the hands together behind the back. Sometimes this causes the shoulders to be pushed forward and the back to bend. If you put your hands this way, or have tension in the neck and shoulders in the walking meditation, we suggest the following position for the hands. First bring the hands forward; roll your shoulders up, around, and back, and settle them completely down. Let the arms hang loosely beside you, so that they are parallel to the body. Bend your elbows, bringing your hands up around the rib cage. Loosely interlock the fingers, and have the thumbs just touching. Make sure that you don't pull the hands in towards the body, as this forces the elbows back and the shoulders to bend forward. We are holding them out a little, and it's as if we're holding something very fragile in our hands. This helps the shoulders to go back, and helps you to support the back with the lower back. With this you may find less posture-related tension arising.

Here are some special hints about dealing with some of the hindrances in the walking.

If you are focusing on the movement of the legs and feet in the three phase walking; lifting, moving, placing; and you find the mind becoming sleepy, tired or feeling restricted: first, note that sleepiness is there "sleepy, sleepy," "tired, tired." Then quicken the pace, go back to the two phase walking or to the simple touch of the feet on the ground "stepping, stepping."

If need be you can broaden your awareness even more. You have been focusing in on the movements and sensations of the feet and legs. This can be similar to the close-up of a camera lens and can build concentration. When the mind is sleepy or feeling restricted, the mind needs to develop more energy. Rather than continuing with the "close-up," you can broaden the awareness for a while to energize the mind.

It is similar to using the wide-angle lens of a camera. Try to bring the awareness to the whole body moving through the air. Feel the air against the body, the feeling of the whole body moving, the vision of things advancing toward you, the "flow."

If you wish, stop and stand at the end for longer than usual. You could bring the attention to the whole body just standing or perhaps simply the feeling of the feet touching the ground. This may strengthen the awareness and concentration, and help you when you begin walking again.

If you start to feel restless, or the mind is thinking, thinking a lot, you can try focusing in your awareness. Walk more slowly, trying to see the subtle changes in the sensations of the feet or legs. Try to mentally note the action more precisely and more continuously. This helps to bring forth concentration. The mental noting may also help to replace the thoughts more easily, helping you to let go.

If you start to feel frustrated or angry, try to note this when it has arisen. Then try to observe how you are walking. Have you ever observed how an angry person walks? The footsteps often are heavy, pounding the anger, frustration, worry into the Earth. How much anger, frustration, worry has been pounded into the Earth?

If you are stepping heavily in this way, consciously try to step more lightly on the Earth. At that moment, try to be as graceful, light and flowing as you can. Try to care for each step, "arriving" in each footstep. It is very difficult to hold onto the anger and frustration when you do this.

As we focus our awareness on walking, we begin to see more clearly the mind states that pull us away from the moment. We can begin to see the nature of their energy and characteristics. We can begin to soften around our habitual clinging; noting, investigating, and letting go of attachment, with Compassion. We can try to work with what arises, seeing what is needed to balance the mind and help us to let go; broadening out our awareness, focusing in our awareness, making our awareness light and compassionate by stepping lightly, gracefully on the Earth. We can see what is appropriate and in this way, we work with the body and mind, seeing their interrelationship.

A few words now about Awareness or Mindfulness of other objects arising in the body and mind.

We have asked you to make mental notes such as; wandering, thinking, hearing, smelling, feeling, etc., whenever these contacts occur. That is, either when you are distracted away from the awareness of the breath, or when these objects become more predominant than the breath. You may have increased your mental noting in order to aid you in being aware of your activities, such as; in the walking, in opening and closing doors, in eating, etc.

Last night I talked in depth about the Five Hindrances. So now when you are aware that the wandering thought is aversion, you can try to note "aversion, aversion" and then gently return to the breath. Whatever the mind states, or contacts that occur, if you can recognize it, try to make more precise noting. It will help you in becoming more objective towards these mind states. Similarly, if the mind goes to the future, you can note "planning, planning," or if it goes to the past, you can note "remembering, remembering." Whatever the mind states, or thoughts that arise, if you can make more precise noting, try to do so. At times, our awareness is not so clear, and you may find it difficult to recognize them. At these times it's quite OK to leave the noting as "thinking," or "wandering." As the awareness increases, you'll be able to recognize them more clearly.

This is quite an important part of the practice, the noting of the mind. In this way we include the mind in our awareness. We usually consider ourselves to be the body and the mind. If we are going to understand the nature of who and what we are, we have to include the mind in our awareness. As we learn to note the hindrances when they arise, we build the ability to observe thoughts objectively. As we learn to observe objectively, it gives the opportunity for understanding to arise. In the beginning, many meditators tend to push the thoughts away, rather than noting them objectively, running back to the breath or the steps. This may build concentration, but it also may build a tendency to avoid looking at the mind. It can also develop aversion, judgment, suppression of the thoughts. That is, running away from the mind, instead of observing it objectively. With this fear, aversion, suppression, or judgment of the thoughts, there is no objective awareness, and the ability to understand the characteristics of the body and the mind, whether they be pleasant or unpleasant, may not arise.

Our main objects of concentration so far are the body, the breathing, and the footsteps. This helps to strengthen concentration and mindfulness, helping to develop a strength and clarity in the mind. Also, because we're trying to stay with one object, we begin to see more clearly what draws the mind away from these objects, and how the mind reacts to these contacts.

In this way we begin to see the different patterns of our thoughts, clingings, aversions more easily. If we can build a more objective awareness, we may begin to understand the energies in the mind that cause us to fall into stress and suffering. This helps us understand more clearly the Law of Cause and Effect in the mind. We can also learn to let go of these attachments, either by objective awareness, or by investigating how these energies affect the body and the mind, developing Compassionate Understanding.

We are trying to develop a moment-to-moment Awareness, to bring ourselves into the actual moment...trying to let go of the past, let go of the future, and experience what is actually happening in the thoughts and in the actions...trying to not get caught in the content of the thought but instead observe their energies...trying to get to know and understand who and what we are.

In this way we can be developing Compassionate Understanding toward ourselves and toward others.

We will now do sitting meditation. As we have been instructing you, please settle into the posture, if you have not already done so. Run your attention through the body, relaxing into the posture. Perhaps a few deep breaths, then allow the breath to become natural. Breathing in and breathing out, rising and falling. Settling back and just watching...like the waves at the seashore.

(end of period)

Yesterday we had a special mindfulness activity of opening doors, going through doorways, and shutting doors. Please try to continue with this mindfulness exercise.

Today we are going to add another special mindfulness activity.

Please put forth extra effort towards mindfulness of washing your dishes. We are going to try to wash the dishes, in order to be aware of washing the dishes; not only to get clean dishes.

So when you are taking your dirty plate, glass, spoon, etc. to the dishwashing pans, try to bring extra awareness to the whole activity, from the beginning until the end. While you are standing in line, try to be aware of standing, then stepping forward, standing, stepping, until you reach the pans.

Try to be aware of placing the dishes into the cold water, feeling the temperature of the water and the action of the hands. Then, try

to be aware of moving the dishes to the pan with the soapy water and wiping the plate with the sponge. You can feel the texture of the soapy water, and the movement of the hands.

Continue the awareness as you move the dishes to the next pan of rinsing water, moving, and rinsing. Then moving again to the next pan, and finally walking to put away your dishes in the racks. If you wish, you can use mental noting to aid in your awareness, such as "washing," "placing," "cold," etc.

Try to be just there, washing the dishes, as best you can.

# EVENING DAY THREE

# COMPASSION AND LOVINGKINDNESS TALK AND GUIDED MEDITATION

Tonight we will be having a talk, a guided meditation and then a little finishing talk at the end. The talks and the guided meditation will be concerned with understanding the importance of Compassion and Lovingkindness, and the learning of some methods by which we can help Compassion and Lovingkindness to grow within ourselves.

On the first day of the retreat, I talked about a relationship that followed like this:

First we see a problem or difficulty, something unsatisfactory. Then we wish to alleviate the problem or remove its cause. This is the arising of Compassion. Then we may wish for happiness to replace the unhappiness. This we refer to as the arising of Lovingkindness.

With our thoughts of Compassion and Lovingkindness, we then try to use Mindfulness to be able to understand the problem or difficulty. When we understand the situation well enough, we then can apply our Understanding to the situation and alleviate the difficulty or remove its cause.

I would like to explain this relationship in more detail. As I mentioned in the beginning talk, for all of us there occur things in life that are not totally satisfactory. These occurrences can be physical or mental. They can range in intensity from only a slight irritation to major suffering. From time to time each of us is confronted with experiences in life that are not totally satisfying.

Chances are that for each of us, there has developed an awareness of some thing or possibly many things that are unsatisfactory in life, and we have the wish to improve these things. Perhaps we have tried to ignore them and have seen that this was not a good enough method. Perhaps we have tried to escape from them and have seen that this also was not a sufficient method.

So here we are at a meditation retreat trying to learn methods that will be more successful. Methods that will help us to learn how to deal with the continual changes in life's situations and our reactions to them. This development of our minds can provide the basis for more Peace and Happiness within ourselves that need not be dependent on external conditions.

It does not matter whether our life has had a great amount of satisfaction or a small amount. It does not matter whether our life has had a great amount of dissatisfaction or a small amount. Each of us, in our own way, wishes to deal with the unsatisfying aspects of life, and find more inner Peace and Contentment. Seeing of the difficulties, problems, etc. and wanting to solve them or remove their causes; this, we have said, is an arising of Compassion.

Compassion, as used here, means a feeling of sympathy toward ourselves or others who are experiencing some type of difficulty. Compassion is a softness, a tender heart that is sympathetic and willing to open to all of life. But at the same time, it possesses a strength that is not weighed down by difficulties or sorrows. A tender heart that sees that there are difficulties and wishes to help in some way.

In many dictionaries, Compassion is defined as "a feeling of deep sympathy or sorrow for another who is stricken by suffering or misfortune, accompanied by a strong desire to alleviate the pain or remove its cause."

For purposes here, we will slightly adjust this definition in two ways. First, to feel the sorrow of an occasion may be beneficial at times, but to be weighed down by it is not. That is, it is better to identify with the difficulty yet to maintain a degree of Equanimity and strength to deal with the situation, for it is only through dealing with the situation calmly and wisely that will produce the best results. If everyone merely feels the sorrow and is weighed down by it, then the best solution will be hard to find.

Secondly, to have Compassion only for others does not include everyone. If one takes a broad view of life, it is fairly obvious to see that separation, change and death are universal. Each of us has misfortunes, difficulties and obstacles. All of us encounter the impermanence of life and things that are unsatisfactory. Our bodies occasionally will get sick or injured. If we live long enough, our bodies will become weak, possibly feeble. We often are separated from what we like. We often have to be with what we do not want to be with. And often, we simply do not get what we want. These things are just facts of life.

In this way, we are not separate from others but interrelated. Each of us is another human being who needs Compassion. So it is important to include having Compassion for ourselves as well as for others.

It also is important to make a distinction between Compassion, as used here, and the word "pity." Although these words often are used interchangeably, pity, in its actual application, frequently indicates a distance between oneself and those who have problems.

Pity can fall short of opening and seeing the interrelationship of human beings, and the universal aspect of impermanence. It can be as if one is in a separate bubble, unaffected by life. Many times, pity is from the outside, looking at them over there.

Compassion is from the inside. Compassion can be the breaking down of this separate bubble, thus creating a feeling of connection instead of separation.

When there is the arising of Compassion with the wish to alleviate difficulties or remove their causes, there often follows a wish for Happiness. This is a very important point for all of us. What is the best thing that we can wish for ourselves or for others in order to have Happiness?

Money? Cars? Houses? Clothes? Food? These things are very beneficial but they are limited in their ability to give Happiness. Going beyond the limitations of material objects lies the most important thing.

It is having Peace of Mind: the strengths, the characteristics, the abilities of mind that can cope with any difficulty and not be adversely affected. This is the most important thing we could wish for.

There are many, many wealthy people who have many, many material comforts who are not happy and peaceful. And there are many, many poorer people with much fewer material comforts who are happy and peaceful. If material wealth could always produce happiness, then this situation, of an unhappy rich person and a happy poor person, could not happen. But material wealth cannot always produce happiness. Indeed, material wealth can be very beneficial, but it is limited in its ability to give people Peace and Happiness.

If we develop the mind with methods, techniques and tools of Mental Development that can enable us to cope with, understand and deal successfully with any experience that we encounter, then we can gain the ability to have Peace and Happiness, whether we are rich or poor, famous or obscure, healthy or sick, young or old, and so on.

If we have developed our mind in beneficial ways, then our problems and difficulties can cease to be problems and difficulties. Instead, we can view them as opportunities to grow in Understanding. One story that may illustrate this point is about a manager of a large and famous hotel. The hotel and its staff were noted for their outstanding service. The manager was being interviewed once and was asked by a reporter, "What do you do when you have problems?"

The manager replied, "Here at this hotel we have no problems. Here at this hotel, we have only challenges."

With the development of the mind, each of us can turn our problems into challenges. This is the best method of dealing with the unsatisfying aspects of life; to develop the mind in beneficial ways.

As I said before, Lovingkindness, as used here, means a wish for Happiness for ourselves and others, often following or connected to the compassionate wish to solve difficulties. The strong connection that can exist between Compassion and Lovingkindness can be understood with the help of the following example.

If a wise, mature parent were to walk into the child's room while a child was peacefully sleeping and look upon the peaceful, sleeping face, then the parent might be filled with compassionate thoughts, such as realizing that the child will have difficulties, obstacles and challenges in life.

And then a wise, mature parent might be filled with Lovingkind thoughts, such as wishing that the child will have the ability to develop in beneficial qualities to be able to cope with, understand and successfully deal with difficulties, obstacles and challenges in life.

The development of Compassion and Lovingkindness has many benefits. One of the most important is that this development will help to overcome anger and aversion, irritation and annoyances. Anger, aversion, irritation, annoyances, etc. are states of mind that often cause difficulty for ourselves and others. These are frequently prime reasons for wars, killings, persecutions, beatings, thefts, confiscations, suppressions, annihilations, and so on. All types of hatreds and prejudices cause so much difficulty for all of us.

It is easy to see the difficulties that aversion causes for others. But it is not always so easy to see the difficulties that we cause ourselves by being angry.

Most of the time, it is fairly obvious that if a person allows their anger to develop into some type of violence, then it will normally cause difficulties for that angry person. As well, when something happens that causes us to get angry or irritated, by getting angry or irritated we actually create an emotional state that gets in the way of clear thinking. And it is only through clear thinking that the best solution to the problem can come about.

But what about when someone is angry or irritated and does not show it outwardly? Some people will hold onto grudges and grievances for days, weeks, years. Most of us have done this to some degree.

Often the story is the same: Someone did something that we did not like. We got angry but we controlled any physical or vocal response. Later, we recreate the incident in our mind over and over, recalling how stupid the other person was, and often wishing bad things to happen to the other person. Minutes are wasted fuming, hours are wasted, days are wasted. Some people will waste months and years building aversion inside toward some person for some event that happened a long time ago. Sadly enough, some people hold onto these aversions for the rest of their lives.

What is the result if we hold onto some past incident in this way? Pain...mental pain...mental pain for ourselves. The other person goes on living their life. We go on recreating a past incident with our "super-righteous" attitude, all the time just breeding more anger within ourselves. Pain. Mental pain.

It has been said that having anger toward someone is like picking up a red-hot coal with the intention of throwing it at that person. But instead, the red-hot coal burns the hand that grabs it. There is no peace in the mind, only burning, causing problems for ourselves.

We do not have to act like this. The development of Compassion and Lovingkindness can help to overcome anger, aversion, irritation, annoyances, and so on. From the large to the small, all of our dislikes will decrease as Compassion and Lovingkindness grow. Anger and aversion are opposite states of mind to Compassion and Lovingkindness. They cannot exist together at the same time. It is not too difficult to understand that if we could lessen the angers and aversions that we have in our life, that this would be a major step in finding deeper Peace and Happiness.

So we see problems and difficulties. Compassion arises toward the problems and difficulties. Lovingkindness may also arise wishing for Peace and Happiness to replace the problems and difficulties. Now, with thoughts of Compassion and Lovingkindness, we try to apply Mindfulness as our tool.

Mindfulness or Awareness. Being mindful, being aware. Knowing what you are doing, knowing what you are saying, knowing what you are thinking. Causing fewer mistakes and less problems for yourself and for others.

Compassion and Lovingkindness are deeply related to Mindfulness. We could say that they can "feed" the growth of each other. Mindfulness, used in this way to lessen difficulties, is obviously a method by which Compassion and Lovingkindness are put into action. By observing closely, we can see where and when difficulties arise and what factors bring them about, and thus discover ways to avoid similar difficulties in the future.

As we said before, the different steps of the growth of Mindfulness can be seen in this way. When you have done something and you realize, afterward, that it would have been better not to have done it; that is one step in being aware, being mindful; realizing after the fact and seeing what has happened. The same types of events often happen again and again.

The more you realize afterward what has happened, the more your Mindfulness will grow. At some time, you will find your Awareness of the same type of event begins to come about while the event is happening. And you may be able to use your past knowledge to help you get out of the situation better than previously.

At some time later, you will find your Awareness comes about when the situation begins to happen. Then you will be in a much better position to utilize your Understanding and possibly avoid much of the difficulty that may follow.

Later, when your Awareness is strong enough, you will actually be able to see when the event may happen and be able to avoid it entirely.

By developing stronger and stronger Mindfulness, our Understanding will grow concerning our difficulties, problems, irritations, annoyances and all types of experiences that we normally consider unsatisfying.

We then will be able to understand when a problem exists or when a problem does not exist. We will be able to understand how the problem comes about and how it goes away. And, most importantly, we will understand how the problem will not arise in the future. Then we can apply this Understanding to our problems and difficulties, and work to alleviate them or remove their causes.

As this type of Compassionate Understanding grows, the wish and the ability to reduce difficulties for ourselves and others also will grow. By practicing in this way, we will then gain more and more Peace and Contentment, and be able to help others gain more and more Peace and Contentment also.

By now, hopefully, all of you have developed a clear understanding of how important Compassion and Lovingkindness are in dealing with the unsatisfactory experiences with which we are continually confronted throughout our lives. Without any Compassion and Lovingkindness toward problems and difficulties, there may be no wish to solve the problems and difficulties. There may be little, if any, desire to practice Mindfulness, and Understanding would be difficult to develop.

What will follow shortly is a guided meditation which can aid us in our growth of Compassion and Lovingkindness. This guided meditation is a type of reflective, contemplative meditation, using thought. It is primarily concerned with the development of Compassion and Lovingkindness. However, one can easily see how Mindfulness and Understanding are beneficial supports.

Awareness of the breath will be used only for the beginning moments of the meditation. Then as soon as I start to talk, let go of the breath and listen to what is being said. There will be several things talked about and several instructions. There will also be periods of quiet. During the quiet periods, try to think about whatever was just mentioned; reflect, contemplate and/or visualize the situations and possible responses of the people involved.

Occasionally there are parts of this meditation that produce odd responses in some people. If you happen to have any odd or difficult response, please try to become aware of this response as to how your mind reacts and how your body reacts. This awareness of your thoughts and body can be a valuable aid in developing Compassion and Lovingkindness.

Keep in mind that your body and breath may react certain ways when the mind is stimulated and other ways when peaceful. Knowledge of these physical reactions is very valuable. So if you feel somewhat uncomfortable with parts of this meditation, then please try to become aware of this uncomfortable feeling both in the mind and in the body. Once you have noted this response, then please continue with the meditation.

SPECIAL NOTE FOR THE BOOK: Reading a guided meditation of this type is probably not as good as listening to it, especially during a meditation retreat, but the following may be helpful to get the most benefit.

When rested, set aside 20-30 minutes, possibly more, and try to arrange matters so that you will not be interrupted.

As you read through this, when you come to a "*****," please shut your eyes and reflect, contemplate, think about whatever you just read. It may also help to try to visualize the situations mentioned and the responses of people involved.

Although the talk had set time spacing, it is not practical, when reading, to try to time yourself. At each "*****" the time may vary that you wish to use. Sometimes 10-15 seconds will be enough, and at other times you may use a minute or more. Try to take your time; there is no rush.

Have two blank pieces of paper or cardboard at least as big as a page of this book. Use them to block out each page, moving it down the page that you are reading line by line and stopping at each "*****." This will help in two ways. First, by not encouraging the disturbance of your train of thought by seeing what is written later, and second, it will serve to keep your place when you shut your eyes.

SPECIAL NOTE: It is not advised to read the following without first having read all of the previous pages of this book, for your own benefit in understanding.

### A reflective, contemplative meditation concerned with helping to develop Compassion and Lovingkindness

Please breathe calmly for a short while, trying just to be aware of the breath, coming in and going out or rising and falling.

*****

Now try to identify with this situation:

A family of two parents and three children are living comfortably in a suburb of a big city. The working parent has a good enough job so that things go smoothly for all. The family is very happy.

One day the worker goes to work and just prior to lunch, gets a promotion. At the same time, a bad fire occurs at home destroying the house, killing the other parent and all three children.

Unknowingly, the worker goes home at lunch to tell the family the great news of promotion.

*****

Now try to put yourself in the worker's position. Try to feel as the worker would driving up to your house with this great news, only to see a complete disaster and all of your family killed.

\*\*\*\*\*

Try to feel with this pain.

\*\*\*\*\*

Great news of promotion? Not very important now.

\*\*\*\*\*

Heaviness. Sadness. Maybe tight stomach. Maybe lump in the throat. Maybe heavy chest. Soft eyes. Maybe something in the lips.

\*\*\*\*\*

Try to raise a feeling inside for this person and this very sad occasion.

\*\*\*\*\*

Many in the world feel a lot of pity for others with problems, especially extreme suffering such as this. But pity can be cold. Pity can be from the outside, looking at "them over there." Try to get inside. Try to get to the feeling of Compassion. Try to let go of some of your conditioning and get to this feeling for this person.

\*\*\*\*\*

A deep feeling of wishing you could help. Wishing things could be different. This is a reaction to an unpleasant situation. Identifying with, then feeling with the pain and reacting; this can be an aspect of Compassion.

\*\*\*\*\*

Out of this Compassion, can come the hope, the wish of Lovingkindness. That this person will be able, one day, to find peace of mind after such tremendous difficulty. Not that this person will get married again and have three more children and a new house. But that this person will find peace of mind. Through some mental development, be able to cope with, understand and accept what has happened.

Try to wish this person that type of Lovingkindness.

*****

May this person, one day, be able to learn, practice and develop methods, techniques, and tools of mental development, so that they can cope with, understand, accept and overcome the difficulties and challenges of life.

May this person find peace of mind.

*****

Now try to identify with another situation:

Two best young friends, we will call Jim and Tom, are out for the evening, doing what for many young friends is quite common. Nothing in particular, having a nice time at a beach disco.

They go out on the pier in a happy mood, feeling good and joking. In the sense of the words, having a good harmless time. Then, jokingly, Jim teases Tom by almost pushing Tom over the pier into the water. But, in reacting, Tom slips and falls in anyway. Although a good swimmer, Tom was not moving much. Jim jumped in and helped Tom to shore, only to discover that Tom was now a paraplegic. Paralyzed.

*****

Try to feel with the pain of this situation.

*****

Best friends. Happy evening. One has now caused the other to become a paraplegic. Paralyzed.

*****

Try to get to that heavy feeling inside.

*****

Something very difficult has happened to both Tom and Jim. This bad accident that has happened to Tom is extremely sad. But, for now, please focus your attention on Jim. Jim has just caused his best friend to become paralyzed. The guilt and self-hatred are vast...enormous...huge.

Feel with Jim.

*****

Try to feel with this pain.

*****

Try to feel Compassion for Jim.

*****

Now let the feeling, the wish, the hope arise that Jim will someday find some tools of mental development to be able to cope with, understand and accept what has happened. And, in Jim's case, that this mental development will also enable Jim to forgive himself, as he will have enormous guilt and self-hatred.

Let this wish, this Lovingkindness, warm feeling rise within you for Jim.

*****

This is a different feeling from Compassion. This is a feeling that can wipe away tears. That there are tools of mental development that can help.

And that Jim will one day learn these tools.

*****

May Jim, one day, be able to learn, practice and develop methods, techniques, and tools of mental development, so that he can cope with, understand, accept and overcome the difficulties and challenges of life.

May Jim find peace of mind.

*****

Now please consider another situation

This one concerns you and another person. This person is obnoxious, very disturbing, a gossip, a braggart, a bully, a cheat, a liar, or whatever else that you do not like. Most of us have known someone whom we did not like. Someone who did something unkind to us.

Try now to remember a difficult person in your past. Try to remember an exact occasion when this person did something unkind to you.

Try now to get back the feelings you had then.

*****

Dislike, irritation, anger, hatred, wishing bad things for that person.

*****

Try to get to that feeling. Try to get to that hatred.

*****

For some of you this may be difficult. For others easy. Try to get to that feeling of dislike for that person who did something unkind to you.

*****

You probably had this feeling as a child. Try to remember. Like Compassion, this feeling of aversion can often have physical reactions as well. Maybe tenseness, maybe changes in the heartbeat, in the breath, the face, the mouth, the teeth.

Try to experience all that you can of this hatred, aversion, dislike.

*****

Now I have had a few difficult people in my past. Consider this one:

I have not seen this person since high school. Several years ago I was told that this person had tried to commit suicide twice. I was told about the upbringing at home, the family life and how bad it was. The parents had great difficulties. Other siblings also grew into sad, miserable people. The details are unimportant. Perhaps you know similar people.

*****

How can I hate my difficult person knowing this?

How can I hate my other difficult people considering this?

Let your hatred give way to Compassionate Understanding. That your difficult people are probably similar to mine, perhaps messed up, perhaps confused. With little understanding of how to bring peace and happiness to themselves or others, unable to control their reactions to life, and often isolated, alone.

*****

This can be difficult. If so, try not to worry. Try to get some of that same feeling that you had a few minutes ago toward the worker and Jim.

*****

Do not force it. It might not be able to come yet. The aversion can be strong. If you continue to develop your mind wisely, the aversion will weaken, the Compassion will grow.

Try to bring forth some Compassion for your difficult person.

*****

Having understood more now about your difficult person's pains and difficulties, try now to let the wish of Lovingkindness arise; Lovingkindness toward a confused person. With Compassionate Understanding, how can you wish anything else, except that peace of mind will arise and this person will cease to be a problem for other people.

The wish that your difficult person will be able to achieve some mental development so that they can cope with, understand and accept the difficulties of life.

*****

May this person one day, be able to learn, practice and develop methods, techniques, and tools of mental development, so that they can cope with, understand, accept and overcome the difficulties and challenges of life.

May they find peace of mind.

*****

Now it is possible that you have met people who are opposite to this. People who are always kind and nice to be with. It only takes a little bit of understanding the mind to know that unless these people are perfect human beings, then they, too, have some difficulties, pains or obstacles. Although perhaps only minor problems for most people; to them, they may consider it to be a major difficulty.

Try now to bring forth some Compassion for these people. People whom you know who are nice and kind. Inwardly at times, you may be somewhat envious of them, but consider this:

They, like you, are still having some difficulties.

They, like you, are still traveling the path of mental development.

They, like you, may stumble and fall.

They, like you, may have obstacles and problems in finding total peace of mind.

They, too, need Compassion and the wish of Lovingkindness. So try now to raise some Compassion for them and then try to wish for them that they will be able to cope with, understand and accept their difficulties of life.

*****

May these people perfect their learning, practicing and developing of methods, techniques, and tools of mental development, so that they can cope with, understand, accept and overcome the difficulties and challenges of life.

May these people find peace of mind.

*****

Now, try to bring forth Compassion for your parents or the person(s) who were your substitute parent(s). Try to identify with the difficulties that they had.

Try to understand how hard things may have been for them. Most likely they did not have a University degree in parenthood. They probably did not know everything and they probably made many mistakes.

Try to get to that deeper feeling of Compassion for them.

*****

There was probably at least one occasion when you were punished and yet you did not even know what you had done wrong. And, possibly, you did not even do anything wrong.

Can you have Compassionate Understanding to realize that your parents or substitute parents were limited in their own mental development?

And like most of us, with limited mental development, we will make mistakes.

*****

Now, with this understanding, try to bring forth the wish of Lovingkindness towards your parents or substitute parents. Wish them that very great wish that they will be able to learn and develop methods of mental development so that they can cope with, understand and accept the difficulties of life. And find peace of mind.

Try to wish this Lovingkindness towards them.

*****

May my parents be able to learn, practice and develop methods, techniques, and tools of mental development, so that they can cope with, understand, accept and overcome the difficulties and challenges of life.

May my parents find peace of mind.

*****

Take the next few moments to consider one or more of your friends. Try to raise some Compassion for them and then the wish of Lovingkindness.

*****

May my friends be able to learn, practice and develop methods, techniques, and tools of mental development, so that they can cope with, understand, accept and overcome the difficulties and challenges of life.

May my friends find peace of mind.

*****

Through practice and experience, you probably will find that there is one person for whom you have the most difficulty raising Compassion and Lovingkindness. For many, if not all of you, you will discover that this person is yourself.

You know everything that you have done.

You know all of the kind, beneficial things that you have done.

And you know all of the unkind, unbeneficial things that you have done.

For many of us, the unkind things play a greater role in our memory. We tend to shy away from thinking about the kind things that we have done. This way of thinking can bring about some major obstacles, such as feelings of guilt, self-hatred, unworthiness, doubt, self-pity, inferiority and many more.

Take a look at your past now, and try to bring to mind some of these unkind things that you have done; things that most of us do not really like looking at too closely.

*****

We have probably all done something that we are not happy about. Stole something. Cheated someone. Lied about something. Even those unkind thoughts that we have had towards someone. Try to think about some of these things.

*****

We may have acted like some of the people that we ourselves dislike. Doing something unkind to others.

*****

Unpleasant feelings may be arising. If so, examine them. There may be difficulty here. Note your physical reactions, the body, the face, the breath.

*****

Can you view yourself when you were a 6-year-old as not being who you are today? It is not too difficult. As a 6-year-old child who did not understand much, who was ignorant of many things and who made many mistakes.

Try now to raise some Compassion for that little 6-year-old who you were.

*****

What about when you were 10 years old? Can you raise some Compassion for that person who you were then, who did not understand much, who was ignorant of many things and who made many mistakes?

Try to raise some Compassion for that little 10-year-old.

*****

What about when you were 15 years old? Certainly not the same person as you are now. Probably did not really understand much, probably ignorant of many things and probably made many mistakes.

Try to raise some Compassion for that 15-year-old.

*****

What about the person who you were last year? Can you view that person as different from yourself now? Probably not really understanding everything, ignorant of some things and still making mistakes.

That person needed Compassion also.

*****

What about the person who you were yesterday? Different in some small way from who you are today. Yesterday you probably did not understand everything, probably still ignorant of some things and possibly still making mistakes.

Try to have some Compassion for the person who you were yesterday, different in some way from who you are now.

*****

What about now? At this very moment, you probably do not understand everything, you are probably ignorant of some things, and you are possibly still likely to make a mistake. You need Compassion as much as everyone else. You have pains like everyone else. You have your own difficulties.

Try to have some Compassion for yourself.

*****

Now, what is the most important thing that you want? What can you wish for yourself that would be most valuable? Is it not that you will have Peace of Mind? That you will have the opportunity to learn, practice and perfect Mental Development, so that you can overcome all of your difficulties, from the small to the large.

Give yourself that wish. Try to turn that kind of Lovingkindness toward yourself. You deserve this Lovingkindness just like everyone else.

*****

May I be able to continue my learning, practicing and developing of methods, techniques, and tools of mental development, so that I can cope with, understand, accept and overcome the difficulties and challenges of life.

May I find peace of mind.

\*\*\*\*\*

\*\*\*\*\*

(end of meditation)

There are many different ways of doing Compassion/Lovingkindness types of meditation. This is one of them.

You may have noticed that certain phrases were repeatedly used. If you wish to do this type of meditation or other similar structured types of meditation that deal with Compassion/Lovingkindness, then it is often advised and can be very beneficial to use certain repeated phrases.

If you recall to mind the example used earlier about the mature parent and the sleeping child; it is possible that the parent may or may not actually have words going through the mind for the feelings of Compassion and Lovingkindness to arise. But for many of us who wish to develop more Compassion and Lovingkindness within ourselves, the use of words, reflections, visualizations and more can be valuable help.

However, it is important not to just simply perform the action of repetitious thought. Try to utilize these techniques to develop that deeper Compassionate, Lovingkind Understanding that all of us have difficulties, obstacles and challenges in life. All of us are liable to get sick, to get injured. If we live long enough, we will grow old and weak. And all of us will die. Just as you wish to avoid difficulties and obtain happiness, so, too, do most beings wish to avoid difficulties and obtain happiness.

When you practice Compassion/Lovingkindness meditation in the future, you will probably want to consider other relatives, friends, teachers, people you like, people you do not like, people you know, people you do not know. Maybe animals and other creatures. Perhaps especially those who annoy you and bring about the hindrance of anger and aversion in you; barking dogs, biting ants, mosquitoes.

Here are a couple of other ways of doing this type of meditation in a more systematic manner:

You could start with yourself, then your parents or substitute parents, then closest other relatives; husband, wife, children, brothers, sisters, expanding to the rest of your relatives, then friends, teachers, and depending on time, you could continue expanding to other people and creatures. When you finish, it can be helpful to come back to yourself.

A second method could be to start with yourself, then consider the person closest to you in the hall, then all others in the hall, then all others at this retreat. Expanding again to all on the island, all in Thailand, and so on. Again, when you finish, it can be helpful to come back to yourself. There are many other ways.

We wish to encourage you now to use the Compassion/Lovingkindness Meditation regularly in your practice, especially the standing and sitting. Sometimes do the breathing awareness for the period, and other times do Compassion/Lovingkindness for the period. Some meditators also like to begin every period with some Compassion/Lovingkindness meditation even if their main time is planned to be on the breath or other subjects. Others will end every sit with a few minutes. And there are some who will begin and end every sit that they do with some Compassion/Lovingkindness meditation.

This is also a technique which can help if you are trying to watch your breathing and a strong hindrance or wandering thought keeps coming back again and again, even if you are trying to just note them and return to the breath. If you find this is happening then you can change your object of meditation; let go of trying to watch your breathing and change into Compassion/Lovingkindness meditation concerning the different thoughts that are coming about so strong.

Perhaps doing some Compassion/Lovingkindness toward the people who are involved in the thoughts. Or to yourself because you have this particular problem at this time. You could then expand and consider the other meditators who have similar problems. Expanding again, you could consider other people, with similar problems who do not even know of any method to help themselves with these types of problems.

As you have changed your object of meditation into Compassion/Lovingkindness you may find that after some period of time, the thoughts and emotions which were giving you a lot of difficulty in the beginning have somehow gone away or faded. And that you are now a bit more relaxed toward them. If you find this happening you may then return to the breathing or, if you wish, continue with Compassion/Lovingkindness.

We would also like to encourage you to use this type of meditation when you are lying down, going to sleep. It has been written in many meditation books and has been the experience of many meditators that if a person develops Compassion and Lovingkindness strongly enough within themselves then certain benefits will come to that person. Among these benefits is the ability to fall asleep easily, wake up easily, and dream few, if any, unpleasant dreams.

Please keep in mind...I am not saying that you can go to bed tonight, do this type of meditation and not have any unpleasant dreams...what I said was "that if a person develops Compassion and Lovingkindness strongly enough within themselves then certain benefits will come to that person." As people change their life style, often they will find that the more peaceful they are in the daytime, the more peaceful will be their sleep and dreams.

Regarding sleeping and dreams: Many people who experience a nightmare or any type of agitating, disturbing dream often find that this affects their mental state for hours after they wake up, and sometimes even for a whole day or more.

If you have any disturbing dream, we recommend that as soon as you wake up, you do this type of meditation toward all of the different people and/or other beings who were in your dream, even if you do not know their names and only vaguely remember their faces.

As well, do some Compassion/Lovingkindness meditation toward yourself at that time. Then do some Compassion/Lovingkindness meditation to all the other people around the world who may be experiencing a nightmare or disturbing dream right at that moment. You may find that this helps you to lessen or let go of some of the anxiety or agitation that is present.

This type of meditation is also a technique which does not have to be done in only a "formal" meditation environment. In simple words, this is just a type of thinking. You can use this at any moment of the day. Any time that you are getting annoyed at someone else, you can reflect similar to how we reflected on our difficult people. Any time that you are getting annoyed at yourself, you can reflect on the segment about yourself. It is probable, too, that you can add more similar thoughts to the ones that I have given here tonight.

If you start to become more aware of the aversions in your life, from the slightest irritations to the most intense anger, and if you try to use reflections similar to those given here, then these reflections can help to remove these aversions. They can all fade away with the use of Compassion and Lovingkindness.

Anger and aversion normally disturb our Peace and Happiness, and disturb the Peace and Happiness of others. Compassion and Lovingkindness normally help to develop our Peace and Happiness, and help to develop the Peace and Happiness of others. The energy of anger and aversion may be strong, but we can bend this unwise energy into the wise energy of Compassion and Lovingkindness.

May each of us grow in Compassion and Lovingkindness.

# MID-MORNING DAY FOUR

# V.R. AND V.V.

This morning I would like to remind all of you about the Five Hindrances. I talked in depth about them two nights ago. Now you have had more time to practice, experience them, and perhaps understand them a little more. Remember there is sense desire, aversion, sloth and torpor, restlessness and worry, and doubt.

I'm going to talk more about the process of noting and investigation, in order to let go of attachment to some of the hindrances. This may help prevent you from building either aversion towards or indulgence in the hindrances, and instead help you develop understanding of the Law of Cause and Effect within.

In learning this process we are able to transform the stress and suffering arising from the hindrances into valuable understanding.

The process can be compared a bit to gardeners who want to grow vegetables. They go out into their garden and see weeds growing among the vegetables. So they pull the weeds out, but they don't throw the weeds away. They put the weeds on their compost heap, make sweet compost, and then feed it back to the vegetables.

In the same way, if we learn to investigate in an objective way, anything that arises can be used to help the growth of Compassionate Understanding. Instead of rejecting the stress and suffering in the body and mind, it can be the spark for increasing Compassion and Wisdom, a way to glimpse the deeper truth behind the mind/body process.

An important first step in this process is objective awareness, the attitude of non-rejection, non-attachment, and the willingness to use the investigative quality of the mind. The investigative quality is a step further than objective awareness, and is a means to develop wisdom.

So if a hindrance arises, we try not to push it away, hating its presence, suppress it or indulge it. This prevents us from learning from and transforming it.

The first step is to simply note what is present. For some energies this may be enough. If we note what is present, and if the mind is truly objective, the thought will pass away, or pass through. At this time, we see the impermanent, impersonal nature of the thought.

If, however, there is a strong attachment, the thought will not pass away, or if it does, it comes back quickly. Although not enough to truly let go, noting does give a little space in the mind, making it possible to step back a little. Then the mind jumps back in again. At this point we need to understand more deeply the result of attachment. This is in order to use the stress present, to give rise to understanding, that is, "using the weeds."

So if a strong hindrance, such as aversion, fear, worry, restlessness or strong craving, is present, we bring awareness to the body. Scan the body, and observe the tightness, the tension, the stress present in the body. Continue to observe it, *without* trying to make the uncomfortable feeling pass away or disappear. This is quite important. Continue to observe the feeling without trying to *make it go away*.

Remember the phrase: "Not the story, but the feeling," to aid you to bring awareness to the feeling arising in the body.

Well, some people may express "How is this going to help me find peace, to look at stress and suffering arising in the body? How is this going to help me let go? Don't I have to resolve the story?"

Perhaps this analogy will help: Suppose there is a room with no windows and only one door. You go into the room, lock the door and then slide the key out under the door.

In the room is a fireplace and lots of matches, paper and wood. You think to yourself, "It would be fun to light a fire in here." So you put paper in the fireplace, pile wood on top and then light the paper. The fire starts to burn, and the flames get higher and higher.

"This is a lot of fun," you think, so you throw more wood on and the flames get higher and higher and higher.

You keep throwing on wood because it is so much fun until finally you realize, "Whew...it's really hot in there. I'd better open the windows. Oh! There are no windows. I'd better get out!" But you have locked the door and thrown away the key.

Now you are very afraid. You look at the fire and feel the heat, then you pick up a piece of wood and start beating the fire, saying, "Go out, go out, go out, go out, go out!" But the wood in your hand starts to burn and then it begins to burn your hand, so you throw the stick down and try to ignore it. But you've dropped the wood on the carpet and the carpet starts to burn. You smell the burning carpet and you realize that if you ignore it, the whole place will go up in flames. So you quickly push the stick into the fireplace, and jump up and down on the carpet to put it out. By this stage, you are *really hot!*

Now you realize, "This way isn't working. I will have to try to understand the nature of fire." So you step back from the fire as far as you can. You sit down. You resolve to just observe the fire. Well, it's still very hot because you have been feeding it for a long time. Yet now you resolve just to be *with the heat* and observe the fire.

After a while, it gets a bit cooler in the room—whew. Still you continue to just observe, not feeding the fire, not beating it. And slowly the room gets cooler and cooler.

If you observe the fire long enough without feeding it, what happens to the fire? It burns low and goes out by itself. You are left with a deeper understanding of the nature of fire. Fire burns from fuel. Not fed, it goes out.

In this same way, we can begin to understand suffering and its true cause: attachment to, and ignorance of, the nature of unbeneficial energies in the mind. With understanding arising, Compassion may arise for ourselves. And then the hindrances can be transformed.

With more subtle hindrances, such as desire, imagining, and planning, we may need to note them, and then reflect a little about the overall dissatisfaction it brings to the moment.

The moment just doesn't seem good enough, does it? We may be like people who want to get the dishes done really fast, so that they can get to the coffee. And all the time that they are doing the dishes, they hate the fact that they have to do the dishes. Finally, the dishes are over. "Glad that's over." They start to make the coffee. They smell the aroma. "Ahh! Wonderful!" They take the first sip, then they start thinking about the chocolate they'd like to have, or the movie they're going to see. And soon, the cup's empty. "Where did it go? Oh well, the chocolate..." They start eating the chocolate, they taste the first bite, and then they start thinking about the movie, "Well perhaps I don't want to see a movie anyway, I mean not much is on really. Maybe I'll just stay home and watch a video."

All the while, they push away the present, and imagine the sweetness in the future.

Or maybe you are like the people who are lying in their hammocks, at the beach. And all the time they're lying in the hammocks, they are thinking about going trekking in Chiang Mai, "Oh, it's going to be wonderful, all the hill-tribe people, it's going to be such a wonderful experience."

They plan it right down to the very last detail. Then they travel to Chiang Mai, and go trekking. While trekking, they start thinking about going trekking in Nepal, in the Himalayas, "It must be more beautiful up there, the mountains are bigger, the snow..."

They start planning their trekking experience in Nepal. Finally they get to Nepal, and they're trekking in the Himalayas, but they start thinking about going back home, "Oh, it's going to be so wonderful to see everybody, I haven't seem them for such a long time. It's just going to be great!"

We start to glimpse dissatisfaction and its true cause: craving, ignorance of the nature of these energies, and the result of attaching to them.

I would like to mention briefly two particular obstacles which many meditators experience while in retreat.

One of these concerns the hindrance of sense desire. This is the desire that builds the V.R. or the Vipassana Romance. At the beginning of the retreat many of you managed to talk with the other meditators here. Some may not have had this opportunity, but now we are all silent. We are trying to concentrate on our movements, on the breath, etc.

Yet, occasionally in retreat people may let their eyes wander to other meditators. They may get drawn to that particular person who attracts them the most—their "potential partner!" They may manage even to make eye contact. This may excite them with the hope that it is mutual; "They are attracted also!" Even if no eye contact is made, it may not prevent them from continuing to build the V.R.

They may manage to come close to this person while walking back into the hall for the next sitting, or in the dishwashing line, or food line. Then they may begin to "seek-out" the sight of them to see how they are doing, watch how they sit, walk, move, do the exercises.

They may get lost thinking about how "perfect" they would be together. "Both meditators, both travelers, we have so much in common. I wonder what else she/he is 'into'." They may start to build their wonderful future together. Or they may simply develop wishful thinking that they could have a future together. They may get lost in daydreams of "if only," or imagine other wonderful romantic situations and pleasant sensations.

Some meditators experience the V.R., the Vipassana Romance, so intensely during a retreat that they even plan the wedding! Right down to the fine details of whom they will invite, what time of the year would be best, etc., before they are able to realize what their mind has created.

Desire is a powerful energy. So, if you get caught in this energy, try to smile at the mind. Realize that you are lost in desire, and try to come back to the breath, your actions, your movements. Try to resist the impulse to gaze around. When desire arises, watch it, recognize it. Try to let go, each time that it pulls you off balance.

The second obstacle concerns the hindrance of aversion. As with the V.R., the Vipassana Romance, people can very easily get lost in the V.V., the Vipassana Vexation. It may start out with a slight irritation at others' restlessness, because they come into the hall late, making a lot of noise, or they leave the hall early, stomping down the stairs, putting on their shoes and stomping away—flip, flop, flip, flop, flip, flop.

Maybe they have particular favorite walking tracks that they have been using all the time up until now. They go out at the end of the sitting, mindfully walking, eyes downcast, in the direction of the track. They are almost there and they look up—the others are using "their" walking tracks!

Perhaps they have favorite spots in the hall. One morning they come in, with their sitting mat, start to go to their place, and "the others" are already sitting there! Agitation and annoyance may arise at these times.

Some may continually take a long time in the food line, or take a lot of food. They may become impatient with them; "They don't have to do things that slowly to be mindful, especially when everyone is waiting to eat!" or "They are so greedy!"

After a while they may start to "focus-in" on a particular meditator, or maybe more than one, who continually irritate them. Then they may start to find fault with all that they do; judging and commenting on the way they dress, wear their hair, walk, eat, and so on.

Or, as I mentioned the other night, the Vipassana Vexation may be directed at yourself; "I can't meditate, all I have is frustration and pain. Everyone else can meditate—I can't. Everybody looks like they're so 'in-to-it'—What's the matter with me?!"

Try to step back and recognize these hindrances when they have arisen and try to let them go. If you cannot let go, try to investigate and open to their energies. See how they affect the mind and body. In clearly seeing the stress and unsatisfactoriness, Compassion may arise for yourself and the obvious difficulties you are experiencing within yourself by attachment to this state of mind. Compassionate Understanding of your conditioning and your stress will help you to gently let go.

Try to resist the impulse to gaze around. And with the V.R. and V.V. you can realize that they are common experiences. Try to smile at this tendency if you are experiencing it. Try to remember that the mind is a product of conditioning; that by recognizing it, stepping back and letting it go, we are creating new conditioning, little-by-little, bit-by-bit. Try to do it gently, with Compassion.

**For this morning's meditation, I would like to start with a guided Compassion/Lovingkindness meditation.** After I finish the guided part, I'd like you to expand this meditation on your own for the rest of the period. This is so that you can gain experience in trying to do it on your own without having it guided.

Please settle yourself into the posture if you have not already done so. Try to make yourself as comfortable as possible. If pain arises in the body it may be better to shift the posture, focusing the mind mostly on the feelings and thoughts you're trying to generate. Start with being aware of your breathing for a short while.

*****

Focus your thoughts toward yourself. Reflect about and bring to mind some of your difficulties, failures or obstacles.

*****

Realizing you may have failed in the past, in your own eyes or in the eyes of others, try now to reflect on the power of the forces of conditioning. How difficult it is sometimes to understand and let go of negative, destructive energies, and to rise beyond them.

*****

May I be able to see that in holding onto self-hatred and judgment, I hold onto pain and my failures, making it difficult to grow beyond them.

*****

Realizing the limitations of my understanding, the pain of self-hatred and judgment, may I learn to forgive myself.

*****

Allow the healing energy of Compassion to arise for yourself. Allow the energy of Compassionate Softness to gently surround and dissolve the painful feelings of lack, and the harshness of self-judgment...heal the pain.

*****

In the warmth of Compassion and Lovingkindness may I learn to accept myself, forgive myself, and grow beyond my limitations.

*****

May I be able to let go of anger, fear, worry and ignorance. May I also have patience, courage, wisdom and determination to meet and overcome difficulties and problems, challenges in life.
    May I find peace of mind.

*****

Direct your thoughts to your parents or a special relative. Perhaps visualize them in front of you. Think of some of their difficulties, problems, failures, and challenges.

*****

Reflect on how difficult it may be for them to understand and let go of negative energies and to rise beyond them.

*****

Allow the spacious energy of Compassion to arise for your parents or special relative. May they be able to learn self-acceptance and forgiveness. In the warmth of Compassion and Lovingkindness may they grow beyond their limitations.

*****

May my parents be able to let go of anger, fear, worry and ignorance. May they also have patience, courage, wisdom and determination to meet and overcome difficulties and problems, challenges in life.
    May my parents find peace of mind.

*****

Now direct your thoughts to one or more of your friends. Reflect on some of their difficulties, obstacles, and challenges.

*****

Allow the spacious energy of Compassion to arise for them. May they learn self-acceptance and forgiveness. In the warmth of Compassion and Lovingkindness may they be able to grow beyond their limitations.

*****

May my friends be able to let go of anger, fear, worry and ignorance. May they also have patience, courage, wisdom and determination to meet and overcome difficulties and problems, challenges in life.

May my friends find peace of mind.

*****

Direct your thoughts to your teachers or to those people who have helped you or taught you something valuable in your life.

*****

Reflect that they may still have trouble understanding, letting go of attachment to negative energies, rising to their challenges or forgiving themselves for their shortcomings.

*****

Allow the spacious energy of Compassion to arise for them. In the warmth of Compassion and Lovingkindness may they grow beyond their limitations.

*****

May those who have helped me be able to let go of anger, fear, worry and ignorance. May they also have patience, courage, wisdom and determination to meet and overcome difficulties and problems, challenges in life.

May those who have helped me find peace of mind.

*****

Continue to expand the meditation in this way, thinking of other people, other living beings, reflecting on their difficulties and problems, in order to get to the feeling of Compassion within, and then wishing them Lovingkindness, the wish for their inner Peace of Mind.

*****

(end of period)

This morning we will be adding another special mindfulness activity. The reason that we are emphasizing these, is so you can practice bringing mindfulness, awareness into your everyday life activities. Then when you leave this retreat, you do not have to consider that meditation is only sitting down on a pillow or mat watching your breathing, walking back and forth, or standing still. Instead, you can think that you can use mindfulness in your everyday activities, strengthening your awareness and understanding throughout the day.

The first morning we asked you to try to be aware of opening doors, going through the doorways, and closing doors. Yesterday we asked you to try to be aware of washing your dishes.

Today we are asking you to try to pay extra special attention to putting on and taking off your shoes. Here we are usually taking them off and putting them on very frequently. As well, we ask you to try to pay extra special attention to walking up the stairs to the meditation hall, and walking down the stairs.

So there is taking off your shoes, and walking up the steps to the hall. Then when you leave, walking down the stairs and putting on your shoes. If you wish, you can use mental noting, trying to get close to each movement.

Becoming aware of the body helps you to come closer to realizing what is going on in the mind.

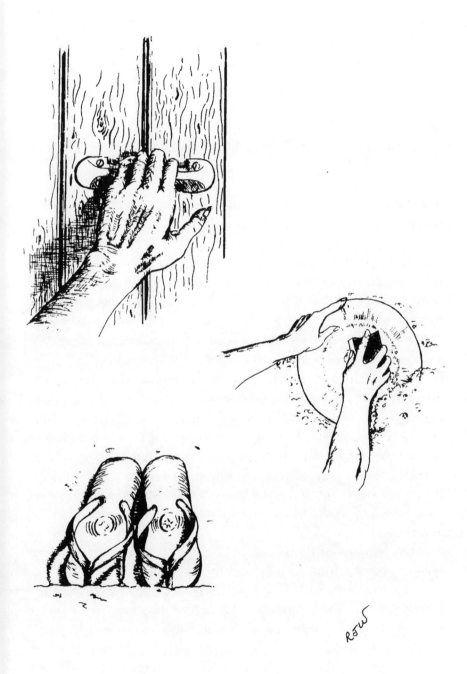

# EVENING DAY FOUR

## UNPLEASANT PHYSICAL SENSATIONS

Tonight's talk will be concerned with unpleasant physical sensations, and how we can work with them, using them as an aid to further our growth of Compassionate Understanding and Wisdom.

All of you probably have experienced many, many types of physical pain. These would include cuts, scrapes, sore muscles, coughs, colds, headaches, sprained ankles, broken bones, sickness, illness and so on. Every part of our body can experience physical pain.

Often when we start to do a meditation retreat, we experience quite a bit of physical discomfort and pain. This may frequently arise in the knees, the hips, the back, the neck, the shoulders. Sometimes it may seem that the whole body is full of pain.

Why does this happen?

One reason is that this type of sitting posture is not what most of you are used to. Sitting in this way, then standing, walking, sitting, standing, walking, sitting. In this aspect, to be able to sit comfortably is similar to learning a new sport. It takes time to learn a proper way of sitting, and to build enough endurance to be able to sit for longer and longer periods.

Occasionally the thoughts may come; "Oh...wouldn't it be nice to have a big soft lounge chair, now then I could sit still for 45 minutes." Or the thoughts; "Why can't I do lying down meditation, then I could stay still for 45 minutes." Or maybe the thoughts; "I wish I had bigger pillows, then I could sit still for 45 minutes."

Actually, no matter what posture you take, no matter how soft or comfortable the pillows or chairs or beds, if you try to stay still for a certain amount of time, then unpleasant sensations will automatically arise in parts of your body. This has been continuously happening to us all of our life. But most of us have never taken the time and effort to examine this.

Here at a meditation retreat, we have a lot of time to learn about unpleasant physical sensations. In fact, understanding and dealing with pain is a major part of Mental Development. Pain, in some form or another, is a key aspect of life to which we are continually reacting, often in unbeneficial ways. If we can understand pain and understand our reactions to pain, then we will be in a much better position to gain Peace and Contentment.

During meditation practice, we may experience two types of physical pain. One is a real, actual pain, coming from an injury or illness. The other we call a "meditation pain." One stays with us after we get up from sitting meditation, and the other goes away.

If you have a real, actual pain, shifting your posture while you are doing sitting meditation may relieve the unpleasantness for awhile, but it will not disappear totally. However if you have a meditation pain, then it normally will disappear with the changing of posture.

It is very important to recognize the difference between these two types of pain. If we have a pulled muscle in our leg, the actual pain in the leg may cause us to shift the leg periodically during meditation. This may continue for many days until the pulled muscle is healed.

A meditation pain may have the same unpleasant sensations as a pulled muscle, but when we shift the leg, the painful sensations disappear.

Learning to work with these meditation pains can be very valuable and can teach us a lot about ourselves. If we continually shift our posture every time that we experience a meditation pain, then it will disappear and we will not get the opportunity to learn from it.

Some people feel that if pain comes while they are meditating, then there must be something wrong, that there has been a mistake. Yet, whenever we try to stay still, this is a natural process of our body; it is not a mistake. Our bodies have been continually producing painful sensations to which we have been continually reacting.

With Vipassana-type meditation practices, we can build awareness of these sensations for the development of Insight and Understanding. Also, we can build awareness of our reactions to these sensations for this same development.

Once you realize which types of pain are only meditation pains, you can then gradually learn how to sit still while you are experiencing a meditation pain, and you will be able to gain this valuable Understanding.

I would now like to explain some techniques that can be used to help you understand more about these meditation pains. We do not recommend using these techniques if you are doing Compassion/ Lovingkindness meditation (or any other reflection meditation). In that case, we recommend changing your posture, letting the meditation pains go away, and continuing with the Compassion/Lovingkindness meditation. However, if you are watching the breathing and an unpleasant physical sensation develops, then the use of these techniques can be very valuable to help you understand more about yourself, and about how you react to life in general.

First, when a meditation pain comes and distracts the attention away from the breath, try to treat it just like a wandering thought. Try just to realize that there exists this unpleasant sensation and then gently return to the breath. Try not to react to the unpleasantness and try not to shift the posture. If you are using mental noting, you could just note "sensation, sensation" or something similar.

Please be very objective with what word you use to note the unpleasant physical sensation. If we note, "pain, pain," it automatically implies we have aversion to it. If we note, "sensation, sensation," it is much more objective.

To give you an example of what I mean: suppose we have a loved one and they come to us and stroke our arm...it feels pleasant. Suppose they continue stroking our arm for four hours!! In the beginning we label it "pleasant," but after four hours we will label it "pain." In both cases it is a "sensation." Try to be objective with the noting. "Sensation, sensation" is very objective.

This may be enough; often the sensation will go away by itself. If not, within a short time, the sensation may distract the attention a second time. Again, try to just note that the sensation exists and then return gently to the breathing. Try not to have aversion toward the unpleasantness. Allow it to be simply as it is, and return again to the main concentration object of observing the breath. Try to do this each time that the sensation distracts the attention.

For most of us, there will be a limit to how many times we can simply note that the unpleasant sensation is present and return to the breath without reacting. Depending on our experience level, we will be able to see the sensation and return to the breath calmly, just so many times, before aversion toward the sensation will arise in the mind.

Then we get all sorts of thoughts. We don't like it, we want it to go away; "Here I am trying to concentrate on my breathing and here is this unpleasant sensation bothering me! Why doesn't it go away?" Or the thoughts may come, "Why me?! Everyone else is sitting like little Buddhas and here I am with all this pain. Why me?"

On and on, our thoughts will sometimes go wild, building and building aversion toward the sensation until finally, we feel that we have just had enough, and we shift our posture. And the sensation goes away.

We certainly do not encourage self-torture, but we do encourage you to try to calmly note the unpleasant sensation and return to the breath as many times as you can. Also, we do not encourage building up aversion and more aversion toward an unpleasant sensation.

Many people will change their posture each time that they get an unpleasant sensation. But we have some other techniques for you to try. These techniques can help you to understand these sensations and use the experience for valuable growth.

The first new technique is to change your primary object of attention away from the breath and focus directly on the unpleasant sensation. Gently soften your awareness around the sensation, trying to keep an open, investigating mind, wishing to learn about the sensation. What is this thing that we normally call "pain"? What is the reality of it? Not just what we *think* it is, but the true reality of it.

Try to examine the sensation in every different way that you can. What is the actual sensation like? Is it hard or soft, heavy or light, burning or cold, pinching, poking, whatever? Try to see very closely the physical characteristics of the sensation.

It may feel like something is pushing into us or squeezing us or other such feelings that are similar to real actual pains that we have experienced in everyday life. Whatever this so-called painful unpleasant sensation is, try to see all of the characteristics concerning it.

Try to see where the sensation is, the exact location. Often we say that we have a pain in the knee. Is it in all of the knee or just part of the knee? The front of the knee or the back of the knee? Sometimes we think that we have a pain in the shoulder, but when we investigate, we may find that really it is in the neck, not actually in the shoulder. Try to locate the sensation exactly where it is.

Try to see its shape, its size. Is it round, is it stretched out? Is it large, is it small? Try to see whether the sensation is made up of different parts. If there seems to be a center spot of more intense sensation and less intense sensations around this center, then try to focus your attention on the center. Perhaps there will be a few spots of intense sensation; if there are a few, then just pick one of them and focus on that one.

Sometimes the spot of intense sensation that you are watching will move. If this happens, then try to follow the sensation as it moves. At times the sensation will shift around in a certain area. At other times the sensation may disappear and seem to arise in a new location.

Another characteristic that can be observed is the changes of intensity that occur within the sensation. The so-called painful unpleasantness may be stronger at one time than at other times. It may be possible to see a type of vibration within the intensity.

When I ring the bell (bell is rung)…Can you hear the wavelike vibration of the sound? (bell is rung again)…. In a similar way, it may be possible for you to observe the wavelike vibration of the unpleasant sensation.

Moment-by-moment watching, observing, trying to learn, trying to understand; "What is this?" Watch the sensation as it changes size, shape, location, intensity. Watch the impermanent nature of the sensation as it arises, exists for a while, and passes away in various different ways.

Try to continue watching as best you can, trying to treat the sensation with interest instead of aversion, with a wishing to learn about it rather than a wishing that it was not there. Occasionally this sensation will disappear by itself. If this happens, then return to trying to concentrate on the breathing.

What we are trying to do with this sensation is to understand not only the sensation itself, but also our reactions to the sensation. We are trying to change reactions of aversion and hatred into reactions of inquiry, interest, acceptance and patience; through Understanding, using Mindfulness as well as we can, to look closely at the sensation.

Watch it arise, watch it exist, and watch it change and/or disappear. We are getting to know the sensation as another impermanent experience that we encounter in life. And we can learn how to have Peace of Mind, even though we have an unpleasant experience.

At first, we label this sensation as "pain." But if we can build our ability to concentrate on the sensation directly, we can see that the word "pain" may no longer apply. It is possible to see the sensation as just a sensation, without the thoughts of "pain" surrounding the sensation.

Often in life we label this "pain," that "pain," this "unpleasant," that "unpleasant," this "bad," that "bad." How often have we labeled things in this way only to change our opinions at some later date? Many times in our lives when we first encounter something, we label it a certain way and later discover that our first perception was not correct.

Within this meditation practice, we are trying to see things the way they actually are, the reality of a certain object, and not just our views and opinions about the object.

With patience and perseverance, we can understand more and more about these meditation sensations. Like everything, this takes practice and with time, our Understanding will grow.

As we each have our own energy and concentration levels, at some point in watching the sensation in this way, we will get tired and our concentration will weaken. This is normal for most of us. At that time, the sensation may be too unpleasant and the aversions toward the sensation will arise. As well there may be other thoughts such as fear and worry in relationship to the sensation. At this time many meditators will change posture, but we have some more techniques for you to try.

Just as we changed our primary object of concentration from the breathing to the sensation, we can also change our concentration to observe these thoughts of aversion, fear, worry as they manifest in our body. Rosemary and I have already talked a bit about dealing with aversion.

The physical reactions can be observed. Tightening of muscles in different parts of the body, such as; hands, stomach, chest, neck, face, eyes, lips, teeth. Also the breath may change and sometimes our heartbeat will change noticeably as well. Many different tensions in the body may come about when the mind has thoughts of aversion, fear or worry.

Run your attention through the body from your feet to your head, from your head to your feet. If your body is bent over, hold the posture and feel it for exactly what it is. Feel the squeezing, and pulling, and twisting, whatever it is. Note it clearly and after you have felt and noted each part then sit up straight. Relax in the posture again. If you find your hand is closing into a fist; note it, open your hand, perhaps wiggle the fingers and then settle the hand again. If you find your teeth clenched tight; note it, then open the mouth, separate the teeth, relax the area. When the eyes are found tight and perhaps the forehead frowning; note this, open the eyes, gently close them again.

By turning your attention to parts of the body and trying to examine again with interest and investigation, we will be providing the mind with an opportunity to let go of the thoughts of aversion, etc. At the same time, we will be learning about the relationship between thoughts and emotions in the mind with reactions in the body.

This understanding of the relationship between thoughts and emotions in the mind with physical reactions in the body is very important. In formal meditation periods, we can see this relationship better because we have less outward distractions. As we quiet and calm the mind we get to see aversion, hatred, worry, restlessness, doubt, etc., as they affect the mind and as they affect the body.

In everyday life, seeing the hindrances in the mind is not as easy, but we can use our awareness of body reactions to help see our thoughts and emotions more clearly. Often when the hindrances arise, they make a "cloud" in the mind and we can be affected by them very easily due to our past conditioning. If we have developed strong mindfulness of the body and of our physical reactions, then this will aid us greatly in letting go of the hindrances.

An example: Suppose we are in a restaurant eating with some friends. A person whom we do not like walks into the restaurant. Aversion arises within us toward this person but we do not see it because we are busy eating and talking with our friends. Also, the aversion has created a bit of a cloud in our mind.

But with aversion in the mind, the body may start to react with tightening and tensions, thus becoming uncomfortable. Our speech may become affected also and we may even display our discomfort to our friends by saying things that disturb them.

If we have practiced mindfulness of the body enough, then within some period of time we will become aware of the unpleasant feelings in the body. Realizing that our body has become uncomfortable we may think, "Why am I feeling so uncomfortable? What is happening here?" At that moment there is a clear seeing, a moment of clear Awareness, Mindfulness, and the cloud in the mind is not so strong. Depending on our level of Understanding, we may be able to see that the physical discomfort has come from the aversion in the mind.

Having now seen the aversion in the mind, as well as the agitation and unpleasantness that has come with the aversion, we then can work toward letting go of this aversion. This is an example of the importance of being able to investigate and understand the physical reactions in the body coming from the thoughts and emotions in the mind. So by examining the physical reactions that come from aversion, worry, fear concerned with the meditation pains, we gain valuable Understanding that will help us find deeper Peace and Balance in our life.

Basically the aversion, fear, worry, etc. had arisen from the thoughts about the unpleasant physical sensation. By continuing thoughts about the sensation in this way, we continue to "feed" the aversions, etc. By changing our attention away from the unpleasant sensation to the physical reactions coming from the aversions, etc., we can stop feeding these unbeneficial thoughts. By doing this, it is possible that the aversions, etc. will pass away by themselves. Also the sensation may pass away, and we can return to the breath.

These are a few ways of trying to work with the so-called meditation pains. Try to understand and be able to see these things as just sensations, coming and going in their own time. Try to avoid the extra concept of pain and the aversions and worries that may arise.

As I said earlier, each one of us will have different levels of ability in dealing with these meditation sensations. What do we do when we reach our limits, and the aversions, worries, fears toward the unpleasant sensation are just too much?

Often at this time, many meditators will change their posture. But we have a little bit more for you to try.

Before shifting posture, try to sit still for just one more minute. Just one, or maybe just 30 seconds. Try to sit still just a little bit more...at least 10 more breaths. Breathing in, breathing out, rising, falling, try at least 10 more.

Then, when you are done with these 10 breaths, check to see if the sensation is still there, and whether or not you still wish to change your posture. If you still want to change posture, then gently note to yourself; and this is very important; gently note to yourself that you have worked as hard as you can at that time and rather than building more and more aversions, you will change your posture and start again on the breathing.

This can be a *very* important aid. Gently acknowledge to yourself that you have dealt with this sensation as well as you feel able to at this time. And rather than build up more and more aversion and frustration, you are going to shift posture and then begin again on the breath.

In this way, you are acknowledging your limits in the present which are due to conditioning of your past. And yet, in this process of observing the sensation for as long as possible at that time, you will be developing new conditioning that will help you in the future to understand more about these meditation sensations and your reactions to them.

Gently, gently; we are not asking you to be supermen or superwomen. When you are working with your breathing and you are distracted by an unpleasant sensation, try to just note it and return to the breathing. After some time, if you find that the sensation is distracting the attention too much and you are starting to build aversion toward it, then change your attention to the actual sensation.

Try to see its characteristics. Its size, its shape, its location. The changes in intensity. Try to examine all that you can about this sensation with a soft, interested mind, open, inquiring, trying to learn about it. Trying not to have aversions towards it and wishing that it was not there. When the aversions and irritations become too strong, try to work with them as they are manifesting in the body.

Then when your energy and concentration levels are getting a bit too weak and you feel that you have had enough, try to sit still for just a little bit more, one minute, 30 seconds, maybe at least 10 more breaths, breathing in, breathing out, rising, falling. At that time, if you still wish to shift postures, gently note to yourself that you have worked with the sensation as best you can at that time, and rather than build more aversions and frustrations, that you will now shift posture and then start again watching the breathing.

When you are shifting posture, try to do it slowly and quietly, trying to be very mindful of each movement. Pay extra attention to the area where the sensation is and watch it carefully as it slowly changes in intensity and gradually passed away, then start again observing the breathing.

By dealing with these types of unpleasant meditation sensations in this way, we will be strengthening our ability to deal with any unpleasant situation of life. With less anger and aversion, irritation and annoyance. With more Patience, Acceptance, Equanimity and Understanding. Developing the ability to see things more clearly as to what they actually are and not just what we think they are.

Again, as I said earlier, there is one type of painful sensation in the body that comes from an actual pain or injury. And there is a second type of unpleasant sensation which is not an actual pain or injury that we call meditation pain. The techniques that I have just talked about are for working with the second type, the meditation pain.

Before you start using these techniques, please be certain that you are working with the meditation pain. If you try to use these techniques on an actual pain while in sitting meditation, it is possible that you can cause some extra physical problems. If you are in doubt as to which type of pain you have, it is best to shift posture and see if it disappears. Get to know the difference, then you can try your best to work with these techniques.

There is one type of physical sensation which can arise during sitting meditation that for some meditators is pleasant and for other meditators is unpleasant. This is when parts of our body become numb or what we normally call "falling asleep." For some meditators, this happens from time-to-time. Often in the legs.

For those who experience this, it may occur for 5-10 minutes every once in a while just coming and going. However, there are a few meditators who experience this numbness for longer periods, sometimes with pain also. And sometimes there is worry and concern about the numbness.

If you happen to be one of these few meditators who have longer periods of numbness and you are concerned about it, then please inform us during the interviews. It is normally not a serious problem and it is possible that just a change in the sitting posture is all that is needed.

Often during meditation an itch will arise in parts of the body, and our first reaction is to scratch the itch. It is possible to use these techniques with the itch. Unless it is a rash or fungus infection, etc., then itches are just small irritations which come and go. They do not last very long, and we do not have to scratch them in order for them to go away.

By not reacting and just watching the itch, you will be developing Understanding, Patience, Acceptance and other beneficial qualities. Just patiently watching the impermanence of the sensation as it comes, exists for a short time and then passes away. Obviously an itch is not an actual physical pain. It is just a physical sensation which comes and goes. We can use itches to help us in our meditation practice.

Insect bites are another type of physical sensation that we may experience during sitting meditation. And they often produce very strong reactions of aversion and hatred. In reality most insect bites are not very painful compared to so many of the other injuries and illness which we have experienced throughout life.

If we can be mindful and just watch, with Patience and Compassion, then we need not develop aversion and hatred. Compassion is very important here: Can we just sit and watch a sensation without making ourselves angry and upset? It is possible.

You may wish to wait to experiment with mosquitoes until you are back in your home country; but if you do try to become mindful of mosquitoes, you may discover that you get more upset when you hear the mosquito "buzzing" around you. Frequently, much more upset than when the mosquito actually "bites" you.

Once again, we are not advising you to perform self-torture nor try to be a super person. We don't encourage the building of aversion either. If insects are a bother to you, then we advise you to use an insect repellent. However, it is possible that the repellent will wear off while you are meditating or that the insects find an area where the repellent was not applied.

During those times, if you wish, you can try to use these techniques and observe the insect bite as just sensation, without the normal reactions of aversion. Watching it arise, watching it exist and watching it pass away. Gently, gently, try your best. This can be a very good part of our Mental Development practice which will help to build Patience, Acceptance, Compassion, Understanding, and other beneficial qualities.

Sleepiness is another often unpleasant physical sensation, especially when we want to stay awake, that may happen to us from time-to-time during the sitting meditation. And for many people when they are feeling sleepy in the sitting they develop a lot of aversion towards the sleepiness. It's possible to use these techniques when you're feeling sleepy.

For many meditators when they're feeling sleepy, it goes a little like this: They may be sitting there, the mind starts to drift and starts to get sleepy. The body starts to move over. It gets just so far and then we feel like falling. We bounce up and we hope nobody saw us. Many of you know this one, right?!

That's what happens to most people, but to work with it in this technique, it's like this: When you do find you're falling asleep and drifting over and you get to that point and you jerk, stay there. "But everybody will see me!" It's okay, everybody else is getting the same teaching. Hold the posture where you jerk. Normally for many people, it is impossible in the beginning, they jerk and bounce straight up. Okay. Put yourself back to where you thought it was. (Sounds crazy, right?!) Hold the posture in this way wherever you thought it was, and feel each part of the posture. Note it clearly. Feel the tightening and stretching, whatever it is, all through the body, the arms squeezing, whatever it is. Note each part however long it takes. Hold the posture there.

After you have done this, sit up and relax in the posture. Perhaps you fall asleep again in five or ten minutes. When you do, if you can, hold the posture. If you bounce up, put yourself back. Note every part, feel it clearly as best you can. In this way, we will be developing the awareness of what a bent over posture feels like compared to sitting up straight. If you think sitting up straight in meditation is painful, try being bent over for forty-five minutes! We start to realize that bent over is a painful posture, sitting up straight is much more pleasant.

After doing this thirty or forty times, (maybe it will take longer, maybe shorter), at some point what is going to happen is this: we are falling asleep, we are drifting off and we are starting to lean over, we get about ninety percent of the whole distance and all of a sudden we feel the stomach tightening. It's like an alarm clock and it wakes us up, "Ding, ding, ding,"—"I hurt," whatever. It wakes us up before we go all the way down and jerk. At ninety percent hold the posture. Feel every muscle, note it clearly. After you are done, sit up, relax in the posture. Perhaps you can understand what will happen now. Maybe we fall asleep in the future, we get about eighty percent of the way, we might feel another muscle stretching. It wakes us up. Slowly we develop this understanding. If we develop it strongly enough, there may come a point where we are sitting in meditation, we start to fall asleep and drift, the head moves maybe half an inch or so and we feel it. It wakes us up. It is very valuable to use these techniques with sleepiness. There is no need to have aversion to it anymore. You can use it in your practice helping you in many ways.

If you are feeling hot during your meditation, then you can also apply these same techniques to the sensations experienced. Rather than having aversion to the heat, we can develop an interest in the slight changes of temperature, such as, when a soft breeze enters the hall. Or, we can try to calmly watch the drips of perspiration as they move along our body. Trying to stay peaceful even though we experience what is normally an "unpleasant" situation.

So these are some ways to work with many of the different types of unpleasant sensations that you may experience while you are doing your formal meditation practice. *Changing your attitude.* Letting go of aversion, fears, and worries. With experience, you will also find that these same methods can be applied in everyday life to help gain Peace and Understanding.

Many of us have experienced some sort of accident or illness during our lives that produced very intense, unpleasant physical sensations. Broken bones, burns, cuts, sprains, etc., are common results of accidents. Illness include a vast range from diarrhea to cancer, each producing its own level of unpleasant physical sensations.

Often when we first become ill or injured, we have to deal with the situation without being able to escape from the unpleasantness and the pain. Even if there are drugs that will provide physical relief, it could be many minutes or hours before the drugs are available or, in rare cases, even days. And if the medicines are used there will probably be periods of time when their effectiveness starts to wear off or disappears entirely. These are times when it is of great benefit to be able to deal with unpleasant physical sensations with a calm, patient mind.

So our practice in formal meditation with observing and watching the meditation pains (that is, those painful-like sensations that are not actual physical pains) helps us to develop the ability to deal with the actual physical pains that we encounter in life from time to time.

Working with meditation pains will help us to have a calmer, clearer, more peaceful mind whenever we have real, actual pains. We can learn to see sensation as just sensation, without the agitation, fear and worry that often comes with an unpleasant physical sensation.

We can discover that we do not have to "run away" from every unpleasant sensation that we experience. We do not have to become upset, angry or sad. Perhaps we will discover that we do not need as many pain-relieving drugs as we once believed we needed. How often do people use drugs when it may not be necessary? Instead, we may be able at times to relieve ourselves with the use of our inner abilities.

This type of practice, of seeing sensation as just sensation, is helping us to see the reality of life, the reality of sensation. We may discover that in a similar way to finding more Peace of Mind with unpleasant physical experiences, we can find more Peace of Mind with unpleasant mental experiences.

We do not have to have aversion, fear, worry or agitation when we encounter unpleasant mental experiences. Can we see an unpleasant mental experience simply as an experience and as another opportunity to learn and to grow?

We do not have to run away from difficulties in the mind. Can we open to them? Can we try to understand them? Can we see them as a challenge and not as a problem?

If we suppress any unpleasant mental experience, turn away from it, become upset and disturbed at its presence, then we may miss a valuable opportunity for the growth of Wisdom and Compassionate Understanding.

If you become very restless during parts of the day, do you find yourself starting to dislike those periods of the day? Do you find yourself wanting to "escape"; go to the toilet, get a drink, go to your room?

Can you try to open to the restlessness, to the aversion, to the doubts or other hindrances in ways that Rosemary and I have explained? Investigating these hindrances as they are manifesting in the body.

Getting to know and understand their energies. And being able to have a Peace and Contentment within, lessening our problems and difficulties. So much of this practice is learning how to work with restlessness, anger, doubt, etc. and then transforming them, learning how to let them go.

If you want your restlessness, you can keep it. If you want your anger, you can keep it. If you want your doubt, you can keep it. But this would normally mean that you do not understand what it is that we are trying to teach.

Sometimes there are a few people doing our retreats or reading our books who are not clear on what it is we are teaching. And there may even be one or two people who think that the development of Compassion and Mindfulness has no real application in normal, everyday life—that it just doesn't help in any way.

And the thoughts may come, "Well, so what if I become more compassionate and loving. Won't change the world! I'll go back home and everyone else will still be aggressive and hate me. What good is it?" Or the thoughts, "This is just some Eastern Asian philosophy. It won't work in the West!"

Well, we are not saying you can do a 10-day retreat and then go back home and fill everyone up with Compassion and Love. And that everybody, everything, will be loving and peaceful. We're not saying that. What we are teaching are methods to help develop *our own* minds, methods to help ourselves lessen *our own* difficulties. Methods to help *ourselves* to find more deep Peace and Balance within.

If you want your difficulties and problems, then that is your choice. But if you do not want your difficulties and problems, then try out these methods the best you can. Put forth the energy and effort.

This is a rare and wonderful opportunity that each one of you has, to be able to learn some of these techniques, to work on them, to develop them inside of yourselves. It is a precious time, a wonderful time, something that most people in the world may never get. Take advantage of this opportunity, this gift that you have given to yourself.

If you really want to have more Peace and Contentment within, and to lessen your problems and difficulties, then it is so very important that you stay open. Try these methods as best you can, put forth the effort and the energy. Try to let go of your views and opinions. Open to reality.

Some people who go to meditation centers have a very strong conditioning toward intellectual thinking, especially regarding Buddhism, meditation and other types of mental development practice. Usually these people have a whole collection of views and opinions about what they think meditation is or Buddhism is. They often are very proud of their book knowledge and thinking knowledge, and have very high opinions about themselves and their intellectual learning.

Usually, these types of people do very poorly with the methods we teach because they are not open. Learning these methods takes much hard work, and often is frustrating and difficult.

People who prefer intellectual learning to experiential understanding often would rather *think* about their views and opinions of the practice instead of actually *doing* the practice. Basically they have become too filled up with book and thinking knowledge. It is not possible for them to develop experiential understanding until they let go of their high opinion of themselves and their attachment to intellectual learning.

There is a little Buddhist story concerning this:

Once there was a person who had a lot of intellectual learning, book and thinking knowledge, and was very proud of it. One day this person went to visit a very famous Buddhist teacher—a very skilled teacher with profound Wisdom and Understanding.

The visitor expressed to the teacher the desire to learn what the teacher was teaching and followed this wish by asking many questions. The teacher answered each one.

Then a pattern developed. After each question and answer, the visitor would immediately come back with views and opinions about the topic with something like, "Yes, but don't you think such and such?" Or, "Yes, but I've read elsewhere this and that."

It soon became fairly obvious to the meditation teacher that this visitor was very fond of intellectual learning, and was very filled up with book and thinking knowledge. This was blocking understanding arising from what the teacher had to say. The visitor was closed, and could not receive the teaching from someone who had experiential understanding.

The teacher realized that this way of teaching was not going to produce any benefit. The teacher asked the visitor, "Would you like a cup of tea? This tea is very rare, not found in any store anywhere around the world. In fact, this tea is so rare, so special, it only grows in an area very close to here. As well, this tea is one of the most delicious teas in the world, and many people come from all over the world just to taste it. Would you like to have a cup of this tea?"

The visitor became quite interested and said, "Oh, yes, I'd love to have a cup of this tea."

The teacher then began to prepare the tea. With keen interest, the visitor saw tea leaves which were unlike any other tea leaves in the world. The tea started to simmer and the aroma filled the air. The visitor thought, "Oh, it's so sweet; it's such a pleasant smell. I can hardly wait to have a cup of this special tea."

When the tea was ready, the teacher put a little table in front of the visitor. On the table, the teacher placed two cups. One cup was empty but the other cup was filled with water right up to the top.

The visitor looked at this and thought, "Well, this is a bit odd, but I can hardly wait to have this cup of tea." Then the teacher put a cover on top of the cup that was full of water. The visitor looked at it and thought, "Well, this is even odder. But, oh well, fill up my empty cup and I'll drink the tea."

The teacher got the teapot and started pouring the tea. But instead of pouring the tea into the empty cup, the teacher poured the tea onto the cup that was full of water and had a lid on it. The tea went onto the lid, then spilled onto the table.

The teacher kept pouring and it went off the table onto the floor. And the teacher kept pouring...and pouring...and pouring.

The visitor got quite agitated and said, "What's wrong with you?

Are you crazy? Are you mad? What are you trying to do? You're wasting this special tea; you're pouring it on this cup that has a cover on it. You can't pour tea into this cup. You're spilling the tea—it's on the table, it's on the floor. This tea is so special that people come from around the world just to get it. It's wasteful what you are doing. Can't you see? You can't pour tea into this cup—it's full. It is closed. You can pour tea into the empty cup, that cup you can pour the tea into. Can't you see?"

The teacher stopped pouring and said to the visitor, "Yes, I do understand that trying to pour the tea into the cup that is full of water and has a cover over it is not possible. It's a waste of this special tea. But it would be possible to pour the tea into the empty cup."

The teacher then continued, "This cup that is full of water and is closed, this is like you. You are full of book knowledge, thinking knowledge. You are closed to my teachings.

"My teachings are special, they are rare. People come from all over to discover them. They are not found in any normal schools. But it is not possible for me to give you my teachings. If you want to receive my teachings, you must empty yourself of your attachment to your intellectual learning and your high opinion of yourself. Then I can give you my teachings."

Perhaps, needless to say, the same is true here. If you want to understand what we are teaching, then you have to be as open and as honest as you can.

As we continue with our meditation practice, we will be watching sensations as well as thoughts, as they arise, exist for some time and then pass away. They all seem to be impermanent; they have their own coming, being and going. Our overall existence is the same: we were born, we now have life and one day we will die.

As we watch this impermanence in our lives, in our experiences, in our sensations and in our thoughts, we will gain the Understanding that is necessary for developing more Equanimity, Peace and Contentment in our lives.

With practice and understanding of what we normally call "pain" in our meditation practice, we can be able to see "pain" simply as a sensation, as an experience arising, existing and passing away. In time our minds can develop the ability to stay calm and patient without the agitation, irritation, anxiety, worry, grief, frustration, sorrow or despair that often accompany illness, injuries and all types of unpleasant sensations and experiences.

With time, with patience, with practice, bit by bit, gently working with small things first, we build our Compassionate Understanding of life. With this Compassionate Understanding we may learn how to have a peaceful, calm, clear mind in any situation in life.

# EQUANIMITY

This morning I would like to give some more detailed instructions on sitting/standing meditation so that you may understand more clearly how you can be incorporating Mindfulness and Investigation into your meditation. And I will explain Equanimity in a little more depth.

As we have instructed you concerning the breath awareness meditation, begin the meditation by feeling the body sitting, or standing, grounding your awareness in the body in the moment. Run your attention through the body relaxing into the posture; either from the feet to the head in sitting, or from the head to the feet in standing. Gently take a few deep breaths and then allow the breath to become normal and natural again. Gently.

Awareness of the Breathing. Breathing in, breathing out, rising, falling.

Just as waves on the edge of the shore flow in and recede out; some long, some short. Try to just watch and not interfere, just observe.

When thoughts arise, gently note them and try to let go or let them pass through. Letting go, return to the breath. Thoughts and images arising and passing away—"bubbles in a stream"—insubstantial, floating through.

If you cannot let go or if the thoughts do not just float through; you start to jump in with involvement; try to note the mind state. Is it clouded by anger, desire, sadness? Note this. Be aware of it and try to let go of attachment, returning your awareness to the breathing, noting the mind states' impermanent, impersonal nature.

If the involvement continues, investigate. Try to investigate the objects in the mind. Angry thoughts, thoughts of worry, regret, doubt, clouds in the mind. First identify them and then investigate the characteristics of their energy. We are not going to investigate the details of the thoughts or what, who the thought is directed toward, or why we have thoughts such as these, or the story line.

This is important. If you become interested in the details, the object and all of the "whys" of the thoughts, then you will often only continue the thoughts or your attachment or aversion to the thoughts. Asking why is a bit like people on a beach who see a tidal wave coming. Then they just stand there and ask all sorts of questions such as, "I wonder why this tidal wave is coming? I wonder where it started? I wonder how long it's going to take to get here?" Rather than getting to high ground as fast as they can and observing it safely.

To investigate the characteristics of these energies, note their effect on the body. Is the body tight, tense? Note the changes in the breath. Has it shortened, has it become rougher? You can also watch the movement in the mind, from slight agitation to intense turbulence.

Try to step back from the attachment and involvement with the thoughts. Try to open to the stress, that these thoughts create. If you can do this, then Compassion may arise for the unsatisfactoriness and the stress that these thoughts produce, and it will be easier to let go.

When you let go, try to feel the spaciousness, the fading away of the stress at that moment. Experience a moment of cessation of the stress. The thoughts arise, they also pass away.

Emotions arising, passing away. Try to watch. Try to observe. Try to step back from continuing to feed them. This allows the old conditioning to hold less power over the mind and develops new conditioning of "non-resistance and non-clinging." It also helps us understand more clearly the nature of these thoughts as impermanent, unsatisfactory, and impersonal, they arise due to conditioning.

If noises arise, drawing the attention, try to note them, "hearing, hearing," and return to the breath. The same with odors, "smelling, smelling." They arise and pass away. If you start to have reactions and thoughts about them, then focus on these reactions. Try to identify the reactions, thoughts and then try to let go. Gently, return to the breath.

Feelings in the body may arise. If they draw the attention, note them, be aware of them and gently return to the breathing. If they continue to distract the attention, try to focus your attention on them. Soften into them and observe, investigate, watch. Try not to get caught up in reaction to them. Instead, try to watch, on a moment-to-moment basis.

Try to notice the sensation's inner characteristics. Is it expanding, contracting, burning, cold, ebbing, flowing, vibrating, whatever it is. Try to see the continual change within the sensation. Peaks of sensations, then fading away—valleys; to rise again—peaks; fading away—valleys.

Try to *rest* in the valleys. Try not to string the memory of the peaks together.

If the sensations recede in intensity or the mind is no longer reacting to them, return to the breath; breathing in, breathing out, rising, falling. Try not to get lost in sensation. As soon as you see a balance return in the mind then start again on the primary focus of the breathing. Sensations arise and pass away. Try to see that attachment causes the stress and suffering in the mind, and that the sensation and awareness of the sensation are different—not the same.

The body and the mind are in continual flux, change, arising and passing away. We try to watch and observe, attempting to develop a non-attached Awareness and Wisdom. We are trying to investigate into the nature of the body and the mind, and to come into harmony with this constant arising and passing away.

We are trying to develop a place of evenness and balance of mind, which is Equanimity. We are trying to develop the ability to feel this balance.

Equanimity is a peaceful, content mind. It is a factor of mind that allows us to be with everything that arises with balance. It allows us to investigate with a calm mind, neither pushing away nor claiming nor trying to manipulate experience to suit our selfish desires. Instead, Equanimity observes things as they are.

The calmness of Equanimity develops through the deepening of Compassionate Understanding. This is different from the calmness that depends on pleasant situations. Compassionate Understanding is based in and arises from the willingness to open to the true nature of the body and the mind with Awareness and Inquiry.

In this way we observe, investigate, see the characteristics of experience and the cause of unsatisfactoriness. Compassionate Understanding begins to see that grasping and clinging to impermanent experiences and unbeneficial conditions of mind only increase agitation, stress and suffering in the mind. Compassionate Understanding is a cause for Equanimity to arise. Without investigation, it is very difficult for it to arise.

In many ways, Equanimity can be seen as the mind coming into harmony with the Laws of Nature, of Impermanence. It is an acceptance that we cannot make permanent what is impermanent, nor make the world conform to what we want it to be.

Equanimity is *not* indifference. Indifference is based in ignorance and does not come from Wisdom. This is *very* important. Many meditators mistake indifference for Equanimity. Indifference often arises simply from suppression or avoidance, from selfishness, conceit or dependence on intellectual cleverness.

Indifference is a lack of Compassion: not wanting to investigate into the roots and causes of suffering, our clinging and aversions, and not wanting to investigate into the results of these causes within ourselves and others. Indifference is based in not caring. It also can come from unawareness or from boredom or aversion. Sometimes it can develop from a robot-like mindfulness practice that is not grounded in Compassion and Wisdom.

Equanimity is based on the Understanding that sees the source of unsatisfactoriness as our ignorant, unwise reactions and the clinging to impermanent conditions and unbeneficial states of mind. We realize that to alleviate our stress, difficulties and problems, we have to learn how to let go; let go of our selfishness, let go of our attachment to greed, aversion and ignorance.

Equanimity is a patient observation arising from the building of keen Awareness and the deepening of Compassionate Understanding.

**For this morning's meditation I'm going to start out leading you through a guided Compassion and Lovingkindness meditation.** Just as you did yesterday when the guided part is finished I'd like you to expand the meditation on your own for the rest of the period. It will give you some practice and help increase your capacity to think in unselfish ways. Reflect on the difficulties of others in order to feel Compassion and then wish them peace of mind to feel Lovingkindness. So please settle yourself into your posture if you haven't already done so. Remember with Compassion and Lovingkindness meditation it's better not to use the unpleasant sensation technique; that is, if pain arises in the body it's better to shift the posture and keep the attention focused on the feelings you are trying to generate. However, it may be helpful to focus on the unpleasant sensation if it is connected with aversion—that is, when you are trying to develop Compassion, aversion arises and you find it difficult to let go of the aversion.

Try to concentrate on your breathing for a short while relaxing into the posture.

*****

Focus your attention on yourself. Maybe you have come to see some of the difficulties that arise in the mind and body, that make it difficult for you to keep your balance. Reflect on some of these things.

*****

Allow the healing energy of Compassion to arise for yourself, realizing the universality that all of us have difficulties. Let the energy of Compassion surround the tension, the feelings of lack, the pain of self-judgment and aversion…opening…softening…healing the pain. In the warmth of Compassion and Lovingkindness may I learn to see things as they are, accept myself and grow little-by-little beyond my limitations.

*****

May I be able to let go of anger, fear, worry and ignorance. May I also have patience, courage, wisdom and determination to meet and overcome difficulties and problems, challenges in life.

May I find peace of mind.

*****

Next, focus your attention on some of your friends. Realize that their mind may be very similar to your mind. They might be experiencing similar difficulties to you, similar mental states arising and passing. Allow the spacious energy of Compassion to arise for them. Feeling with them. Understanding the pain of self-aversion and the clinging to stress. In the warmth of Compassion and Lovingkindness may they learn to see things as they are, accept themselves and little-by-little grow beyond their limitations.

*****

May my friends be able to let go of anger, fear, worry and ignorance. May they also have patience, courage, wisdom and determination to meet and overcome difficulties and problems, challenges in life.
　　May my friends find peace of mind.

*****

Now direct your attention to people whom you do not know very well. Perhaps people whom you meet only occasionally in the store. Someone you know from a distance. Reflect that they may have a mind very similar to your mind. Having their own difficult states of mind to deal with.

*****

Try to allow the spacious energy of Compassion to arise for them, feeling with them; living beings with hopes and wishes for happiness the same as you. In the warmth of Compassion and Lovingkindness may they grow beyond their limitations.

*****

May these people be able to let go of anger, fear, worry and ignorance. May they also have patience, courage, wisdom and determination to meet and overcome difficulties and problems, challenges in life.

May these people find peace of mind.

*****

Now focus your attention on a person whom you do not like. Try to remember when you formed this dislike or hatred. What were you reacting to? What mind state did that person have at that time. How would it feel to have that mind state in your mind? What expectations did you have of them that were not fulfilled? Try to realize that person may have problems with dealing with difficult states of mind.

*****

Having seen the pain within yourself of anger, jealousy, isolation and self-aversion, and how difficult it is to understand, let go of these negative energies and rise beyond them, may you try to understand those whom you do not like. From this understanding try to allow Compassion, Forgiveness and Lovingkindness to arise for them. If you are experiencing resistance focus on yourself. Feel the pain of this resistance within yourself and try to have Compassion for *yourself.*

*****

In the healing energies of Compassion and Lovingkindness may they rise beyond their limitations, learn to let go of destructive emotions and negativities. May they learn self-forgiveness and in the warmth of Compassionate Understanding discover inner peace, the fading away of suffering and the warmth of loving.

*****

May those I do not like be able to let go of anger, fear, worry and ignorance. May they also have patience, courage, wisdom and determination to meet and overcome difficulties and problems, challenges in life.

May they find peace of mind.

*****

At this point, please continue to expand the meditation.

*****

(end of period)

On the first morning, we asked you to pay special attention to going in and out of doorways. The next day, we asked you also to pay attention when washing the dishes. Yesterday we added putting on and taking off your shoes, and walking up and down the stairs.

Today we would like you to add to these special mindfulness activities, the awareness of raising your body, getting up. When you are sitting in meditation and you finish, the action of standing up. When you are eating at the tables and you finish, the action of standing up. When you are lying down, waking up in the morning or after a rest, and then you get up from the lying posture. Try to be aware of changing to sitting and then changing to standing. After you finish on the toilet, the action of standing up. Every different time during the day that you change from a lower posture to a higher one, try to be aware of the action.

Try to be mindful of how your body moves; where your arms go, where your hands go, how your back bends, how your head tilts. Try to watch. Try to learn. Try to be right there...right there in that moment with the action of raising your body.

# EVENING DAY FIVE

# SATIPATTHANA SUTTA
# THE FOUR FOUNDATIONS
# OF MINDFULNESS

Tonight I would like to talk more in depth about Mindfulness.

Steve has talked about the Compassion that can motivate one to practice, in order to alleviate suffering, stress, difficulties and problems. As we have said, Mindfulness is one of the tools we use to apply our Compassionate Motivation.

We have asked you to try to become mindful, aware, of your breath and whatever you do. Now I would like to give you a broader view of what Mindfulness can cover in your practice.

Vipassana (or Insight) meditation is based largely on a teaching given by the Buddha in the scriptures, called the Satipatthana Sutta, or the Four Foundations of Mindfulness.

In this teaching, the Buddha covered four aspects of ourselves to direct our attention toward and to investigate into, in order to see into the nature of ourselves and to develop Wisdom. There is Mindfulness of the Body, Mindfulness of Vedana, or Feeling, Mindfulness of States of Mind, and Mindfulness of Mind Objects.

There are hundreds of books on the subject of Buddhism. Even if we only consider the scriptures and discourses of the Buddha, there are dozens of books. Some people could become a little overwhelmed if they thought that they had to know everything in these books to be able to practice. Please try not to worry; if you start to understand this particular teaching given by the Buddha, then you will have a firm foundation for practice.

At one time the Buddha likened all the knowledge in the world,

and all the knowledge he knew, to a forest. And he said that in order to liberate the mind, one needs only a "handful of leaves" on the floor of the forest. The Four Foundations of Mindfulness are considered to be within this handful of leaves.

**Looking at the first Foundation of Mindfulness, the Buddha said to contemplate the body. How do we do this?**

We have instructed you to become aware of the breath. This is the first part of contemplation of the body. The Buddha encourages us: to know when the breath is long, as one breathes in and out; to know when the breath is short, as one breathes in and out; to know the whole breath-body, as one breathes in and out; and to calm the activity of the breath-body, as one breathes in and out. One is to see the breath as it is; long, short, the whole breath, and how it influences and affects the body.

But further, one is to see the breath in its aspects of arising and passing away. To be aware of its constant change, the impermanence within the breath. This is what is called Clear Comprehension or Wisdom-in-Action.

We have not only asked you to try to be aware of the breath. We have asked you to try to be aware of your postures, all of your activities and everything that you do. These are the next factors of the body to contemplate.

To know when one is sitting, standing, lying down, walking back and forth, or being in whatever posture one is in. One can also be aware in seeing, bending, stretching and performing all movements of the body, and in dressing, eating, drinking and tasting, going to the toilet, falling asleep, waking, speaking and keeping silent.

In order not to be on automatic pilot, we try to build Awareness and Clear Comprehension. If we are to know who or what we are, then we have to look closely. We have to try to bring Awareness to all that we do, bringing our Mindfulness toward helping to investigate into the moment and the actuality of things as they are. Clear Comprehension sees how these activities arise and pass away, the flux of activity.

This phrase "Clear Comprehension" implies more than just Mindfulness. Mindfulness can be very sharp and aware—yet only sharp and aware, just watching. That is, Mindfulness can be present while we are doing something unbeneficial and lacking in Wisdom. We can be mindful of doing something unbeneficial and be unwilling or unable to discern the possible results of the action. Through this lack of Wisdom and Understanding, we may continue to do the unbeneficial action.

When Mindfulness is linked to Clear Comprehension, then if we become mindful of doing an unbeneficial action, investigate into it and understand the possible unbeneficial results of it, then we try to change the action or to prevent its arising in the future.

This is Clear Comprehension, clearly knowing what is happening. It is the willingness to use the sharp awareness of Mindfulness to aid in discerning the possible results, possible effects of things, the characteristics of things, and not just the simple, basic process. Another term that often is used for this is "Wisdom in Action."

Two other factors of the body contemplation we have not mentioned yet, as they involve more of a reflective investigation of the nature of the body, using the thought processes, the analytical processes of the mind. These reflective investigations are especially helpful when experiences arise when reflection seems to be beneficial and appropriate, helping to deepen our understanding or lessen our attachment to unbeneficial states of mind. They can also be used in formal practice, for concentrated investigation into the nature of the body.

Their purpose is to counteract the common view that we normally have of our own body or the bodies of others, to help balance unbeneficial attachment that we have to the body. This is done by investigation and reflection on the body's true nature.

The first reflection is to reduce the body into 32 parts; bones, hair, nails, teeth, flesh, blood, skin, and so on.

Excessive attachment to the body comes from the concept that the body is beautiful. This is a type of "positive" attachment. Excessive repulsion to the body comes from the concept that the body is ugly. This is a type of "negative" attachment.

What this reflection can do for us is to see the body as a collection of parts rather than the whole thing. This may help to reduce the positive or negative attachments toward the body so that we neither excessively like nor dislike it. Instead, we may develop more Equanimity, evenness of mind, toward it.

The second reflective meditation of the body is the cemetery meditations. If we see a corpse, in any stage of decomposition, we can contemplate and reflect that our own body is of the same nature; "I will also die and my body may come to be like this."

In the days of the Buddha, they had what were called charnel grounds where they simply threw dead bodies, so it was common to see corpses. In Thailand, it is very common for people to be encouraged to view a dead body, and to contemplate and reflect on it, before the cremation. Death seems a more open subject here than in the West.

Unless, of course, you happen to come from Australia: One day I was traveling back to the island on the express boat, and I happened to meet a Thai man. We got into a conversation, and the usual things were asked: "What's your name, how old are you, and where do you come from?" When he found out I was from Australia, he was quite excited, because he had spent about two years in Australia, and then he became very serious. He looked at me and said, "One thing I don't understand about Australians." I said, "What's that, perhaps I can help you understand?" He replied, "Why are they so preoccupied with death?" "They are?," I said, "They seemed to be like normal Western people last time I was home, they didn't want to talk about it! What do you mean?" "Well, everywhere I went, everyone kept on asking me, 'How are you tod'y?' 'How am I tod'y?' 'Yes, how are you tod'y?'…"Well, I don't know how I'm going to die…so what could I reply?!"

Of course, he was joking. But maybe this can be of help to us, especially if we happen to be Australian. The next time someone asks you "How are you tod'y?" perhaps you can direct that question deep into the mind. How are you going to die?

The cemetery reflection often is misunderstood to be a morbid, depressing reflection. But it is done to remind us of the reality of life. Our bodies will die, and we cannot escape from this fact of existence.

We have a lot of conditioning in the West that glorifies the body.

This encourages people to go to excesses in pampering and preening it, or in worrying about it with not a lot of thought given to the development of the mind.

This excessive attachment causes enormous stress for many people. It often brings the fear of aging—the dread of seeing gray hairs or wrinkles appearing, perhaps the hairline receding—even though this is a normal process of life and the body.

Because we can identify so much with the body, if it is not as we wish it to be, we can develop tremendous complexes about it. Often people spend hours a day trying to "fix it up" or worrying about it. Sadly, this is in order to feel good about themselves.

We certainly do not neglect our bodies; we try to keep them healthy. The body is our vehicle. Yet the body cannot provide lasting happiness; it is unstable, uncertain and full of change. Sometimes it is just right; we are supple, the right weight, healthy. We feel good about ourselves. Next week, we may have a few extra pounds, or we are too skinny, or perhaps some pimples appear. We do not feel so good. We may start to hate ourselves.

If our happiness or positive self-identity depends on always having a perfect body, then that happiness is unstable, uncertain. Understanding this, reflecting in this way, allows us to slowly shift our focus in life away from the body to the development of the mind. It helps us to let go of our complexes about the body, which burden the mind with stress and which cause us so much difficulty.

The Buddha instructs us when we see a corpse to apply this perception to our own body; "Verily also, my own body is of the same nature, such it will become and will not escape it."

Even though it may not be common to see human corpses, there are certainly many occasions when we see other creatures' bodies cast away—insects and small animals that were once living and breathing as we are. Following the Laws of Nature, they pass away. Even the leaves on the trees follow these laws—they bud, they shade us and they fall. We can use these examples to reflect on our own impermanent nature.

If we contemplate in this way, we may begin to balance some of the conditioning that we have had toward the body and bring it more in line with the reality of life and death. We are part of Nature and are subject to its Laws; we were born and we will die.

A meditator friend of mine told me how this reflection process had been helpful. One day while walking along the beach, quite soon after hearing about this reflection, my friend happened to come upon a dead animal. The immediate, instinctive response was to turn away with repulsion, not wanting to look at it.

But the Buddha's instruction was quite fresh in the mind and came up at that time, encouraging my friend to turn back, to look at the animal, and contemplate. Turning back and contemplating in this way, the repulsion left. And at that moment, a certain amount of letting go began, with the arising of Equanimity, Compassion and acceptance of the death of this animal and of death being a normal, natural occurrence in life.

Another body contemplation is the contemplation of the body as being composed of the four great elements: earth, water, wind and fire. There are many ways to do this, both in an analytical way, or in the moment-to-moment investigation. What seems most appropriate tonight is to talk about the moment-to-moment investigation. When we do this contemplation, it can be on a sensation level, as various sensations arise within the body.

Each element manifests as certain characteristics of sensation in the body. The earth element manifests as heaviness, hardness. The water element manifests as humidity, wetness, cohesion; the wind element as vibration and movement, expansion and contraction; the fire element as temperature, heat and warmth.

When unpleasant sensations arise in the body, we can notice their characteristics: Are they hard, heavy, burning, vibrating, etc.? Pleasant sensations also arise in the body. They, too, have certain characteristics—perhaps lightness, coolness, a flowing sensation.

Both types of sensation occur, and the characteristics can be seen as the elements manifesting themselves. This is natural. The body is part of Nature. We try not to react excessively to the sensations or to claim them. Instead, we try to see them arise and pass away, and to see the nature of the body as the elements in constant flux.

This is a subtle level, the body manifesting in sensations. It may allow us to break down somewhat the concept of the body as a solid, unchanging, fixed thing. And it may help us to experience it on a deeper level, that of constantly changing sensations, arising and changing due to cause and effect.

So in the afternoon, when the sweat is pouring down, that's the water element manifesting. When we feel hot, that's the fire element manifesting. If you feel heavy, that's the earth element manifesting. If you feel light, vibrating, this is the wind element manifesting. You may see that they arise due to various causes, and even if you like them, or do not like them, they pass away in their own time. Cause and Effect: it is quite impersonal.

The cemetery contemplations are contemplations on the impermanent nature of the body on a lifetime scale. The contemplation of the body as a manifesting of the four elements is a contemplation on the impermanent nature of the body on a moment-to-moment level.

So the first foundation of mindfulness is contemplation of the body. However, we are more than the body, so we have to investigate further.

**The next Foundation of Mindfulness is contemplation of feeling or Vedana.** Vedana is the ancient Pali word used in the scriptures. In English, the word "feeling" is used to describe various things: thoughts, emotions, physical sensations. The English word "feeling" also has been used to describe the meaning of Vedana.

Vedana is the immediate feeling of pleasantness, unpleasantness or neutrality that arises in the mind when the senses come into contact with their objects: the eye with sights, the ear with sounds, the nose with odors, the tongue with tastes, the body with touch and the mind with thought.

Why do we want to become aware of this feeling/Vedana? This is a very important point in our practice. It is the step in the process of our contact with the world that comes just before our reaction of liking, disliking or neither liking nor disliking something. As we have said, being mindful of our reactions is very important, to help us let go of unbeneficial qualities, and help increase beneficial qualities. If we lack wisdom, we may fall into grief, aversion, fear, worry.

These reactions may throw us off balance and into the creation of thought-streams and emotions. These reactions, thought-streams and emotions can be the source of our problems, our stress and our suffering.

Mindfulness of the Body and Mindfulness of Vedana are very closely related. Being mindful of our sense contacts is Mindfulness of the Body. From our sense contacts comes Vedana, or feeling. So if we develop strong Mindfulness of the Body, we have a better foundation for developing Mindfulness of Vedana.

Together these two foundations of Mindfulness can aid us greatly in letting go of so many of the problems we cause for ourselves from our reactions.

During one retreat, we had a number of retreatants who became ill, and Steve had to switch around some of their jobs to get the important work done. He wanted one retreatant to switch from sweeping leaves to cleaning toilets.

Speaking in the language of the teaching, this person didn't like to clean toilets due to the aversion to the Vedana arising whenever there was eye and nose contact with cleaning toilets.

So Steve asked, "Would sweeping and washing the steps be a problem for you?" "No, that's fine," came the reply.

Steve said, "Well, when you clean the steps, the body moves this way and that, the arms move this way and that, the head moves this way and that, the eyes see sights with their color and form, and the nose may smell odors. Do you think you can do such a job?"

The retreatant replied, "Sure, fine, that's easy."

And then Steve said, "Well, the person sweeping and washing the steps is not ill. Another person whose job also requires sweeping and washing, is ill. In that job the body moves this way and that, the head moves this way and that, the arms move this way and that, the eyes see sights with their color and form, and the nose may smell odors."

The retreatant laughed—and went off to clean the toilets.

Being aware of the body. Being aware of Vedana. Being aware of reactions.

By becoming aware of Vedana, we can bring Awareness and Clear

Comprehension (Wisdom in Action) to this point and try to prevent the reactions that cause us to have stress, difficulties and problems.

We try to become aware of the arising of the Vedana and the passing away of the Vedana. We try not to react immediately or compulsively to it. This will enable us to learn how to have peace and balance when feeling arises.

When a pleasant feeling arises, try not to get carried away and overpowered with excessive desire, or with grief when it passes away. When an unpleasant feeling arises, try not to fall into aversion, hatred and impatience with its existence. When a neutral feeling arises, try not to react with indifference and dullness.

Instead, try to be aware of pleasant, unpleasant and neutral feelings as they arise, stay for awhile, and pass away, seeing the impermanence of feeling. Try to see it for what it is, with objective, unattached awareness. Try not to add extra, unwise reactions, which may overpower and control the mind.

Some people may say, "Well, I can understand having Awareness and Clear Comprehension concerning unpleasant feelings, but there is really no need for it when a pleasant feeling arises—why can't I just enjoy it?"

It is a matter of reflecting on the danger of unawareness to pull us away from wise decisions and instead lead us to unwise reactions and actions. For example, a retreatant once told me this story about drifting with pleasant feeling and the results of it.

During this retreat, there was a lot of loud music in the valley and it was drifting up during walking meditation. The retreatant had already learned a lot, realizing the benefits of being here, so at first just noted "hearing, hearing" and went back to the footsteps. But after a while, the thoughts started to drift into the sound of the music and the pleasant feeling arising from listening to the music.

This started a long chain of thoughts that just drifted along until suddenly the retreatant realized what the thoughts were. The thoughts were of leaving the retreat, going to the beach, and being with the music.

This drastically interrupted the daydream. This retreatant didn't want to leave the retreat and thought, "How did this happen? I don't want to leave. Oh, I've been drifting with the pleasant feeling from listening to the music. And these thoughts led to my thoughts of leaving the retreat. Oh!" The retreatant quickly returned to the footsteps and started to be aware of lifting, moving and placing, noting "hearing, hearing."

Often, drifting in pleasant feeling can cause us to do things that we really don't want to do, if we don't have Awareness and Clear Comprehension to balance this. You can easily apply this to your everyday life. How often have you drifted with pleasant feeling and done things that you later regretted?

In a deeper way, having Awareness and Clear Comprehension with feeling also can help us to start to understand the process of the workings of our mind.

If we continually react with liking or disliking to the arising of this Vedana, we won't be able to understand clearly the process of the workings of our mind and the causes of stress and suffering, and be able to let them go.

Consider a scientist who wants to understand the cell samples beneath the microscope. If the scientist always wants to see only a certain type of sample, there will be the continual liking and disliking instead of just looking at and seeing what is there. This attitude could cause the scientist to throw away some cell samples through aversion. In this way the scientist will never be able to understand the workings of the cell and the causes of disease.

If we are able to bring wise attention, as well as the Compassionate Wish to end problems, stress and difficulties, to the Vedana that arises from our contacts, then we are able to give ourselves the opportunity to react in a skillful way.

In this way, we do not fall into difficulties and we are not sowing the seeds for the arising of difficulties in the future. This gives us the opportunity to develop a level of Peace that does not depend on pleasant feelings.

The Compassionate Motivation can strengthen our wish to become mindful. It also can help give us the strength to try to step back, watch and learn, try to understand what causes us to fall into difficulty.

By opening and learning, we may be able to treat the practice as a "Journey of Discovery." We may begin to let go of the wish to claim what cannot be claimed. How can we claim things that are arising and passing so quickly? The desire to do so stems from unawareness and not understanding the nature of things. And the effort to do so is a source of our difficulties.

We can understand this on an intellectual level. The process of meditation gives us the opportunity to understand it on an experiential level.

By seeing the causes of stress and difficulties and strengthening the Compassionate Wish, we can start to let go, bit by bit, of unskillful reaction. In our normal life, we may not have the strong awareness to be aware of every feeling that arises from our sense contacts. But during times of retreat is a very valuable opportunity to use the retreat conditions to gain insight into this process. Then we can bring this strengthened understanding to our everyday life, to know where to look for the source of our difficulties and problems—the excessive wanting, wanting, hating, hating, that arises from our sense contacts, and the feeling arising from them. In doing so, we may experience the fading away of stress, difficulties and unsatisfactoriness.

Some people become quite concerned that Awareness will make them become quite dull and boring, lacking in energy and losing the so-called joys of life. With this in mind, consider the example of two groups of people—one group with Awareness, the other without Awareness—who decide to go to different mountaintops to watch a sunset.

The people with awareness decide to try to watch all the changing colors, not missing a single one. They try to be with every color, not holding onto the last one but flowing into the next one. And so they are with each color, and when the last color disappears, they flow into the descending darkness, not clinging to the sunset.

The people with unawareness go to watch a similar sunset. Immediately they get very excited and start looking around for more people: "Hey, there's a sunset going on here. Come on, come and have a look at it. Oh, there's no one else around. Oh well, we have to look at it all by ourselves."

Then they look at the sunset and begin comparing it with the one they saw last week: "Well, it isn't as beautiful as the one we saw at the beach. Oh, the one at the beach had pink and orange in it, yeah, it was really beautiful.

"We're going to Tibet next month. Wow, what will the sunsets be like in the Himalayas, with the sun reflecting on the snow? It is just going to be wonderful. Oh, the sunset is changing. There is more gold and orange, it's so beautiful now. We really should take a picture."

They fumble in their bags and, "Where is the camera? Nobody brought a camera?! Oh, that is just so stupid. Now we won't be able to send a picture of the sunset back to the people at home to show how beautiful the sunsets are here."

Swayed by the future and the past, they are unable to see the moment before their eyes. And when the darkness descends, they are left longing for the sunset in the Himalayas.

Who is able to experience the sunset more?

Project two similar groups of people into another situation, a difficult situation with unpleasant feelings arising.

The people with awareness try to see the moment to moment change in the experience and try to keep their minds balanced. They know that when the condition that caused this experience to arise passes away, it will pass away. And they try not to suffer with the experience, trying to keep their minds balanced, understanding that it doesn't follow their wishes, but the Law of Cause and Effect.

The people with unawareness and ignorance meet the same situation and immediately they may react with aversion, pushing it away: "No, I don't want this experience."

What is the result of this? Stress arises in the body and the mind suffers with the experience, and they may even fall into grief and despair. The people with unawareness don't understand that the experience will pass away when the condition that caused its arising passes away. It follows the Law of Cause and Effect and does not follow their wishes.

It is also helpful, at this point, to mention that, in other teachings in the scriptures, the Buddha went into more depth with explaining Vedana. He said that in order to overcome attachment to worldly pleasant and unpleasant feeling, we cultivate "spiritual" pleasant and unpleasant feeling. In order to overcome neutral worldly feeling, we cultivate "spiritual" Equanimity.

We cannot let go all at once. It simply is not possible. Try to realize that it is a gradual awakening, and we cannot force the awakening. It may start out shallow like the beach shore, but as we move out into the water, it gets deeper and deeper.

Some people develop concern, even fear, with this teaching of Vedana: "If I lose my pleasant worldly feelings, there will be nothing left but suffering or even just emptiness." At these times they are focusing more on what they think they are losing, rather than considering what they may gain by understanding the nature of the body and the mind, and life.

Consider this story: There once was a village in a valley. Most of the people in this village thought that there was nothing more to be known about the world than what they knew from the valley, that there could never be a more beautiful and expansive view than the view from the valley.

So they simply stayed in the valley and didn't go anywhere else, even though some felt inwardly that perhaps one could find out more or get a better view of the world from the mountain in the East.

Two people finally decided to take the journey to try to climb that mountain. Although they were not able to reach the top that time, they were able to learn quite a lot even from half-way up the mountain. They saw the ocean in the East and the Earth curving away. They saw the forest on the other side of the mountain. They were able to get a clear view of the sky and the stars they were not able to see from the valley. They also observed that the weather and the wildlife in the valley were affected by the ocean in the East and the forest on the other side of the mountain. They understood the interrelationship of things. They learned all this and much more as they observed from their viewpoint on the mountain.

After a while, they began reflecting upon the people in the village and the limited view of the world they had. They felt compassion, and decided to go back and tell the people of the village about the wonderful, expansive view from the mountain and what they had learned from the mountain. But the people in the village didn't believe them: "No, there can't possibly be a more beautiful and expansive view than the view from this valley. I don't want to lose this view from the valley."

So, in our practice of contemplation of the body, we try to become aware of our breath, our actions, our postures. This sharpens the mind and we may begin to see the impermanence of the body. As well, it may lead us into a clearer awareness of the contacts that we have with the world through the sense doors.

As we become more aware of the Vedana arising from the contacts of the senses with their objects, we may be able to see the impermanent, unstable nature of Vedana. We may begin to understand that to attach to it, wanting it to be as we wish, wanting it to continue or to vanish "right now!" only causes us extra stress. With Compassion for ourselves, we can begin to avoid getting caught in unwise reaction. Remember, "We *try* not to get caught," not "We *should* not get caught."

So there is contemplation of the body and contemplation of Vedana/feeling.

**The third Foundation of Mindfulness is contemplation of states of mind.** What is meant here by "states of mind"?

Picture a container filled with clear water. This represents the mind. If we take specks of dye and drop them into the water, they dissolve and tint the clear water. The specks of dye represent thoughts, and emotions—the contents of the mind. When dropped into the mind, they tint the clear water of the mind creating the states of mind through which we experience life. For example; if anger or desire arise in the mind, they are the objects of the mind and they are also like the dye, they tint the container, the mind, and create mental states through which things are experienced.

Many of us have probably experienced days where we woke up in a "bad mood." We may not have been aware enough to know what thoughts created this mood or state of mind. Then throughout the day, all of our experiences were tainted by this mood. We had to "drag" ourselves through the day.

On the other hand, many of us may also have experienced waking up in a "good mood." The day, the experiences may have been just the same as the other day, but we viewed it from a mind of joy and lightness, coloring our experiences with this state of mind.

With the developing of this foundation of mindfulness, we apply Bare Awareness, without aversion or indulgence and try to become aware of states of mind. In the scripture, the Buddha lists 16 states of mind to be aware of. I will not list them all but just mention a few; the state of mind with greed or without; with hatred or without; with ignorance or without; concentrated state or unconcentrated state. So when the mind is unconcentrated: Bare Awareness, we simply know that it is unconcentrated.

With becoming aware of our state of mind, we are trying to be aware of it simply as it is—objectively seeing, trying not to bring up self-hatred or grief. Self-hatred and grief only hinder clear seeing, block understanding from arising and prevent the letting go of unbeneficial states of mind by creating more unbeneficial states of mind.

This is a very simple teaching. Yet many people feel that it is not enough or even that this part of the practice is useless. This often is because they think that Concentration and Mindfulness are the same thing, or even that Concentration and Wisdom are the same thing. This is wrong understanding.

As we observe more objectively, we may begin to see the impermanent nature of states of mind. As we become aware of the impermanence, the arising and passing of states of mind, the understanding may arise that forming self-images based on an impermanent mind state is wrong understanding.

That is, saying, "This is me, this is mine" is like saying that the clouds in the sky, which arise due to conditions and pass away due to conditions, are the sky. Or that the waves in the ocean, which arise due to conditions and pass away due to conditions, are the ocean.

So there is contemplation of the body, Vedana/feeling, and states of mind.

**The last Foundation of Mindfulness is contemplation of mind objects.**
In this Foundation of Mindfulness, we are going to investigate

the laws that govern the mind/body in order to understand how they work. This uses both present moment investigation and also the analytical processes of the mind.

**The first in a list of five subjects to contemplate is the contemplation of the Five Hindrances.** I talked a great deal about them on the second night.

We are to try to know when any of the Five Hindrances are present: sense-desire, aversion, sloth and torpor, restlessness and worry, and doubt. We also are to try to know when they are not present. We are to try to realize how the arising of the hindrances occurs. And, if they have already arisen, how they are abandoned. We also are contemplating in order to know how they will not arise in the future.

As you can see there is more involved here in investigating of mental objects than there was with bare awareness of states of mind.

In order to aid us in abandoning the hindrances that already have arisen, we may see that we need the Compassionate Motivation to end difficulties, stress and problems. It can help us to let go of attachment to these things by seeing that the nature of their energy is stressful.

I talked a lot about this in my talk concerning the Five Hindrances. I did not talk much about the last aspect, which is knowing how they will not arise in the future.

This understanding can arise in two ways. First we can use various analytical reflections to reach and transform the wrong view that causes the hindrances to arise. We change wrong view gradually into *right* view.

In the moment to moment practice, understanding comes from our increasing awareness, and compassionate investigation. We try to observe how we react, trying harder to build awareness closer to the actual moment of reaction. As we do this, we come closer to the Vedana/feeling that precedes our reaction. This we talked about in the contemplation of Vedana/feeling.

We try to come closer to the reaction which we have to the feeling, that is dependent on our past conditioning. As our Awareness and Understanding of our mind becomes deeper, we will know which situations, events and conditions cause us to react unwisely, and to fall into difficulty. Then we can bring Compassionate Understanding to these events and situations.

We try to learn how to de-condition the urge to react instinctively, and we try to bring about more skillful and wise reactions.

Here we need Honesty, Patience and Compassionate Softness, that gentle, caring attitude. We try not to view things as problems, but just seek to learn new ways of looking at things and new ways of dealing with the experiences that we have. We constantly try to uncover the balancing energies of Awareness, Wisdom, Compassion and Equanimity. The seeds of these lie within us all.

Try to allow the old unbeneficial conditioning to lose the fuel it feeds upon—unawareness and attachment, the claiming mind. Try to realize that we have to care for the "plant," *and in caring for it,* it will grow and bloom.

If we go about with an aggressive quality—suppressing, pushing away, judging ourselves and condemning who we are, rather than trying to step back, understand and let go based in Compassionate Understanding—then we will only increase our suffering.

It is like trying to rip open a flower in order to make it bloom, rather than patiently caring for the plant. We could only end up destroying the flower.

If we do not care enough, we may never apply our minds. If we don't understand the causes for our difficulties, we will not be able to let them go. It is like neglecting a plant; it never has a chance to bloom because it shrivels up and dies from neglect.

**Another contemplation within mental objects is contemplation of the five aggregates.** What does this mean?

This contemplation can go fairly deep, and is also the subject of a lot of differing views and opinions within Buddhist circles. I will only touch on it lightly.

Basically, we are going to analyze the body and mind process, in order to see its dependent arising nature, and understand the governing characteristics of the body and the mind. For this investigation we can use the moment to moment investigation and also the analytical processes of the mind. In Buddhism it is normally considered that the body and mind processes are composed of five parts.

There is body, material form and there is mind. Within mind, there is consciousness, Vedana/feeling, perception, and mental formations. Consciousness is the knowing quality of mind that arises when the six senses come in contact with their objects. For example, ear-consciousness arises when the ear comes in contact with a sound and it passes when another sense contact becomes stronger. Eye-consciousness arises when the eye comes in contact with a sight and it passes when another sense contact becomes predominant.

Vedana/feeling, I have already talked about. It arises from the contact and the knowing of consciousness.

Perception is the labeling quality of mind, the process that recognizes and labels things as this or that. For example, the eye sees color and form, perception labels it as a tree.

Mental formations—these are the thoughts that we often create about perception, what we have already labeled. Perception says that it is a tree, then mental formations take over... "That tree reminds me of a tree back in my own country... It is a really beautiful tree... There is a whole forest of them in the mountains near my village... I remember one day last summer Dave and I went there together... It was such a beautiful day... The sun was shining through the leaves casting shadows all around... It was magic... That was when Dave and I were still together... It's such a pity we had to break up... He is probably in India with someone else now"... Mental Formations!! As you can see, it often starts out very pleasant, but if unguarded, without mindfulness, it can often lead into suffering.

Although Mental Formations can be used to help develop the mind; i.e. reflective meditations; many of us have probably come to realize by now that Mental Formations of an unmindful, rambling nature can be a source of stress and difficulty.

When we contemplate, we take a closer look at the different parts that make up our mind and body processes. We try to analyze their nature. This may enable us to see the characteristics of the mind-body process; see their impermanent, unsatisfactory, impersonal nature. This may help in breaking up the concept of the self as an unchanging, static identity and enable us to see it as a process of Cause and Effect.

The third contemplation is to focus on the senses and their objects, and to see the problems arising which are dependent upon the contact. For example, if the ear comes in contact with a sound and it's unpleasant, we may start to react developing aversion and hatred. We try to see how this problem arose dependent on the aversion arising, which arose dependent on the ear coming in contact with the sound, which arose dependent on having senses, which arose dependent on having a body, which arose dependent on birth.

But more, we are instructed to contemplate in order to know how to let go of the problems that have arisen. And, to develop the Understanding of how the abandoned problems will not arise in the future.

To do this, we have to develop a keen Awareness and Wisdom. The first three contemplations are interrelated. It is more a matter of where we focus the attention, what we are trying to discover from investigation, and how fine or deep the investigation becomes.

The fourth aspect of contemplation of mental objects focuses on beneficial qualities of Mental Development. These are called the Seven Factors of Enlightenment. They are Mindfulness, Investigation of Mind Objects, Energy, Joy, Tranquility, Concentration and Equanimity.

*Mindfulness, Awareness:* In order to understand ourselves and life, we have to try to become mindful, aware; we try to develop a watchful, careful, awake mind.

*Investigation of Mind Objects:* With a more awake mind, we can begin to investigate into the nature of things using both present moment investigation and various analytical meditations in order to develop Wisdom.

*Energy:* In order to contemplate and meditate, we need energy—the energy to make the effort to be mindful and investigate, to continually start again, and to let go.

*Joy:* Without Joy, it is difficult to renew or increase Energy. Joy can arise from being mindful, and from the gradual lessening of the problems that arise from not being mindful. Mindfully aware and awake, we begin to experience fully and more freshly things that we often used to take for granted. This fresh seeing can help us to find

Joy in simple things, in being more present and discriminating in the moment. Joy also arises from contentment in, acceptance of and non-resistance to the moment. As well, it can arise from the ability to concentrate.

There is also what I call "Vipassana Joy," which arises from the increasing of Compassionate Understanding. It is realizing that we are not getting caught up in stress and difficulties as much as we did before and that, at times, we are finding the Inner Balance and Peace that depends less on external things and more on the deepening of one's wisdom. Joy can also arise from reflecting on confidence inspiring objects, which I plan to explain in more detail near the end of the retreat.

*Tranquility:* A Joy coming from Contentment often deepens into a tranquil mind, a calm, quiet mind.

*Concentration:* Concentration helps to add strength to Awareness. The ability to concentrate is like the focus of the mind. Awareness is able to see the characteristics of what concentration focuses on. Concentration can be fixed on a single object or it can be working in balance with Awareness, focusing on changing objects. The concentration that is balanced with Awareness is what Vipassana meditation seeks to develop. This is in order to develop understanding of the mind/body or of the characteristics of what concentration focuses on.

*Equanimity:* Equanimity allows us to be *with* anything that arises with Balance—not pushing away or claiming, just observing things as they are. It allows us to have a Peace that is not dependent on outward things, but on our inner reaction to experience.

With these Seven Factors of Enlightenment, we are instructed to try to know when they are present; when they are absent; if they are absent, how they can arise; and if they are present, how we can develop them.

The beneficial mind objects of the Seven Factors of Enlightenment arise in the course of our practice from time to time. Many of us experience them, and when they pass away, we are left not knowing how they can arise again—as if their presence was a bit of a "fluke" or chance happening.

Here, we are encouraged by the Buddha to pay attention, to try to understand what conditions brought them about and what factors of mind aided in bringing them about. Also we are encouraged to try to see how they can arise in the future and continue to be developed by applying this understanding.

With this and all of the investigation objects, the direction is to develop Wisdom.

**The last contemplation on mental objects is the contemplation of the Four Noble Truths.** We have explained much about difficulties, stress and problems; how difficulty arises, the ending of difficulty and how to end the difficulty. This is, in essence, what is referred to in Buddhism as the Four Noble Truths.

*The First Noble Truth is the existence of unsatisfactoriness, difficulty and suffering.*

*The Second Noble Truth is the cause of unsatisfactoriness, difficulty, and suffering*—ignorance, unwise reaction, and craving.

*The Third Noble Truth is the cessation of unsatisfactoriness, difficulty and suffering*—that there is the ability to experience the end of these by developing Wisdom and by giving up unwise reaction and craving.

*The Fourth Noble Truth is the path leading to the ending of unsatisfactoriness, difficulty and suffering*—the methods by which we end these.

In this contemplation, we investigate into the difficulty, (or stress, or suffering) when it is arising. We investigate to see the cause of the problem and how to give it up. By applying various methods to help let go, we may experience the ending of difficulties, stress or problems in that moment.

Buddhism is based on these Four Noble Truths. If we see the understanding of them occurring within the framework of our practice, we can feel confident that we are practicing correctly. This may help to end doubts about how to practice.

The Compassionate Motivation enables us to keep our practice directed toward seeing difficulties and problems, and toward the cessation of difficulties and problems.

Many other motivations may be misdirected. The motivations

to achieve, to become powerful or famous, to obtain psychic powers or to be "great" meditators are not directed correctly. This is because there is not enough understanding about the problems involved with creating a bigger self-image. If we do not understand, instead of the practice being directed toward the end of suffering and the purification of the mind, our practice may actually increase the sense of the separate self, selfishness, and ego, therefore increasing suffering, difficulties, and problems.

The Compassionate Motivation is a strong energy directing the mind toward awakening itself. It asks: Is there difficulty? How does it cease?

With a wish to solve stress or suffering, we can try to bring non-attached awareness to investigate the characteristics of the body and mind. We do this in order to experience the fading away of stress and suffering, and to help purify the mind by the lessening of attachment to greed, hatred and ignorance.

The Satipatthana Sutta, the Four Foundations of Mindfulness, is an in-depth and vast teaching of the Buddha. It helps to give you an extended overview of the practice of Vipassana meditation. It may also help prevent you falling into a common tendency. The tendency of limiting the Buddha's teaching, and especially the concept of Vipassana to a single technique. Instead it may encourage you to continue to contemplate all aspects of the body and mind, so that you may begin to understand the nature of yourself and life.

From this teaching, you can see that it is impossible to section off part of your life and say "this" is meditation but "that" is not meditation; that concentrating on the breath is meditation but one cannot be meditating when going to the toilet; that concentrating on walking back and forth is meditation, but seeing a leaf fall, reflecting on death and impermanence, and applying this perception to one's own body is not meditation. Actually, it is all meditation.

One can be practicing contemplation in the course of everyday life—watching the mind, seeing how difficulties arise, seeing how they pass away—as well as while one is sitting and watching the breath.

The benefit of formal sitting, standing, and walking meditation is that it helps to build strong awareness and the ability to concentrate. This may enable us to see the nature of the body and mind more clearly and develop understanding.

We then can apply this strengthened concentration, awareness and understanding to watch ourselves in all aspects of life: to see impermanence, to see stress and difficulties, and to see how we cannot claim what is impermanent to be ours. Not seeing, and not understanding, the laws of nature, causes us to react unwisely to experience, to try to cling to and grasp things that cannot be held onto. From this ignorance, unwise reaction, or grasping, we experience stress, difficulties and problems. Meditation helps us to build Awareness and Compassionate Understanding. This will enable us to experience the Peace of letting go and living in a non-grasping harmony with things as they are.

# COMPASSION

I would like to compliment all of you on the fine work, fine efforts that you are putting into this retreat. Your efforts to keep silence, your efforts to come to all of the sits, the standing and the walking.

Try to keep these efforts going. Try to maintain the efforts that you have built up. Try to increase them if you can. Keep trying.

Keep your silence going, it is so very beneficial. Come to all of the sits and standing, come to all of the walks. Just keep trying. Any effort that you put forth in this direction is going to produce some beneficial results. Any effort, no matter how small you may think it is.

This practice of trying to learn who and what we are, this type of Mental Development, is the hardest thing in the world to do. It is extremely difficult. It is not easy. It takes hard work. But the rewards of this work are well worthwhile, so very valuable.

Much of the practice is basically just to try—to keep trying, gently, bit by bit. There are some people who feel that "try" is a negative word. And indeed, as some people use it, it is negative because some people may try once, twice and then that's it, they quit.

But we are not saying to try once, twice, and then quit. We are saying to try, to try and to keep trying. If we keep trying, we keep learning and we keep growing.

In the Thai language, there is an expression—"Tee la lek la noi." This means "little by little, bit by bit." Just keep trying, keep trying.

We try to watch, watch ourselves, watch our minds. With Patience, with Compassion, with Lovingkindness, with Understanding, we try to learn who and what we are. We try to learn why we react in certain ways.

Not only do we try to understand which parts of ourselves are unbeneficial, that we would like to correct, but also to look at the parts of ourselves that *are* beneficial, the good qualities that we have. Often many people do not look enough at the good qualities that they have. Try to take some joy and happiness that you have these good qualities, and try to work to increase them.

The more we can understand ourselves and our minds, the more we will grow in Compassion, Lovingkindness, Understanding, Patience, Equanimity, and many more beneficial qualities. The more we can grow in these qualities, the more we might be able to help others grow as well.

Try to add a Compassionate Intention to whatever you are doing throughout the day. When you are coming into the hall, if there is already someone sitting in meditation, out of Compassion, try to be as quiet as you can. Try to be on time, out of Compassion for others so that you do not disturb the people who are already sitting.

Out of Compassion for yourself and others, try to sit as well as you can during the talks. It is so very beneficial. If you get too relaxed, if you lay down, then the mind gets too relaxed, the mind lays down, too. And then it cannot concentrate as well as when sitting up in a meditation posture.

If you are having a lot of discomfort when sitting, then talk to us about it in the interviews and we will show you a few other ways of sitting. Try your best, especially during the talks to sit as well as you can. Trying to keep a bright mind, an awake mind. So that you can understand more and be of more value.

Out of Compassion for yourself please try to be very mindful of another aspect of aversion which often manifests for many meditators. This is sometimes called "Yogi mind." But it is not a true yogi, true meditator's mind. It is more of a pretend yogi, immature meditator's mind. It is one who does not yet understand the essence of this type of Mental Development practice.

Perhaps some of you have already experienced this type of mind. Some examples of the "immature Yogi mind" are; "The schedule is not right... There's too much walking... There's too much sitting... The walking tracks are not right... Those are too short... Those are too long... Why do they ring the bells so loud?... Why don't they ring the bells louder?... Why can't we watch the sunset?... Why can't we do more exercises?... The teachers should not do this... The teachers should not do that ..." And on and on.

This is a type of mind that is continually trying to find fault in the schedule, the environment, the teachers, the other meditators. This type of immature Yogi mind is not pleasant and is fueled by aversions continually pointing outside, pointing outside to somehow justify one's own problems. This can cripple your practice and slow down, even stop any growth of Understanding and Compassion because the mind is spinning; spinning and breeding more and more aversion.

If you find you are having a lot of these little aversions, then that is a good time to remember why you came here: to work on yourself, to develop methods and techniques within yourself. Methods and techniques that will help you to let go of your problems and difficulties that you cause for yourself.

You did not come to change the outside things here: the schedule, the environment, the teachers.

Out of Compassion for yourself try to keep your attention inward, watching yourself, watching your *reactions* to life. This is where the work can be done in the most constructive manner. If you get continually caught up with aversion toward outward things here and other people here, you will be wasting a valuable opportunity.

Please be careful and try not to fall into this type of immature Yogi mind. It can be very disruptive for your own practice as well as very disruptive in your relationships with the other meditators, with myself and with Rosemary. Out of Compassion, try to be mindful of these aversions.

Often the immature Yogi mind is caused by self-pity, feeling sorry for oneself. This is a very negative quality that some people find very hard to let go of because it can build a powerful sense of self-identity, even though it is so full of pain and grief.

Last night Rosemary mentioned the Four Noble Truths that are very much the basis of this type of Mental Development: That there are difficulties, problems, unsatisfactoriness in life. That the cause for much of our problems lies within ourselves. That there is the possibility of ending problems through developing Wisdom. And lastly, the Path which leads to this Wisdom.

Some people focus their attention on only the first two Noble Truths. They see problems, difficulties and unsatisfactoriness, and they see that frequently it is something within themselves that causes the problems.

They then blame themselves, thinking they are terrible, and do not look any further, just getting lost in self-pity. They may think that they deserve to suffer, that they are not worthy enough to be without these problems.

Even if these people are told methods and techniques of how to solve their problems, they will refuse to listen or to try the methods and techniques. Many times these people will claim, "Oh, that might work for someone else, but it does not work for me"—even if they have not yet tried it.

Compassion is not self-pity. Self-pity is a type of self-hatred. Compassion can help to reduce and let go of self-pity, but only if one wants to let go. To understand how painful self-pity is, one must try to see it for what it is, and not get lost and indulge in it.

Often those starting out on the path of mental development are like people who have not taken very good care of their home. Through a lack of Wisdom, they neglected to clean and care for it properly. Now they decide to clean it. But if they walk around the house with their eyes closed, can they properly clean it?

Opening their eyes, using Mindfulness and Compassion, looking at the house, trying to understand what is dirty, what needs to be cleaned—these things are important.

Sometimes this is unpleasant and very hard work. We may open the door to one room, see how dirty it is, and then immediately close it again. And some people see the whole house and get so overwhelmed by it that they just sit down and feel sorry for themselves. This does not help; it actually slows down, even stops, one from continuing. There *are* tools to clean the house. If we know the proper tools and know which tool is needed for which situation, then we apply our energies, getting on with the work, the house can get cleaned.

Keep in mind, as I use this example, that we do not have only dirt in our house. We also have beautiful paintings, nice furniture, trophies, etc., which may need only a bit of dusting and polishing. We have both beneficial and unbeneficial.

How do we increase the beneficial? How do we decrease the unbeneficial?

If we wax and polish a wooden table, that is an appropriate method and we get it clean. But if we wax and polish the cotton curtains, well… If we use the vacuum cleaner on the floor, then that is one way to help clean the floor. If we use the vacuum cleaner on the silverware…! Learning the proper methods to use, coming to understand the situation and then applying the proper method to help in each situation.

Try to be aware of self-pity when it arises. Try to learn how to lessen these thoughts. Focus your attention on all Four Noble Truths, not just the first two. Out of Compassion, you will be helping yourself and thus be able to help others.

By sticking to the schedule, you are showing Compassion to yourself and to others. By keeping silence, by trying to sit as well as you can, you are showing Compassion to yourself and others. By watching over the immature Yogi mind, by watching over self-pity, you are showing Compassion to yourself and to others.

So for the most possible benefit for yourself and to help others, try to keep to the schedule, keep it going. Keep your efforts going. Keep the silence going and just keep trying.

Any effort that you make to try to increase beneficial qualities and to try to decrease unbeneficial qualities, any effort in this direction is going to produce beneficial results.

The more we understand ourselves, the more we will develop. The more our Compassion will grow inside us. The more we will be of benefit to ourselves and the more we will be of benefit to others.

**I would now like to lead you through some Compassion/Lovingkindness meditation.**

Just before beginning I would like to mention a few words about the Compassion/Lovingkindness wish and the phrase we use here. In particular, in reference to the words, "peace of mind," we do not mean a "piece of cake." In other words we do not mean a piece of cake, money, cars, homes, anything material, anything outside of ourselves; but a deep inner peace that comes from within ourselves. Generally most of you will understand that, but on occasion we have some people who have a very limited understanding on what they think peace of mind means. In one interview during a retreat here, I was talking with a person about peace of mind. The conversation went a bit like this:

The meditator said, "I feel that I have many moments in my life where I experience peace of mind."

I asked, "What types of experience are you calling 'Peace of Mind?' What was actually happening?"

The reply, "I feel I experience peace of mind whenever I am riding my motorcycle on a mountain road."

Well, this type of normal peaceful time, for this person, depends on a motorcycle, a mountain road and quite a few other things. I merely asked, "What happens to this type of peace of mind if one of your arms gets cut off?"

The meditator looked at me first a little bit stunned but then thought much more about what I just said. This person then realized that what we were referring to as peace of mind was much, much deeper than just riding a motorcycle on a mountain road.

So if you have any doubts in your mind, please be very clear when we use this phrase "peace of mind." We do not mean a piece of cake, money, cars, homes or anything material, anything outside of ourselves. But a deep inner peace coming from within ourselves. Now please settle yourself in your posture for a few moments.

*****

Please try to consider your own difficulties and challenges that you have in life. Try to raise some Compassion and Lovingkindness towards yourself.

*****

May I be able to learn, practice and develop methods, techniques and tools of Mental Development so that I can cope with, understand, accept and overcome the difficulties and challenges in life.

May I find peace of mind.

\*\*\*\*\*

Now please try to consider some of your relatives, reflecting upon the difficulties and challenges that they may have. Try to raise some Compassion and Lovingkindness towards some of your relatives.

\*\*\*\*\*

May my relatives be able to learn, practice and develop methods, techniques and tools of Mental Development so that they can cope with, understand, accept and overcome the difficulties and challenges in life.

May my relatives find peace of mind.

\*\*\*\*\*

Try now to consider some of your friends, reflecting upon the difficulties and challenges that they may have. Try to raise some Compassion and Lovingkindness towards some of your friends.

\*\*\*\*\*

May my friends be able to learn, practice and develop methods, techniques and tools of Mental Development so that they can cope with, understand, accept and overcome the difficulties and challenges in life.

May my friends find peace of mind.

\*\*\*\*\*

Now, try to consider some of your teachers or other people who have helped you in life. Try to think about some of the difficulties and challenges that they may have. Try to raise some Compassion and Lovingkindness towards these people who have helped you.

\*\*\*\*\*

May those people who have helped me be able to learn, practice and develop methods, techniques and tools of Mental Development so that they can cope with, understand, accept and overcome the difficulties and challenges in life.

May those people who have helped me find peace of mind.

*****

Please continue expanding the Compassion/Lovingkindness meditation at this time.

*****

(end of period)

So far we have asked you to pay extra attention to the activities of going in and out of doorways, washing your dishes, taking off and putting on your shoes, coming up and going down the stairs. Yesterday we asked you to pay extra attention to the process of your body rising.

Today we would like to add paying extra attention to the process of your body lowering. Whenever you find yourself changing from a higher posture into a lower posture, be aware, be mindful, realize how your body is moving.

So when you come into the hall and sit down on your mat, try to be aware of the process of your body lowering, the movement of your back, moving of your arms and hands, head bending this way and that way. When you are going to the toilet, try to be aware of the action of squatting or sitting. After you have taken your food and are sitting down, try to be aware of the action of sitting down. When you are going to lie down for a rest or sleep, try to be aware of the changing from the standing, into the kneeling or the sitting and then into the lying down posture. Or anytime during the day when you find yourself changing from a higher posture into a lower one, try to be present, try to be aware. See if you can let go of future thoughts, past thoughts, worries, fears and such; and find a peace and a balance that can exist just in the simple movements of lowering your body.

# LETTING GO

Tonight I would like to talk about achieving, letting go, and the difference between gaining and giving.

Often when we first become interested in anything new, in developing our knowledge and skill in that area, we "gather up" the energy to achieve something that we do not yet have.

Acquiring knowledge, education, wealth or status means that we add these things to what we already have, building a self-image. We may acquire a new skill for our livelihood. We may acquire friends, a family, material possessions. And most of our society judges us on the end product of our efforts.

This has deeply conditioned us into the thought of acquisition—the "gathering-in" mind. We often direct our energies toward the result of our actions, working purely for the result. The result of our work may become the most important thing to us, not how we approach our doing.

We may not even have questioned this way of looking at things. We may see Peace, Enlightenment, Wisdom or whatever goal we have as something that we are going to achieve. One of the reasons that we may be having difficulties with meditation is because the meditation process is not so much one of the acquisition of Peace and Wisdom, but of Letting Go. This is really the letting go of the obstacles to that potential Peace that lies within us all.

It is a letting go of our habitual reactions, views and opinions of how life should be or what we think life is all about—and, instead, investigating into what life really is. It is letting go of the factors of mind that block Peace and Wisdom from arising.

In your efforts to develop Concentration and Mindfulness, you may have noticed that when there is a strong desire to be concentrated or mindful so that you can gain a particular state of mind, this energy of the acquiring mind actually may prevent you from being concentrated.

What it often brings up is a lot of restlessness, tension, frustration and doubt. We may not be content, then, to be with each breath, each step, each movement in the moment. Instead, we have this image of Mindfulness and Concentration as some goal to achieve in the future, thinking that we are doing the necessary drudgery in the present to obtain it. It will be the reward for our efforts now.

With this attitude, we may miss the peace of the acceptance of, and non-resistance to, the moment; the experience, even if only brief, of the relief of letting go and the peacefulness of absence of desire; the contentment just to be with whatever is happening. With the letting go of the hindrances, concentration will occur.

Concentration is not a goal or reward. It is a natural arising from a continual letting go and coming back to the moment. This is a different kind of effort and energy. It is the effort and energy to continually let go and come back to the *moment*, not the effort and energy to achieve in the *future*.

When you do walking meditation, is it in order to achieve some wonderful experience in the future? Are you walking just to get through the period, thinking that by doing so you will deserve some reward?

Or is your effort in walking more directed toward being with each step, each movement, perhaps experiencing the few moments when you actually are *there*, free from future concerns, free from unwise reaction and free from wanting?

The following analogy may give you an idea of the actual energy of the acquiring mind, the achievement/reward-oriented way of practice, compared with the effort and energy that may be of more help to you in your practice.

Two groups of people want to climb a mountain. They both wish to reach the top. This initial desire gives them the energy to begin. However, each approaches the climb in a different way.

One group is filled with longing; their deepest desire is to be on that peak. They start to climb, continually looking up with this longing, never content with where they are on the mountain. They keep stumbling on obstacles in front of them, then come back grudgingly to the actual drudgery of climbing, continually holding the image of the top of the mountain in mind.

This longing burns and consumes much of their energy. There is no time to stop, enjoy the scenery, the fresh, brisk air. The climb becomes something they have to suffer through in order to get to the top. They may be so consumed by the image of the top of the mountain and their future fame, praise, etc. that they stumble and fall often. They continue make unwise decisions and may even make a fatal mistake.

The other climbers become interested in the actual climb. They may look up occasionally to the peak to gain inspiration, yet they become interested in the actual process of climbing as well: the limits of endurance, the feeling of the body. "How can one approach this steep incline in front?" "Can this crevice be avoided?" "How can energy be conserved and not depleted?"

When they get to a level area, they take in the environment: the fresh air, the widening view, the actuality of being there. There is more to climb, but they try not to allow it to overwhelm them, thus consuming the energy needed to continue.

Climbing becomes an art of discovering new territory, not just something that they have to do in order to get to the top of the mountain. When they climb a sharp incline and make it to the next level, they take joy with just this, trying not to think about how many more difficult cliff-faces or crevices there will be.

Their skill is increasing; their knowledge is increasing. When they come to a difficult obstacle, they investigate different routes around it, concentrating on just this obstacle. After they investigate, making use of their past understanding, they take the way that they are capable of doing, realizing their limitations.

Most of us will be able to identify the achievement drive in ourselves. In the Western world, great value is placed on achievement. From when we were small children, we often were conditioned to

believe that if we achieve this or that, are successful and show this in material acquisition, name, fame, status according to the values of our society, then we are valuable, useful, worthy human beings.

As children, it is often like this: If we do things well and achieve something, then we are worthy of love and praise. So, often, the achievement mind gets mixed up with, "If I'm successful, I'll be worthy and be loved."

Then when we do not achieve, we may feel we are unworthy, useless and unlovable. We may not like feeling this way, so the desire to achieve, succeed and show the results may become a major drive in us...so that we can be worthy...and be loved.

This may start out early in life, when we try to learn how to do so many of the basic things in life, and when the approval of our parents is so important to us.

For example, while quite young we may have been playing in the backyard and there was a big muddy puddle. Intrigued, we headed toward it, wondering, "What is this?!" Investigating, we timidly put our foot into it...it sinks down...the mud oozes through our toes. Delighted, we crouch down and slap our hands in the muddy water...it spatters all over us. Thrilled, we shout with joy.

Our parents, upon hearing our shrieks, hurry out to check on us. We look up, our face bright with delight. Yet they frown and groan: "Look at you, you bad child. You've got all your clean clothes filthy!" They scoop us up, rush us inside to be changed, as we cry and look longingly back at the mud.

Often we are left with the feeling of failure, yet we were only doing something quite natural.

Perhaps we were normal students in school; we "got by." Some teachers are only interested in the high achievers. They get all of the teachers' attention, all the gold stars; they are asked all the questions. And we sit forgotten, along with all of the other average students and low achievers. We may have been able to answer some of the questions, but we are just not quick enough. So we see that through achieving we could get praise, attention and love.

If we were the high achievers, we notice that we get a lot of attention by achieving and we see that those who do not achieve are forgotten. So we may want to achieve continually through fear of losing this attention.

We may have been brought up by parents who wanted us to achieve so they could feel worthy in the eyes of others. They may have wanted us to be the best students, the best athletes, the most beautiful or handsome, or to pursue a certain professional career. They may have placed great demands on us to achieve so that, when we did not, we felt like a failure, unworthy, useless.

These are only a few examples. Looking back into your own experience, perhaps you can remember some situations that resulted in your feeling that by achieving this or that, you would be loved. You may have created the ideal and continually pushed away what you were.

"If only I could do this or that, achieve this or that, then I'd be loved and be happy." "I should be this way or that way." An ideal may have been continually held up, a gap between what you would have liked to be and the actuality of what you were.

Now you may be comparing the imagined end result of your practice with the person in the present. Naturally, if you set up such an ideal and continually compare the actuality with it, you often will feel lacking, thus feeding your sense of unworthiness and your self-hatred.

You may find it very difficult to let go of this obstacle of idealism and investigate deeply, compassionately. You may then miss the small growths, the moments of Understanding; they may never feel good enough. Dissatisfaction may arise because you are only able to be mindful for some parts of your walking, your sitting, your eating, your sweeping.

It is very helpful to illustrate the pessimistic view that idealism may create. This dissatisfaction may color all experiences. It is a bit like the people who, while eating lunch, look at their glass, and note, "Oh, it's half-empty."

Other people may get inspired by small growths, small moments of Understanding, small moments of being there. This allows joy to arise in the practice. As you may recall, joy is a Factor of Enlightenment, a necessary part of mental development. Joy gives us further energy and inspiration to continue. It colors experience with a lightness and optimism. It is like the people who, while eating lunch, look at their glass, and note, "Ah, it's half-full."

With the obstacle of idealism, we may go into each moment with preconceptions: the breath should be this way or that; the mind should not react this way or that; "If I were a good meditator, then I would be able to destroy all of these wandering thoughts." So if we get lost and wander a lot, we may feel that we are failures.

Actually, the unworthiness mind creates more and more self-image, self-identity. "I can't do this... I am like that... I can't meditate... I'm a lousy meditator... I can't do walking meditation—it's impossible!"

We may take from the mind different moments and start to build the self-image again, this time concerned with "the meditator." We may try to freeze it into a solid image of ourselves, an opinion or concept that is almost unshakable and unchanging. At the same time, we may set beside it the ideal.

The trouble with this is that forming solid, static images of ourselves is directly opposite to the truth, to the Laws of Nature. Everything appears to be changing, arising and passing away. When we start to investigate the mind and body, we may see that within a short time there is constant change. Thoughts are coming and going, feelings in the body are arising and passing away. The mind is in constant flux. Mindfulness is arising and passing away. The Hindrances are coming and going...some of you may say "more coming and not going away fast enough!"

We may have created an image that is not in line with the actuality of things as they are. Sometimes there is brightness, Compassion and Lovingkindness; and sometimes there is the opposite floating through the mind.

What we may be doing is jumping into the flow of the thoughts in the mind, and selecting this or that, creating a solid, static image of ourselves—trying to "freeze" the flow.

Negativity in the mind may tend to see only the so-called "bad" things, and forget about the positive, bright spots. We may want to hold onto this image as it gives us a sense of security, even if it is painful. We may have become used to this painfulness and find it very hard to give up.

However, Vipassana meditation is the giving up of self-images and concepts, and the investigation into the actuality of things *as they are* with as much Equanimity and Compassion as possible.

The reward-oriented mind also may create a tendency in us to build concepts and opinions about other things. We may try to work out what ultimate reality is like with our intellect, building concepts of Voidness, Enlightenment, Ultimate Truth, etc.

We may tend to push away the present—"It's just *too* mundane!" We may be the person who would rather have the glamorous ideas of what the result of Concentration will be, what enlightened beings we will become. We may create the longing to become "Spiritual Beings" seeking the Truth, Reality, Enlightenment, union with God, etc.

This may negate the present and push away the purification process that has to be done in the present, the process of letting go of opinions, views and selfishness. We may mistakenly think that if we want Peace, Concentration, Enlightenment enough, and suffer enough in the present, we will somehow deserve it.

What this may do is create a huge burden for ourselves coming from the desire to gain. Creating concepts and longing only increases our dissatisfaction and suffering. We may miss the point that we have to "empty" ourselves of concepts and longing, and try to open ourselves to the characteristics of the body and mind as they are, without preconceptions of what we think they should be.

We can try to learn how to let go of our opinions, views and self-images, and open ourselves to "not knowing." Try to let go of the wish for security in forming ideas about reality and come back to the actual work of being with each moment as it is: investigating, seeing what is true in the present moment, letting go rather than acquiring.

The achievement mind is a very deep conditioning that most of us bring here. A mind that is probably continually judging and commenting on what we see arising, and often does not even know that it is doing it.

Although the achievement mind can hinder us coming into the present it is not altogether unuseful. It has a certain energy and drive—a "gung-ho," "go-get'um," energetic attitude that gets us started into something new.

We can start to bend this energy. First we can turn it into small achievements. We can achieve Concentration and Mindfulness in the next five breaths or steps. We can succeed in seeing this hindrance clearly. We can succeed in being able to sit with restlessness, investigating, until the final bell.

We can succeed in considering only the next sit, and not overwhelming ourselves with the rest of the afternoon or the rest of the retreat. Try to continually reduce the future down into smaller time spans. And then we can go about transforming this energy.

Many of us, when we started to do something new in the past, began with an initial "gung-ho" energy, but later found that we may have lost interest. Unless we can transform this initial energy into something deeper, then this energy may burn out, taper off. We may start to lose interest or develop the idea that it is just too difficult, and we may even drop the whole thing.

Can we transform the tension, almost paranoia in the effort to achieve; "I'm going to be mindful if it kills me!" attitude to the energy of Mindfulness that settles back and is gentle and caring. Even if in the beginning the caring Mindfulness is greatly outweighed by the other paranoid effort to be mindful.

We would like to be able to transform the energy to achieve into the effort to let go.

Even with these words, we have to realize that we do not mean letting go of everything. Letting go has to be based in Right Understanding, Right Intention and Right Effort. Then it is a balanced effort.

In the scriptures, the Buddha compared the effort needed to walk the path of meditation to the tuning of a stringed instrument. If one tunes the strings too tightly, the instrument will not bring forth beautiful music. If one tunes them too loosely, the instrument will not bring forth beautiful music. When one tunes them neither too tightly nor too loosely, then it is possible to bring forth beautiful music.

The too-tight often comes from the energy of wanting to achieve, the reaching out with desire for the fruits of our practice, which brings tension and unbalanced effort. The too-loose is not enough effort, letting the mind wander and drop into laziness and dullness.

Letting go is not dropping into dullness, but having a vital, energetic mind. It is the energy needed to return continually to the breath, the walking; the energy to pull oneself up when the mind starts to wander off, when it starts to seek results.

It is the energy to let go of thoughts, even if they are pleasant and enjoyable, and to let go of restlessness, fear and worry. Or to be with them, observing their energy, until one can let go. It is trying to let go in the moment.

Another very important thing to realize about the term "letting go" is that it is not meant to imply that one can let go of responsibility for one's actions, speech and thoughts. Simply letting go of the guilt associated with unpleasant emotions and unskillful actions does not mean one can avoid the repercussions and results of them.

To do so is a bit like believing that if one throws a stone into a lake and then forgets about the stone as soon as it is thrown, it will not drop into the lake and make ripples in the water. This is impossible.

Letting go of and having Compassion for our anger, jealousy, desire, tendency to judge others, etc. does not mean we do not try our best to heal any damage that these tendencies may have caused, if it is possible to do so.

Compassion investigates and wishes to learn from the ripples that anger, desire, unskillful actions, or thoughtless speech have created. We look into stress and suffering and see their causes, so that we may develop the understanding of how to *avoid* stress and suffering for ourselves and for others in the future.

This protects the "letting go" from falling into a very dangerous attitude of indifference and ego-centered practice. The idea that, "Well, I've forgiven myself, realized it is just due to my conditioning and I've let go of it… What's the matter with you?… Can't you let go too?!"

Compassion and Wisdom protect us from this ego-centered practice. Compassion and Wisdom do not seek to justify anger: "It's just due to my conditioning; I didn't know any better." Compassion and Wisdom realize that we do not have to be slaves to our conditioning. We have the power to investigate, change and transform these energies in the present.

Compassion and Wisdom open to and see clearly the unskillfulness of these actions, speech and mind states. Compassion and Wisdom do not wish to justify them, to allow ourselves to become indifferent to them, or to try to escape the results of the suffering that we have created for ourselves and for others.

One acknowledges the unskillful, unbeneficial things as they are—unskillful and unbeneficial—and seeks to alleviate any suffering or difficulty that has been caused. Unpleasant feelings may be connected with this. These unpleasant feelings are part of the healing process and growth of Compassionate Understanding. Acknowledging our unbeneficial, unskillful actions, speech and thoughts, and their results, and opening to our part in the creation of suffering for ourselves and others, means having to open to one type of unpleasant spiritual feeling that many people do not like feeling. This is often referred to as Moral Shame or Remorse.

In opening to it, we may experience quite a lot of unpleasant feelings, yet Compassion and Wisdom impel us to do so. It is a step in transforming unbeneficial things into beneficial things—honestly seeing things clearly as they are.

After this step may arise the wish and the understanding of how to prevent these things from arising in the future. An energy based in Compassionate Understanding will arise. And then the true letting go process begins.

We have opened to the pain that the ripples of our actions may have created. We also wish to heal the pain by humbling ourselves and by letting go of our selfishness, justifications and depreciating judgments of others. This is the genuine letting go based in Compassionate Understanding, not the false letting go based in indifference and selfishness.

It is very dangerous in the meditation and mental development practice to impose the many intellectual conceptions of ultimate reality that are floating around—voidness, no-self, etc.—onto the process of purification at the level of practice most people are working.

Some people may become quite amoral through thinking they have somehow gone beyond the need to purify their actions, speech and thoughts, or thinking they can escape their consequences because, "Well, you don't exist, I don't exist, it's all illusion. When you reach Ultimate Reality, you have to go beyond good and evil." They may think that training themselves on the morality level is simply for people who are not as "brilliant, intelligent and enlightened" as they consider themselves to be.

This is like thinking that one can somehow put a roof on a house before one has even laid the foundations!

Goodness, evil, beneficial and unbeneficial become merely opinions, concepts and limited viewpoints to these people. They close their hearts to the interrelationship of life and the suffering created by unbeneficial action and speech, and by intellectual coldness.

In letting go of intellectual brilliance, cleverness and the conceit connected to these, we can investigate into the stress of unbeneficial mind objects, intellectual games, selfish desires and egotism. We can open to their difficulty within and we can begin to alleviate it.

So please be careful to understand what I mean by "letting go." Letting go has to be based in Right Understanding, Right Intention—the Compassionate Motivation—and Right Effort.

Otherwise, this misunderstanding may be of great harm to you and to others. It could build more and more ignorance, egotism and indifference within you, creating more suffering and difficulties for yourself and for others, and more suffering and difficulties in the world…a world that is so in need of Compassionate Understanding.

With Wrong Understanding, our conception of Compassion to ourselves and others could become self-pity or pity, self-indulgence or indulging in others' conditioning, or a wish to experience only pleasant feeling.

In that way, there would not be the wish to open to the unpleasant spiritual feeling that is necessary for our purification. This would amount to a wish to escape responsibility for our actions, speech and thoughts, a wish to forget about and deny the stone that has been thrown into the lake.

Compassion to ourselves is the willingness to transform unpleasant worldly feelings into the sometimes unpleasant spiritual feelings coming from Compassionate Understanding and Wisdom. This can cut through our egotism, our indulgence, our selfishness. Then the heal-

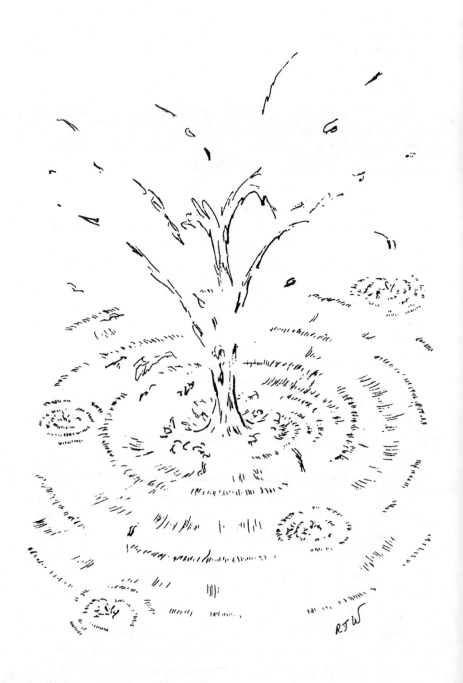

ing brought about by the real, genuine letting go begins to take place.

How can we transform the initial energy of the achievement-orientated mind into the effort to let go? The first thing is to become aware of it. Try to be aware of the mind that is reaching out, is doing something in order to get something, or the mind that may wish to achieve in order not to feel unworthy in the present.

Unless we become aware of it, it may motivate all of our actions and efforts, and continually hinder us. Sadly, it may eventually cause us to "burn out"—to exhaust ourselves.

Try to pay attention to the energy behind your efforts throughout the day, both in formal meditation practice and in doing the necessary chores like sweeping, washing dishes, cleaning your room. See if you are seeking the result of the action—the reward. We have usually approached work in our life in this way, never interested in the process.

When we are able to see the reaching-out, achievement-oriented, gaining mind, we can investigate its energy, its particular uneasiness. We can see the pushing away of the present, the deep tensions and unsatisfactoriness of it. We try to be aware of the tightness and aggression in the mind.

If we have the courage to investigate in this way and to be able to feel deeply the particular stress and suffering involved in it, then the wish to be free of problems, stress and suffering may arise. That Compassionate wish will deepen into a Compassion that has much Strength and Energy—the Strength, Energy and Wisdom that will let go.

When we can let go, we see our tensions fade away. We see the importance of good intention and awareness in the moment. We realize that we can live each moment without the burden of the ego-satisfaction that we seek from obtaining the result. We can experience the Peace of being in the moment in a non-resisting way, making each action important.

We can enjoy the results when the work is finished. But we also have the potential to be at Peace simply with the process of doing. We can try to sweep in order to sweep, wash the dishes in order to wash the dishes. That is, we sweep simply to be aware of the process of sweeping, not only to have a clean yard. We wash the dishes to be aware of washing the dishes, not only to have clean dishes.

This is important to remember when we do repetitive tasks, for big results do not come, and we do these tasks over and over every day. Rather than generating boredom, they can be viewed as an opportunity to use the repetitiveness to aid in the Mindfulness process, helping to develop Awareness and Concentration. In this way, our life becomes fuller and not so dependent on gaining something. We can try to drop the burden of worry and dependence on results.

This also can help in preventing what is a common occurrence in the West—the feeling of futility, of working and wondering what is the purpose of it all. We can use work and all of our actions as the means to purify the mind, rather than working just to make our living, leaving so much of our life unsatisfying.

If we become interested in *how* we do things, then nothing is wasted and we do not separate our life into compartments, living only for the "uppers" and "highs" of reward. We may be able to live all of our life more fully, so that our lives have more richness and Peace.

This also can mean that when the results are not tremendous and wonderful, we can protect the mind from grief and frustration, the sense of failure and unworthiness. This is because what was important to us was *how* we did it. If we tried to work with awareness and good intentions, then the blame or lack of results just does not have as much ability to throw us off balance. In this life, there will always be praise and blame, no matter how well we do things.

The Compassion arising from seeing the stress and difficulty of the gaining, achievement-oriented mind, which helps us to let go, also can transform the intentions and motivations behind our actions. When the gaining idea arises, Compassion can transform that strong energy into a wish to alleviate difficulties for ourselves and for others.

This Compassionate Intention strengthens our efforts, not in order to *achieve* for ourselves, but in order to *ease the burden* for ourselves and for others.

When we can find Peace in the process of working or meditating, when we live more at Peace, then we spread Peace, rather than spreading boredom, frustration or paranoia to others.

Compassion greatly strengthens the ability to be honest with ourselves. It strengthens the willingness to change and it gives us the power to let go. It is a healing energy. It is the difference between *gaining* something for ourselves, the selfish motivation, and the *giving* energy, the Compassionate wish.

Through Compassion to ourselves, we soften around our conditioning, investigating, seeing the tensions deeply and through Compassion, we gently let go. As our Awareness gets stronger, we are able to see the difference between the gaining, reaching out, seeking results energy in the mind and the feeling of letting go as it occurs. Little-by-little we can drop that burden of unworthiness and the need to achieve...learn to live each moment in compassionate awareness.

The gaining, achieving energy is uncomfortable, contracted and full of tension. The energy of Compassion is spacious, broad and healing. The more that we feel Compassion, the more that it is renewed within us, and the more it renews our efforts, resulting in a consistency and a "never giving up" attitude.

Compassion can give us the ability to work through difficulties and obstacles without giving up until we are able to go deeper and discover the causes. The gaining energy does not have this power because it is based more on an ideal of the future, a mind-made, dreamlike wish. When it meets obstacles, it may not have the courage, endurance, patience, and ability to step back, observe, investigate and be truthful. We may merely want to add Peace to our self-image, rather than let go of habitual responses, or our cherished views and opinions about ourselves, others and the world. The achievement motivation is usually aggressive.

The letting go based on the Compassionate Motivation is gentle but also powerfully strong. It adds a gentleness and kindness to our efforts, yet it will not allow us to indulge or delude ourselves. This is because it is based on the wish to alleviate our own and others' suffering and difficulties, coming from the Wisdom of clear seeing.

We see the cause of suffering lying within our selfish reactions to experiences. Compassion then impels us to investigate and to open to the suffering without justifications. We begin to heal the pain through letting go of attachment—through Compassion to ourselves and others.

The Compassionate Energy can be renewed and renewed, because Compassion comes from seeing stress, unsatisfactoriness and suffering and having the wish to alleviate them. With investigating into ourselves, there is no lack of areas in the mind that can activate Compassion. When we see in ourselves the different levels of subtle unsatisfactoriness, frustration and stress, we also begin to understand more clearly the minds of others, and Compassion begins to open out to other living beings.

It seems clear that in order to really understand and deeply feel Compassion for others, we need to first investigate into and understand the causes of difficulties within and feel Compassion for ourselves.

Compassion can allow the separate self to slowly dissolve because Compassion reduces selfishness. We may gradually be able to see the interrelationship between ourselves and others, the effects that our actions and speech can have on others, and we can begin to purify our intentions.

We can try to be mindful of our actions, speech and thoughts through the understanding of unsatisfactoriness, suffering, stress... through the wish to alleviate them in ourselves and others...through Compassion...through *giving* rather than wanting to achieve.

## EARLY MORNING DAY SEVEN

# ONE WORD, ONE WORD

With five billion people, what does it mean?
    When you read about wars, how do you feel?
You hear about a murder, what do you think?
    Another person is starving, why?

When one person cries, there is someone else crying.
    When one person laughs, there is someone else dying.
    When one person is sick, somewhere a baby is born.

And the forest looks lovely, such colors, so fresh,
    the flowers, the birds, the rocks and the grass.
    If that is all you see, watch out for the snake.

The world has its balance of pleasant and not.
    And many don't care.
Few it is indeed who open their heart,
    Their Compassion, their Love.

It is not easy; the way to open one's heart.
    Conditioning is such one may start, one may stop.

Perhaps one word, perhaps one word
    may be all we can change.
Yet the value may be great,
    like in the heat a soft gentle rain.

And many will think, "What can I get?"
    How often comes the thought, "What can I give?"

One word, one word.

# EMOTIONS

It is very normal in a retreat such as this to experience a lot of different emotions arising. A lot of thoughts about the past, thoughts about the future. Each in their own way helping to create different reactions, different mental states. These can be a bit overpowering at times, like giant waves in the ocean compared to little ripples in a lake.

Try to keep in mind that this is just normal, that there is no good, no bad in the sense of the words regarding the emotions coming up. That it is a normal process due to our conditioning.

If we label such and such emotion as "This is bad, this is terrible," then we have just reacted causing more stress, more problems for ourselves. Try to realize that everything coming up, especially thoughts of the past, thoughts of the future, are all just due to our past conditioning. Just natural.

We are what we are because of the past. It is in our reactions and in learning how to be wiser with our reactions that we create new conditioning for more Peace and deeper Happiness in the future.

There are a lot of different ways that a meditator will react in a retreat like this. Rosemary talked earlier about what are called "V.V."s and "V.R."s, having anger towards others or having desire towards others. Yesterday I talked about the "immature Yogi mind."

It can go toward the other meditators. We can be thinking, "Oh, so and so is doing this. So and so is doing that." We can be thinking about the schedule or we can be thinking about the monks and nuns.

Many times we are going outward, pointing outside, pointing outside.

It is important just to be aware that this is a normal process of our mind. Often trying to point outward for the cause of any diffi-culty, any problem.

Try to see it for what it is. See it as a conditioning, a thing that we have been doing much of our life, and a thing that most humans often do. Try to relax around it. Try to have Compassion towards this type of conditioning, this type of difficulty that we all go through. Try to understand it for what it is.

Try not to jump on it with more aversion, thinking that it is terrible. And try not to indulge in it either by getting carried away with it.

It is not the thoughts and the emotions that are the main prob-lems. This is an important point to try to understand and remember. It is not the thoughts and the emotions that are the main problems— it is our reactions to them. This is where we can do our work.

Basically there are three ways to react to thoughts. We may in-dulge them; we like thinking in that way so we just keep doing it.

We may have aversion to the thoughts; we don't like thinking in that way, and yet the aversion often stimulates the thoughts so they keep coming.

Or we may try to have Equanimity and Compassionate Under-standing toward the thoughts, trying just to see them for what they are, without being attached to them in either a positive or a negative way.

Last night Rosemary was talking about Letting-Go through the development of Compassionate Understanding and Wisdom. With this in mind, try to view the practice in the following way: It's as though we've been holding onto fire all of our lives, and yet we never really knew it for what it was. Now we start to examine it; "Hmmm. Fire."

In the beginning we may not be aware enough, intelligent enough, wise enough, to know the extent of the damage and the difficulty that fire actually brings—the burning, the painfulness and so on. In fact, we may simply feel that it's been part of us for all of our lives, and we like it for that reason; "It's me, it's me. It's mine, it's mine." This is a type of positive attachment.

A second way, when we start to look at this fire, is to react with aversion. We don't like it; we don't want it to be there. So we hit at it and beat at it and try to drive it away. But often the aversion present is quite exciting. And so although we hit at it and beat at it with one hand, we hold onto it tighter with the other, so we can do more hitting and more beating at a later date.

Again, in an odd way, we like it. It has become part of us; "It's me, it's me. It's mine, it's mine." This is a type of negative attachment.

A third way to react is to try to see it for what it is—"Fire, fire." In the beginning, we don't understand it clearly. So we have to examine it again and again, "fire, fire," and see its characteristics—the burning, the pain, the heat. Trying to understand fully the difficulties, the stress, the problems that holding on to fire causes.

As we develop a bit of understanding, we may start to let go a little—maybe one finger, maybe two. We may even think we have let go entirely, and become a bit surprised later when we see it's still there. But as we develop our understanding, as we fully comprehend fire for what it is, as we truly understand the pain of holding onto these types of thoughts and emotions, we will want to let go.

It is not the thoughts and emotions that are the main problems. This is an important point to try to understand and remember. It is not the thoughts and the emotions that are the main problems—it is our reactions to them. This is where we can do our work.

It is all due to our past conditioning. The anger comes up. The aversion comes up. The restlessness, and everything else, comes up. Just naturally coming up due to past conditioning. But it is in the present moment, and being wiser with our reactions in the present moment that we create new conditioning for our future.

The more we can settle back, watch and learn, the more we will grow in Compassion, Understanding, Patience, Endurance and many other fine qualities. By practicing in this way, we will get to know who we are, and get to feel that it is all right who we are, in the sense that we are who we are due to the past; then trying to work *with* who we are, not *against* who we are.

The more we practice watching with Patience, with Compassion with Understanding, the more that the different unbeneficial emotions, the different unbeneficial thought patterns will gradually diminish, gradually fade away. If we do not "feed" them with anger or indulgence, if we just watch, then these things will have a chance to pass away of their own nature.

We then will create new conditioning for our future, which will enable us to find more Peace and Contentment. And, in the same way, we may be able to help others find more Peace and Contentment.

A very common way to react when you find that you have been lost in a mind-spin for maybe half an hour, is, "Oh, crud. Lost again for half an hour!"

How does that reaction compare to this one?... "I'm aware again. It was only 30 minutes."

Try not to feed any unbeneficial mental state with more aversion, thinking that you are terrible. This type of mental development practice is the hardest thing in the world to do. Try to take some Joy when you are aware. Joy will help give you more Contentment. With Joy and Contentment, you will have more Energy. With Joy, Contentment and Energy, your Concentration and your Mindfulness will grow.

Aversion will only feed your unbeneficial mental state. It will hinder your Concentration and your Mindfulness. Even if you are lost for three hours... "I'm aware again. It was only three hours." Even if you're lost for three days... "I'm aware again. It was only three days."

How you react, how you react to whatever experience you have. It was the same situation; the mind was lost for some period of time. But you can react in different ways. Start again, start again, try to create new beneficial conditioning for your future.

Some of you may not actually be aware of some other ways that you may be feeding your unbeneficial thoughts and emotions. Concerning restlessness and worry in particular: If you are getting lost in it and allowing it to overcome you, you will probably find that you are having trouble staying still in the sitting meditation and even more trouble, perhaps, in the walking meditation.

This is now Day Seven of the retreat, and many of you have settled down nicely in your walking meditation, putting in the effort, continuing to walk for the entire period, and using the same walking track or one in the same area.

But some of you have not yet settled down in your walking meditation. And those of you who are fairly settled may have periods when the restlessness is getting fairly strong. You may find at those times that you feel like going to the toilet even though there is no need...or getting a drink of water even though you are not really thirsty...or perhaps you feel that there is something that you must do back in your room...wondering if the clothes are dry ...

Maybe you find yourself wanting to go up to the lookouts...or you may get interested in watching the ants and millipedes; sometimes it is much nicer to watch them do their walking than to watch our own!

Not always feeling comfortable in this formal walking stuff, just going back and forth, back and forth...a nice long walk on the beach would be much more pleasant.

Often the basic reason for this physical unrest and agitation is the restlessness and worry in the mind, and the lack of putting enough effort into being mindful of the Hindrances. If you find that this is happening to you, then we strongly encourage you to try to make more use of the mental noting of your wandering mind. Try to put forth more effort so that you will not be overpowered by these giant waves of thoughts and emotions.

It will also help you to make a type of resolution to yourself to stay in the same walking track for the entire period, and to go to the toilet or get a drink only at the beginning or at the end of the period. If you are getting tired during the walking, then you can do standing at one end for as long as you like. If you really feel like you need to, it is OK to sit down for a couple of minutes and then get up and try again.

However, if you do feel you need to and want to sit down, before you do please consider about old antique car engines. Sitting down frequently, going to your room, having a drink of water for ten minutes, etc., giving in to one's laziness is not going to help you get the car engine started. Cranking and then stopping, cranking, stopping, cranking, stopping.

If you want the car to get going then it is important to keep your efforts going, and not indulge your sloth and torpor or your restlessness. Try to put in the effort. Rosemary mentioned that the effort needed is like the tuning of a stringed instrument. Try to be aware when your strings are too loose.

For those of you who have been trying hard in the walking meditation, it is possible at times that your strings get a bit too tight, especially those of you who are walking in the driveway or in front of the hall.

Often the dogs are walking through "your" walking track...often the Thais are walking through "your" walking track...and often some of those restless meditators are walking through "your" walking track. Try to be aware of the change in your attitude comparing when the dogs or the Thais pass through and when a restless meditator is wandering around and passes through.

Try to guard against the V.V. arising and having aversion toward them and their restlessness. Try to make more use of the mental noting, using any and all experiences for the growth of Patience and Compassionate Understanding.

Can you be walking on your path when another meditator passes through, and not make yourself angry and upset??! It is possible.

Whether your strings are too loose or too tight, try not to be overpowered by the giant waves of thoughts and emotions. Try not to always blame the outside for the cause of your own restlessness or aversion. Try to make more use of the mental noting to see more clearly that it is just another paper tiger coming to try to push you off balance. Keep trying. Keep putting in the effort.

When it comes to most of our mental difficulties, if not all of them, they simply arise due to unwise reactions and wrong thinking. If we can develop wise reactions and right thinking then our mental difficulties will end. Learning how to think wisely, training our minds to think wisely.

Tonight we intend to introduce you to five other topics for reflection meditation. Training our minds to think wisely. Concerning this I would like to mention that one of the most important conditions necessary for this wisdom development is to live with good, kind, wise spiritual friends. In the scriptures the Buddha talked about this importance time and time again.

One little story which illustrates this was the time he was having a conversation with his attendant monk whose name was Ananda. Ananda had a habit of whenever he wanted to ask a question, he didn't actually ask a question per se. He would make a statement and see if the Buddha agreed with the statement or point out where the statement was wrong. On this occasion he came to the Buddha and a conversation similar to this took place; "Sir, as I understand the practice at least 50% of the whole practice is to have a good, wise, kind spiritual friend." The Buddha replied, "No, no, Ananda, no, no, don't say that. A 100% practice is to have a good, wise, kind spiritual friend."

**I would now like to start this morning's sitting with a little bit of Compassion/Lovingkindness meditation.** Please settle yourself if you have not already done so. Focus on your breathing for a short while, relaxing into the posture.

*****

Please focus your attention on yourself. Try to consider some of your difficulties and challenges that you have in life. And then try to raise some Compassion and Lovingkindness toward yourself.

*****

May I be able to learn, practice and develop methods, techniques and tools of Mental Development so that I can cope with, understand, accept and overcome the difficulties and challenges of life.
    May I find peace of mind.

*****

Try now to turn your attention to someone whom you like. Try to consider some of the difficulties and challenges that this person might have. And then try to raise some Compassion and Lovingkindness toward someone whom you like.

*****

May this person whom I like be able to learn, practice and develop methods, techniques and tools of Mental Development so that they can cope with, understand, accept and overcome the difficulties and challenges of life.

May this person whom I like find peace of mind.

*****

Try now to reflect upon someone who is neutral to you, you do not like them and you do not hate them, perhaps someone in a store who sold you something. Try to consider some of the difficulties and challenges that this person might have. And then try to raise some Compassion and Lovingkindness toward this person who is neutral to you.

*****

May this person who is neutral to me be able to learn, practice and develop methods, techniques and tools of Mental Development so that they can cope with, understand, accept and overcome the difficulties and challenges of life.

May this person who is neutral to me find peace of mind.

*****

Now try to think of someone whom you do not like. Try to consider the possible difficulties and problems, challenges that this person has. The deep problems that they may have which cause them to do unkind things to others. And then try to raise some Compassion and Lovingkindness toward this person whom you do not like.

*****

May this person whom I do not like be able to learn, practice and develop methods, techniques and tools of Mental Development so that they can cope with, understand, accept and overcome the difficulties and challenges of life.

May this person find peace of mind.

*****

Please continue expanding the Compassion/Lovingkindness meditation.

*****

(end of period)

So far, for special mindfulness activities, we have asked you to pay extra attention to going in and out of doorways, washing dishes, putting on and taking off your shoes, coming up and going down the stairs. Then the last two days were the processes of raising and lowering of your body. Please continue with these.

Today's activity to pay extra attention to is scooping water and pouring it. So when you are in the bathroom and after you have used the toilet, try to be aware of the process of scooping the water and pouring it into the toilet. Try to be aware of the hand grabbing the scooper, putting it into the water, scooping, raising it out of the water, turning and pouring.

When you are doing your laundry, try to be aware of scooping the water and pouring it into the laundry buckets. When you are having a bath, try to be aware of scooping the water and pouring it over your body.

Try to be right there with the contact of your hand with the scooper and the process. If you wish, you can use mental noting. Try to bring yourself right there, letting go of the past, of the future. And, finding the peace that can exist right there in the moment of scooping water and pouring it.

# FIVE REFLECTIONS

Earlier in this retreat, we explained a way of meditating on Compassion/Lovingkindness. This is one type of reflective or contemplative meditation. Tonight we will introduce five more topics that can be used as reflection meditations. Reflecting on these five topics has proven to be extremely beneficial for many people.

**The first of these reflections is to develop the understanding of just how fortunate we are.** That we have a very precious opportunity with our life.

In what ways are we fortunate?

If we compared ourselves to not only most of the Thai people, but to most of the people of Asia, Africa, the Middle East, Central America, South America and many parts of our so-called western affluent countries, we will easily see that money is a first way in which we are fortunate.

Just to be able to buy a plane ticket from Europe, America, Australia, wherever, and come here to Thailand indicates that you are richer than many. The fact that you can stop work and have an overseas holiday also indicates that you are richer than many.

Traveling freedom is another way in which we are fortunate. As probably all of you know, there are countries which do not grant their citizens the freedom that all of us obviously have. To get out of some countries is almost impossible for some people.

Those of us living in the so-called western affluent countries have many benefits that many in other countries do not have. Generally speaking, we have many more educational opportunities. Generally, we have higher levels of health and sanitation. Medical facilities are usually superior.

Although there are rare cases of food poisoning, few people in the West ever worry about eating spoiled food or drinking bad water. Drinking water from nearly any tap or faucet is hardly a concern. But in much of Asia, Africa, South America and many other parts of the world, the situation is quite different. Many people become ill or die due to contamination of food and water.

With our normally high level of educational opportunities, most of us, perhaps all, are fairly well educated. We have many freedoms. At the present moment we are free of work and free of many normal obligations.

Here we are at this very nice little Wat (Thai monastery/meditation center) on what some people would call a "tropical island paradise." The environment is very pleasant. There is no war. There is no famine. The nuns and monks have been extremely kind in helping set up this retreat and in taking care of us. The food is fine. Many, many ways that we can view our life and see just how fortunate we are, having so much more than most people.

As fortunate as you may be in these material ways, what is even more important is that you have come in contact with and learned some methods and techniques of Mental Development. How very, very fortunate each of us is. If we practice and develop these methods and techniques, we will be able to develop a Wisdom and Understanding that will aid us in gaining Peace and deep Happiness.

Whether rich or poor, healthy or sick, in feast or in famine, during times of war or peace, if we have developed enough beneficial qualities of mind, then we can have Peace of Mind in all situations of life.

Just having the opportunity to learn some of these methods and techniques seems to be rare. How many of your relatives have learned anything about Mental Development? How many of your friends? How many of the people from your hometown? How many of the people from your country?

Here we are with this wonderful opportunity to learn some very valuable methods and techniques that can help us throughout our lives. There are many people who would like this opportunity but have not yet had the chance. And there are others who, even if they had the opportunity, would not want it. How very fortunate we are with a very precious, wonderful opportunity in our life.

Part of a food reflection that we teach covers the aspect of having such good food, and plenty of it, at a time when others in the world are starving. Many of us were told something similar to this by our parents when we were children, whenever we did not want to eat our food.

As children, we did not have the understanding that we have now as adults. Now we can use these thoughts, these reflections to aid us in our Mental Development, helping us to have more Peace and Contentment with whatever we experience, knowing that there are many others with far less than we have.

These reflections can help encourage us to make the most of each opportunity and experience that we have in life. The human life is very fragile. At any time, accident or illness can happen. We can never be sure what will happen tomorrow, next week, next month. We are very fortunate now—try to make the most of it now.

During these seven days, many of you have probably experienced some moments which were somewhat depressing, when you were feeling a bit down. Perhaps different mixtures of sloth and torpor, doubt, restlessness and worry, or aversion.

If you reflect often enough on how fortunate your opportunity in life is, you may discover that negative states of mind slowly will decrease and fade away.

Reflecting like this can help to produce Joy and Contentment. It also can help to stimulate Energy in your practice. With the development of Joy, Contentment and Energy in the mind, you will have more ability to gain Peace in any situation.

This type of reflection can be especially valuable when you are waking up in the morning. Just as we recommended doing Compassion/Lovingkindness meditation before falling asleep, we also suggest that when you wake up, you use the reflection on How Fortunate You Are, and the valuable and precious opportunity that you have.

This can help you to have more Joy, Contentment and Energy as you are waking up, thus giving you much better conditions to start off the day in a beneficial way.

So the first reflection for tonight's talk is reflecting on How Fortunate We Are, and the valuable, precious opportunity that each of us has with our life.

### The second reflection is on Death and Impermanence.

On the fifth day of the retreat Rosemary mentioned that within the Satipatthana Sutta, the Foundations of Mindfulness, it is written that the Buddha taught us to reflect whenever one sees a dead body with words such as: "Verily, also, my own body is of the same nature; such it will become and will not escape it."

Another way of reflecting upon death is to ask yourself three questions: Is death definite? When is death coming? And, at the moment of death, what has any meaning?

First, is death definite?

There is only one certainty in life. Each of us, all of our relatives, friends, all of the people in our home country, everyone in the world, all animals, every living being will eventually die. We were all born, we are now living, we will all die.

Death is a natural event. Our bodies are impermanent. All living beings are subject to change. The buildings are impermanent also. Cars, machines, all that we see around us.

It is very beneficial for our Mental Development if we reflect on this fact of life. Everything that we see around us is impermanent. Each thing had its own birth. It now has its own life. And eventually each thing will have its own death.

So, in answer to this first question, "Is death definite?" the answer is certainly, "Yes, death is definite." Even though death is definite, not many people like to think about it or plan for it. We make plans for many possible future events...plans for tomorrow, plans for next week, next month, next year. Sometimes plans for many years in the future, plans for future events that may not even happen. But the one event that will definitely happen, most people do not wish to think about.

The second question: "When is death coming?"

Tonight? Tomorrow? Next month? Next year? In twenty years? Forty years?

Generally we do not know when death is coming. For most of us, there is no certainty. We would like to believe that we will live until we are 70, 80, 90 years old, but if we open our eyes and look around us, we will see that this may not happen.

By reading the newspaper or walking through a cemetery, we will see that people of any age, all ages, have died. People younger than us, people older than us, and people the same age.

Even if someone has terminal cancer, that may not be the way that death comes. Even someone trying to commit suicide may not die in that way.

For most of us, we simply do not know the time of death.

The third question: "At the moment of death, what has any meaning?"

Do our homes have any meaning? Do our clothes have any meaning? Do our jobs have any meaning? Homes, clothes, jobs, friends, relatives, fame or fortune? None of these things seem to be important at the moment of death.

In many ways, depending on how much attachment a person has towards these things, they can actually be a problem at the moment of death, causing agitation, worry and fear, so that there is no peace in the mind.

If anything has any value at the moment of death, it would appear to be how we have actually lived. How we have developed in beneficial mental qualities. How we have developed in Compassion, Generosity, Lovingkindness, Patience, Understanding and many other such qualities.

As we have said before, what you are now is a result of your past conditioning. Your thoughts and mental states are due to your past conditioning. If you wish Peace in the mind, Compassion and Lovingkindness in the mind, Patience, Generosity, Understanding and other beneficial mental qualities, then you must produce certain conditions for these qualities to arise or become stronger.

How we have actually lived is so very important. Nearly all of the

world's meditation practices and religions teach that how we have lived our life is the cause for benefits or non-benefits in a future existence.

How we have lived and developed mentally also will determine whether we die with Peace and Contentment in the mind or with fears, worries and agitation in the mind.

It is healthy to keep in mind the following saying: "If a rich person dies without Peace of Mind and a poor person dies with Peace of Mind, then the poor person was actually far `richer' than the rich person."

How we have actually lived; how we have developed in beneficial mental qualities such as Compassion, Lovingkindness, Patience, Generosity, Equanimity, Understanding; how much Peace and Contentment we have brought into our life; these things seem to be very important at the moment of death, as well, very important in each moment of life.

Last night Rosemary talked about Letting Go. Reflecting on Death and Impermanence can help us in the letting-go process. Letting go of the things that we do not have to hold onto.

Some people become so attached, let us say, to a particular shirt, that when the shirt wears out, develops holes, becomes torn or stained, these people become angry, upset, sad.

Why?

In reality the shirt was produced, it has a certain life span and eventually all shirts will wear out or get torn or stained. This is just a simple truth. There is no need to become angry, upset or sad.

If people reflect in these ways, whenever any of their possessions wears out, is torn, etc. then they can remain with a peaceful and calm mind, without agitation and grief. Knowing that every one of their possessions is of the same nature. That is simply a fact of our existence.

By realizing that each of our possessions is impermanent, we often may find a change in our concern and care for our possessions. An attitude of non-attachment can develop.

Yet when I use this word "non-attachment," I do not mean noncaring. Our Compassionate Caring actually can become stronger as our non-attachment grows—but this is not a type of caring that is centered in selfishness.

We cannot stop the shirt from eventually wearing out, but what we can do is to care for it. We can wash and clean it. We can help to protect the shirt in certain ways so that the shirt provides as much usefulness as possible. And then, when it wears out, that is OK.

In this way we can view our possessions with a clearer Understanding of the reality of life. We can apply similar thoughts to our bodies and the bodies of other people, and animals also. This is not as easy, but slowly we can gain more Understanding which will give us more Peace of Mind.

Remember that the development of non-attachment does not mean non-caring. Compassionate Caring can be extremely valuable when our relatives or friends are dying—as well as when we ourselves are dying.

All of the techniques that we are giving you can be used to develop more Compassion, Lovingkindness, Understanding, Equanimity and Peace of Mind. Our Compassionate Caring can grow with a clear mind that is fit and ready to help in life's difficult situations. Not a selfish type of caring that becomes agitated with worry, fear, aversion, etc., but a strong mind that tries to understand fully a difficult situation so that a suitable solution can be discovered.

Death and Impermanence reflection can help your Compassionate Caring and Understanding to develop. And in so doing, it can enrich your life here and now. Your relationships with relatives and friends, enemies and even people whom you do not know, can grow in the richness of Compassion and Lovingkindness with the use of this reflection.

How is this? Let us suppose that you have an argument with a close loved one or friend. Both of you get quite excited, angry and frustrated at each other. Normally, after some time, the two of you will let go of the anger and frustration and resume your close relationship. In extreme cases, the relationship may not be resumed for years and possibly for the rest of their lives. With many people, though, this anger will last no more than a few days; with others maybe just one day or only a few hours.

For those who develop the reflection on Death and Imperma-nence, this anger either will not arise or, if it does arise, it probably will go away much quicker than normal. Why is this?

If we reflect that death may come at any moment, we realize that our loved one or friend may die soon—or we ourselves may die soon. If we truly care about our loved one or friend, the thought of being angry at them and having them die before we resume our relation-ship is not a very pleasant one. As well, the thought that we might die with these angry thoughts toward our loved one or friend also is not pleasant.

How we say good-bye becomes very, very important; we may never get another chance to talk to that person. With this attitude in mind, trying to have good relationships with others becomes an ex-pression of Compassionate Caring, which can come from this type of reflection on Death and Impermanence.

An English phrase that many of you may use when you separate from others is, "See you later." But you never know for sure. That moment may be the last time that you see each other.

In the West, talking about death is not very much in fashion, and many people find it to be a morbid, depressing topic. Although in-terest in death is growing in the West, I think most people feel that it interferes with their living. Here in Thailand, being a predominately Theravadin Buddhist country, the reaction is quite different. Death is talked about much more openly, with less fears and worries toward it.

And, you may see that rather than interfering with our life, this reflection on Death and Impermanence actually helps us to live life more fully, with deeper, richer relationships, with more Compas-sionate Caring.

Reflecting on How Fortunate We Are. Reflecting on Death and Impermanence.

**The third reflection is on Actions and Results of Actions.** Often the Pali or Sanskrit words Kamma or Karma are used here. And some-times the reference to the Law of Conditioning or the Law of Cause and Effect.

This can go pretty deep, but let us just look at this lightly. Basically, simply said, from every action will come a result.

There is a saying in the Buddhist scriptures that goes like this: "Do good...avoid harm...purify the mind. This is the teaching of all Buddhas." This also is the teaching of all wise people.

From some of the actions that we do, the result may be difficult to see. But from many of our actions we can see the results. Doing good will normally have beneficial results. Doing harm will normally have unbeneficial results.

Often we will have immediate results, we do not have to wait for some time in the future. If we perform some very kind and helpful actions, we can often see that the results can help others as well as ourselves. If we perform some unkind and harmful actions, we can often see that the results will hurt others as well as ourselves.

By using Mindfulness, we can learn about our actions and the results of our actions. As we understand them, we can work toward increasing the beneficial actions and work toward decreasing the unbeneficial actions. In this way, we will increase beneficial results and decrease unbeneficial results.

Most of us wish to have Peace and Happiness, and to avoid difficulties and unhappiness. But it is not enough just to wish for these things. We must try to develop our thoughts, speech and actions in beneficial ways. The results will then be beneficial and we will be better able to deal successfully with any type of problem, difficulty or unhappiness.

As we have said, we are conditioned by everything that we have encountered in the past. By working in the present, we will help to condition the future.

It also is important to realize that each of us has the ability to try to direct or change our own thoughts, speech and actions. Each of us is responsible for our own thoughts, speech and actions.

We do not always have the ability to direct or change other people's thoughts, speech and actions. And we cannot always be responsible for how others think, speak and act.

Taking responsibility for our own actions, speech and thoughts is a very important part of developing Compassion and practicing a type of Mental Development that is founded in Right Understanding.

To know the difference between beneficial and unbeneficial, proper and not proper, skillful and not skillful. These are extremely important. Without this knowledge, how can we develop beneficial qualities? How can we lessen unbeneficial qualities? How can we do good? Avoid harm? And purify the mind?

It is not considered very wise to look at these words and think that they are all just views and opinions and therefore unimportant. People who are not willing to investigate into their actions, speech and thoughts in these ways are not ready for the type of Mental Development we are trying to explain.

These people will continue to cause difficulties for themselves and for others, but unfortunately they will not be able to understand this. Instead, they will try to point outside for the cause of their own difficulties, refusing to accept the fact that their actions will produce results and that if they perform unbeneficial actions, then unbeneficial results normally will arise.

Our actions will have results; like a rock that is thrown into a lake, ripples definitely will happen. If we throw the rock, then it is important to take responsibility for the ripples. If we have caused difficulties through our actions, speech or thoughts, then using Mindfulness, we try to understand these actions, speech and thoughts, and try to understand their results. With Moral Shame based in the Compassionate wish to lessen difficulties, we try to correct any harm or difficulty that we have caused.

Earlier, when I talked about using Mindfulness to develop Understanding, I mentioned that the beginning stage is to see an event after it has happened and if it was not a skillful or beneficial act, then to try to see how it will not come about again. We must have some awareness of a difference between skillful and unskillful, beneficial and unbeneficial, in order to apply this teaching.

During Rosemary's talk about the Satipatthana Sutta, the Foundations of Mindfulness, she talked about Contemplation of Mental Objects with regard to the Hindrances and the difficulties arising dependent upon the sense doors. She said that the Sutta teaches us to try to become aware of these things in order to understand how these will not come again in the future. The teaching also instructs us to try to become aware of the Seven Factors of Enlightenment in order to understand how they will arise again and become stronger in the future.

It is so important to understand what is a hindrance, what is a difficulty, what is unbeneficial, what is unskillful and what is not proper. And it is so important to understand what is a Factor of Enlightenment, what is beneficial, what is skillful and what is proper.

It is not considered Right Understanding to think that we can perform an action and not be responsible for the results that come from that action. Is it possible to throw a rock into a lake and not have ripples? It is very important that we accept the responsibility for our actions, speech and thoughts. It is a very important part of developing Compassion and practicing Mental Development with Right Understanding.

We have mentioned how Compassion/Lovingkindness can help us when we come into contact with difficult people, perhaps those who refuse to accept responsibility for their actions, who may be continually causing difficulties for themselves and others. We also can reflect on this aspect of the Law of Cause and Effect, that each of us is responsible for ourselves, our actions, our speech, our thoughts.

We can help others but only if they want our help. If we meet with a difficult person who does not want any help, and this person is causing problems for us or others, then the best thing that we can try to do is to guard our reactions to this person. To be mindful of our own mental, verbal and physical reactions.

With one person already performing unbeneficial actions with unbeneficial results, let us try not to add more unbeneficial reactions with more unbeneficial results. Let us try to work on our conditioning to aid in developing more Compassionate Understanding and Peace.

An example of this: Say we go from the monastery to town in a taxi and the normal price is 20 baht (60 cents). But when we get to town, the driver and the assistant both say, "Thirty baht." So we recognize that the driver and the assistant are being greedy today. But we do not have to get angry. If they are greedy, that is their problem. If we get angry, that is our problem.

Another aspect to keep in mind when we meet difficult people is that this opportunity is actually very valuable in our Mental Development. How is this? Well, here we are trying to learn methods so we can be more kind, compassionate, loving, understanding, patient, calm, peaceful, etc.

When we meet with other people who also are trying to be kind, compassionate, loving, etc., then normally very little difficulty will arise and our relationship will be fairly peaceful and happy. However, when we meet with a difficult person, can we still remain kind, compassionate, loving, patient, calm, peaceful? These opportunities can be very valuable.

Another consideration also comes in here. It concerns looking at our past actions. Too often, we look at our past actions and think especially about the negativities, the things that we did that we are not pleased about. Not enough time is spent considering the positive and beneficial things we have done.

There are some meditators who see nothing but their negativities: "I'm no good... I did this and that... I'll never amount to anything... No one is as messed up as me!" and on and on. And yet there they are, trying to meditate, trying to become a better person. What wonderful, good actions they are doing.

And all of you here, wanting to become a better person, interested in Mental Development, coming to a meditation retreat, learning some methods and techniques of Mental Development in order to help yourself as well as others.

What wonderful, good, kind, beneficial actions you are doing, right here, right now!

Whenever you are feeling a lot of negativities toward yourself, try to reflect about the positive things that you have done. Try to be open to seeing both sides of yourself. We are not just full of negativities; we have done a lot of beneficial things in our life and we are continuing to do more beneficial things.

One of the biggest negativities that many meditators have toward themselves comes from their view of the practice, and from not having enough patience. With this in mind, perhaps you can identify with this story:

Once there was a gardener, a very good gardener, who could grow and take care of all types of plants—trees, shrubs, vines, flowers, fruits, vegetables, all types of plants. One day this gardener was given a special seed. The gardener was told how to plant the seed, how to water it, how to fertilize it, how to take care of it, but the gardener was not told what type of seed it was or what kind of plant it would grow into. So the gardener took the seed, planted it, watered it and fertilized it, following the instructions exactly.

Later I happen to see the gardener with this plant, and I notice that extra special care is being given to this little plant, which by now is about 4 inches high. I want to know what type of plant it is. I look at the plant and I look at the gardener and then I say, "I've seen you with this plant. It looks a bit special; you've been working with it special. I'd like to know—what kind of plant is it?"

The gardener looks at me and says, "Oh, I'm sorry. I don't know."

I say, "You don't know?"

Again the reply comes, "No, I don't know."

I say, "Well, you are a very good gardener. I've seen you with all sorts of plants, bushes, trees, flowers and all. You mean to tell me you are growing a plant and you don't even know what it is?"

The gardener says, "No, I'm sorry, you see, this plant is special; someone gave it to me and told me how to take care of it, water it, fertilize it, but did not tell me what kind of plant it is."

I say, "Oh, I see...well, how big is it going to get?"

The gardener says, "Oh, no, you don't understand. I don't know what kind of plant it is and I don't know how big it will get. I just water it and fertilize it, which helps it grow, and then I have to be patient and wait."

I think about this water and fertilizer helping it to grow, and I say, "Well, why don't you put a whole lot of water and fertilizer on it and make it grow real fast?"

And the gardener says, "No, no, no, you don't understand. If I put a lot of water and fertilizer on it, I'll just kill the plant. It won't grow at all. I just have to put on the right amount, not too much, not too little. Then it will grow into a strong, healthy plant. And the rest of the time, I have to be patient and wait."

I think about this "waiting" business and I say, "Wait? Wait? What do you mean, wait? Do you just go sit under a tree and watch?"

The gardener says, "No, no, you still don't understand. You see, sometimes I water it, sometimes I fertilize it and then other times I am patient and wait."

I say, "Oh, ok," then I go away. I come back later and now the little plant is a little tree. I look at the tree and I look at the gardener, and I say, "Oh, now you know what kind of plant you have—you have a tree."

The gardener says, "Yup, now I know what kind of plant I have. I have a tree."

I look at the tree and I look at the gardener and I say, "Well, is this as big as it gets or does it get bigger?"

The gardener says, "Oh, I'm sorry, I don't know. I wasn't told. It may keep growing or it might stop now, but I'll just have to put on the water and the fertilizer, and be patient and wait. It will grow by itself, and when it stops growing, then I'll know."

I say, "Oh, ok," and go away.

I come back later and now the tree has lots of flower buds all over it, little green round buds. I look at the buds and I look at the gardener and I say, "Oh, it looks like you are going to get flowers."

The gardener says, "Yup, looks like I'm going to get flowers."

I look at the flower buds—none of them are open yet—I get very exited and say, "What color are they going to be? How big are they going to get? And when are they going to open?"

The gardener says, "Oh, look, I'm sorry. I don't know. I just water and fertilize the tree and I have to be patient and wait. They may open in a day or two, maybe next week, or even they may all fall off without opening and I'll have to wait until next year to see how big they are and what color."

I think about this business of maybe having to wait until next year, and I say, "Why don't you just rip some open and see what's inside?"

The gardener says, "No, no, you don't understand. If I rip them open, well, the color inside may not be the same color as when it opens, and I certainly won't know how big they will get. I just have to be patient and wait. Put on the water and fertilizer and be patient and wait."

I say, "Oh, ok," and I go away. I come back later. The flowers have opened up, nice big flowers all over the tree. I look at the tree and I look at the gardener and I say, "You've got nice flowers."

The gardener says, "Yup, I've got nice flowers."

I look once more at the tree and I say, "What kind of fruit are you going to get?"

And again the gardener says, "No, no, you don't understand. I don't know what kind of fruit I will get. I wasn't told. But I water it, fertilize it in just the right ways. I take care of the tree. It will grow; it will flower; it will fruit in its own time. I take care of it the best I can and I'm patient and I wait."

With your meditation practice, take care of it the best you can. Have patience and wait. Water it, fertilize it, protect it. It will grow; it will flower; it will fruit, we hope, in its own time, but you take care of it the best you can, and be patient and wait.

Apply the Compassion, give it Lovingkindness, protect it with Mindfulness, take care of it the best you can. If you do this, you will be doing good, kind, beneficial deeds for yourself and perhaps be able to help others as well.

Whenever you are feeling a lot of negativities toward yourself, it can be very helpful to reflect on the good, positive things you have done. Try to be open to see both sides of yourself.

Reflecting on our good actions can help to bring more Joy and Contentment into our practice, giving ourselves some renewed Energy. This Joy arises from the Contentment of knowing that yes, we have done some beneficial actions and are continuing to do more. This in turn will help to give us more Energy for our future work.

This is not a normal, everyday type of joy, but deeper. It is a type of Sympathetic Joy—having sympathy with our own efforts. It also can be a type of Vipassana Joy, arising as we see our own development of Wisdom and Compassionate Understanding.

We are not full of only negativities. We all have our positive sides also. Just our being here proves that. And it is very beneficial to reflect in this way.

Reflecting on Kamma, actions and results of actions can aid us in our dealings with unpleasant people. As well, this reflection can help us to realize the important benefits from doing good and avoiding harm. Reflecting on how important it is to be mindful of our actions, speech and thoughts, in order to increase our beneficial qualities and produce more beneficial results for ourselves and for others. Also that it is important to take responsibility for our actions, speech and thoughts.

As well, to reflect upon our good Kamma, our good past actions, in order to balance any tendency of only looking at our negativities. And to help bring more Joy, Contentment and Energy into our practice, helping to replace depressed, agitated and unbalanced states of mind.

So we have reflections on How Fortunate We Are, on Death and Impermanence, and on Actions and Results of Actions.

**The fourth reflection is on Dukkha, often referred to as stress, unsatisfactoriness, faults of existence.**

This Pali word used to be translated only as "suffering." But the word "suffering" does not always imply all that is meant by Dukkha. The word "unsatisfactoriness," although very long, seems in general to be closer to the meaning of Dukkha.

Within the Buddhist scriptures, Dukkha has a very long definition that includes: "Illness, decay, old age, death, sorrow, lamentation, pain, grief, despair, being separated from what we like, having to be with what we do not like, and not getting what we want."

Basically, this word Dukkha includes everything that we normally call unsatisfying: problems, difficulties, sufferings, stress, etc. From the smallest mental and physical irritation to the largest mental and physical suffering, they are all included in the word Dukkha.

A very important aspect of Dukkha to reflect upon is that Dukkha is natural and will occur countless times throughout our life. Continually, we will encounter Dukkha in some form or another.

This is basically due to the fact that everything around us, our bodies and our thoughts are all impermanent. They all have their arising, existing and eventual passing away. This is simply a truth of our existence. Due to this fact of Impermanence, different types of Dukkha will arise.

Many people become upset, irritated, angry or agitated in some way when they encounter different types of Dukkha. But this type of reaction normally only causes more and more Dukkha.

If we can come to an acceptance of life as it really is and not how we wish it to be, then we can come to an acceptance of Dukkha also, in whatever form we experience it.

Earlier in the retreat, I told you of the story about the hotel manager and that in their opinion, the hotel never has any problems, but it only has challenges. Dukkha may come in unpleasant ways, but if we can deal with it as a challenge, as an opportunity for growth, then we will create less Dukkha for the future.

An experience in life may be called Dukkha and may be unpleasant, but it is our reaction to the experience that determines whether or not we stay peaceful and calm or become unpeaceful and agitated. Being mindful and understanding our reactions is a very important part of Mental Development.

Pleasant experiences will come to us. Unpleasant experiences will come to us. Neutral experiences will come to us. We cannot always decide what will be the experiences that we encounter. But we can try to work to develop the Understanding and Wisdom to know and decide what type of reaction we will have toward our experiences.

If we can accept the fact that Dukkha, unsatisfactoriness, will be encountered in many forms throughout our life, then this acceptance will aid us in developing a more peaceful and calm, wise and compassionate reaction, no matter how unpleasant the experience may be.

I also talked earlier about the example of a person with a broken arm. The broken arm is one type of Dukkha. And any agitation, worry and fear about the arm is another type of Dukkha that is caused in the person's reaction to the broken arm.

I am fairly sure by now that most of you can understand that if we develop strong enough Compassionate Understanding and Wisdom, then this second Dukkha does not have to arise. As well, most of the time this only causes more difficulties and stress.

To accept the broken arm and get on with the proper procedure for repairing the arm with clear thinking, not clouded by anxieties, is certainly the best thing to do.

By reflecting on Dukkha, unsatisfactoriness, in these ways, we will develop more of an acceptance of unpleasantness, being able to find more Peace in our life, no matter what type of experience we have.

So we have reflections on How Fortunate We Are, on Death and Impermanence, on Actions and Results of Actions and on Dukkha, or unsatisfactoriness.

**The last reflection for tonight's talk has to do with understanding the relationship between Compassion and Equanimity.** In understanding Compassion and Equanimity, it can be seen that Compassion is an important aspect for the growth of Equanimity, and that Equanimity is an important aspect for the growth of Compassion.

I heard this quote some years ago: "To care and not to care." By using this quote, the relationship between Compassion and Equanimity possibly can be better understood.

The first part of the quote is "to care." Compassionate Caring, Compassionate Understanding is so much a part of our Mental Development. Seeing our difficulties and problems, and wishing to alleviate them. Seeing our good qualities and wishing to strengthen them. Seeing difficulties and problems that we experience and seeing difficulties and problems that others experience, and wishing to help in some way to lessen the Dukkha that all of us encounter.

When we defined Compassion earlier, we said that Compassion means a feeling of sympathy toward oneself or others who are experiencing some type of difficulty. A softness, a tender heart that is sympathetic and willing to open to all of life. But at the same time, possessing a strength that is not weighed down by difficulties and sorrows. That is, one can identify with the difficulty but maintain a degree of Equanimity and Strength to deal with the situation calmly and wisely in order to find the best solution.

Equanimity is the balancing agent for Compassion, the strength that enables Compassionate thoughts to be put into action in the most efficient manner. With this degree of Equanimity, Compassion is strong. Without this degree of Equanimity, Compassion can become weak and turn into anger, sorrow, grief or despair.

When I say the words "to care," this can mean Compassionate Caring with the strength of Equanimity. So what do I mean by the words, "To care and not to care?"

Consider these situations: Let us suppose that we meet with some people who are having a difficult experience. We react with Compassion and wish to help in some way. We offer to help and possibly we know of a solution to the difficulty. This offer is accepted by the other people. We give the help that then solves the difficulty. The other people are relieved and thank us very much for our assistance.

All of us have benefitted from this experience. The other people are relieved of their problem, and we have done good, kind deeds that will help us in our own growth. As well, this can give us a sense of joy and satisfaction in seeing others relieved of their difficulties with the aid of our Understanding. This is one possible outcome of meeting with people who are having a difficult experience.

Now suppose again that we have just met with some other people who are having a difficult experience. We react with Compassion and wish to help in some way. We offer to help and possibly know of a solution to the difficulty. But in this case, our offer is not accepted. The other people do not want our help. We have a Compassionate Caring attitude and we may even know the perfect solution to the problem, but the other people are not interested.

What do we do then? We could offer our help again. But again, it is rejected. Again we offer; again it is rejected. And by now the other people are even getting angry at us. What do we do?

Well, one way to respond is to get angry back, telling them that they are foolish, stupid, etc. But this does not usually help the situation. Normally, trying to force our help onto people who do not want it is useless and often creates more problems in the process.

Here Equanimity is important. To allow things to be just as they are. Out of Compassion, we try to help but the others do not want our help. If we see that our continual offering of help is only creating more difficulty, then again out of Compassion toward this new difficulty, we try to accept the situation and try to have Equanimity—simply realizing that the best solution at that time is to let go of trying to help the other people.

We still have Compassionate Caring, but with our offer to help being rejected, then having Equanimity is far better than developing aversion toward the others. As well we need not feel hurt or dejected simply because they do not want our help. This is an aspect of "not to care." That is, not to get upset simply because our offer is rejected.

Time and time again, many of us will encounter similar situations. Sometimes our help will be accepted and sometimes our help will be rejected. The most important aspect, which is the same in both situations, is our Compassionate Caring, wishing to help. Equanimity is of added importance when our help is rejected.

This often happens with children. Parents may see their children having some difficulty and will offer to help. Many times children will reject this help largely because they want to do whatever they are doing all by themselves. Even though they may get hurt in the process, they may not realize it because usually they do not have the knowledge that their parents may have.

So, often parents will watch their children having some difficulty, offer to help, be rejected, and then wait and watch. With Equanimity and Compassion. Knowing that at that moment they must allow their children to test their abilities. And yet, be ready and willing to help as soon as their children wish to be helped.

Whenever our offer to help is rejected, we can try not to allow the rejection to affect our Peace of Mind. To care and have Compassion towards the situation, but to not care and have Equanimity towards the rejection.

This understanding is extremely important for people who become involved in meditation, especially Westerners. We may have experienced for ourselves the benefits that Meditation and Mental Development can produce. And we may wish to help others discover this also.

Usually most of our relatives and friends do not understand a great deal about Meditation and Mental Development. Although the interest in meditation is growing in the West, still most people back home do not know much about it, or often the information that some do have is not correct.

It is important to be careful with wanting to help our friends and relatives learn meditation. As we said, it often is not possible to help those who do not want our help.

Some meditators, when they return home from a retreat, immediately start telling all of their friends and relatives about the benefits of meditation, often nearly forcing them to go to a meditation center: "Hey, you should do meditation, it'll help you! You know, you should go do a course, a 10-day retreat, it will help you! You got problems, can't you see?! Get on with it, come on!"

If they do not want our help, if they are not interested, then this can cause negative results and instead of helping our friends and relatives, this type of action can produce harm.

Other meditators, when they return home, simply go about trying to practice what they have learned, trying to be Mindful, Compassionate, Lovingkind, Patient, Understanding, etc. When their friends and relatives see such fine qualities, and are impressed by these fine qualities, then the friends and relatives may want to know what it was that has produced such pleasing results. With the people interested, then the meditator can tell them and in this way benefit may come more easily.

Always willing to offer our help—but trying to understand when others want our help and when they do not want our help.

Praise and blame are a pair of opposites that we will encounter throughout our life. To care about doing beneficial actions, speaking beneficial words, thinking beneficial thoughts. With this attitude we will grow in beneficial qualities and be of benefit to ourselves as well as others. Praise, if we know that it is deserving, can be accepted and used to develop joy in ourselves and in others.

Blame, if we know that it is not deserving, can be confronted with Equanimity and we can leave the words of blame with the person who speaks them. We do not have to develop aversion towards this person. We can try to use Compassionate Understanding and realize that this person is making a mistake at this time, and keep a degree of Equanimity and Peace within our minds.

By reflecting on this relationship between Compassion and Equanimity, we can actually strengthen our Compassion and Equanimity. They can work together and support each other, helping to give us a greater ability to deal successfully with any experience in life.

In the same way that we can use Compassion/Lovingkindness meditation, we can use these Five Reflections. We can do an entire sitting period with some or all of these reflections. We can do a few minutes at the beginning of a period or at the end. Some meditators use these reflections as well as Compassion/Lovingkindness at the beginning and end of every period that they do. It can be long, short, whatever.

As well, similar to Compassion/Lovingkindness, we can use these reflections in the middle of a meditation period when a strong wandering mind or hindrance is coming up.

Perhaps a lot of "planning mind" is coming up; we can try to reflect upon Death and Impermanence. This may allow us to let go of these strong thoughts. As I mentioned, if a lot of negativities towards ourselves are arising, we can try to reflect upon our good Kamma, on the good actions that we have done. We can try to reflect upon How Fortunate We Are to help us get out of many of the depressions that we find ourselves in.

So when you find that there are certain thoughts which are creating much disturbance and agitation, you can try using these different reflections. You can let go of your main object of concentration and change into one of these reflections. Try to "bend" the energies of these unwise thoughts that are disturbing you into the wise energies of these Five Reflections.

I also mentioned that the reflection on How Fortunate We Are can be very helpful when you are waking up in the morning. And you may wish to do these other reflections at that time also. Again, these do not have to be done only during formal meditation periods. They can be used at any time of the day when you see that thinking in this way will bring you more peace and balance.

I would like to very strongly encourage you now to use these techniques regularly. We would like for you to use them in your formal meditation practice just like trying to do the awareness of the breath or, trying to do the Compassion/Lovingkindness meditation. They are not just techniques to help us solve problems after they come. If we use them regularly in our practice then they will prevent problems from coming up in the future. As I mentioned this morning, "Training our minds to think wisely." So then our reactions will be wiser. If you do not use these regularly as part of your formal practice and you only use them to try to solve problems, then it may be that you get out of that taxi and you go to driver and the driver looks at you and says, "30 baht." Then you stand there and go, "uh, uh, what did Rosemary and Steve tell me to do about this one?" Don't wait for difficulties to come, use them regularly in your practice and it will help avoid difficulties from coming in the future.

More methods of Mental Development. Reflecting on How Fortunate We Are; on Death and Impermanence; on Action and the Results of Actions; on Dukkha, unsatisfactoriness; and on the relationship between Compassion and Equanimity.

More techniques, more tools to help each of us gain more Peace, more Contentment and deeper Compassionate Understanding in our life.

I would like to end tonight's talk with a quote of the Buddha from the scriptures concerned with the importance of Wise Reflection. In Pali, wise reflection is termed "Yonisomanasikara." Frequently in the scriptures, the Buddha stressed the importance of wise reflection. The following is a quotation from the "Sabbasava Sutta," which in English is called "Getting rid of all anxieties and troubles."[1] The Buddha is recorded to have spoken thus:

"Followers, I say that the getting rid of anxieties and troubles is possible for one who knows and who sees, not for one who does not know and does not see.

"What must a person know and see in order that the getting rid of anxieties and troubles should be possible? These are wise reflection and unwise reflection.

"For a person who reflects unwisely, there arise anxieties and troubles which have not yet arisen, and in addition, those which have already arisen increase.

"But for a person who reflects wisely, anxieties and troubles which have not yet arisen do not arise, and in addition, those already arisen disappear."

[1]An adapted translation of the Sabbasava Sutta, which is Sutta #2 in "The Majjhima Nikaya" of the Theravadin Buddhist Scriptures. Readers may want to explore "The Middle Length Discourses of the Buddha," translated by Bhikkhu Nanamoli and Bhikkhu Bodhi (Kandy, Sri Lanka: Buddhist Publication Society, 1995) or "What the Buddha Taught," by Venerable Dr. W. Rahula (Bangkok: Hawtrai Foundation, 1990.)

# BE KIND TO YOURSELF

This is day eight. On this day of a retreat there is a common occurrence in many retreatants. You may start to let go. But it is not the letting go that we have been talking about in this retreat. It is more a letting go of the effort and energy.

You may relax a little too much, and start thinking in this way; "I've done a lot, maybe I'll just do lying down meditation here and miss the first sit," or "I'll just skip this walk, it's OK, it's through compassion to myself." Maybe you think, "I'll just lie down before the walking," and it extends into 15-20 minutes.

The continuity then is broken. And you may have to work much harder at "cranking up" your mindfulness to get yourself going again.

Many of you may find that you are starting to have thoughts arising about the end of the retreat. What you will do. Where you will go. Who you will see. What you will eat. How long you are going to sleep the day after the retreat! The "tape" may start to roll on and on, and you may become engrossed in it, not realizing that you are getting lost. And many of you may be starting to worry and be concerned about how you will possibly be able to keep the meditation going "out there."

Try not to get upset if this is starting to happen to you. Try not to just relax and drift into the thoughts either—relaxing too much.

Try to be kind to yourself. You have given yourself the opportunity during this retreat to meditate, go inward, learn, develop understanding of how to let go of the things which give you difficulties, to let go of the future, of the past.

Sometimes the process of meditation does not feel very comfortable. You may pull back thinking that something is wrong because "meditation is supposed to make me feel good." You may stop. Doubts may arise.

True, deep Compassion will enable you to open to the uncomfortable energies and begin to understand them. This opening is the first stage of the healing process. You may have been running away from and suppressing these things for most of your life.

If you start to open, start to understand these energies, and through Compassionate Understanding, you may learn how to let go.

Try to realize how precious this opportunity is. Try to find the courage to continue to open. Try not to wish away the present; it will pass quickly enough.

And try not to worry about the future. Concentrate on strengthening the mind in the present. Not many people get the opportunity to drop future demands for a period of ten days and be encouraged to go inward, to learn.

Be kind to yourself. Allow yourself to experience these last days fully without wishing them away or wasting the opportunity. It may be your last opportunity. Who knows what the future holds for us?

The present moment is all we have. The future is just mind-created, the past is gone. If this is your last opportunity, or the last opportunity for some time, then you will have lived it fully.

Try not to push away the present by worrying about something that may not be or situations that may never occur. We all have to make plans and we need to do that, looking at the intentions behind the decisions. That is the moment also, and a practical necessity of life. But try not to worry and develop fear about all of the possible outcomes. They are endless.

The Compassionate Motivation can purify our intentions. After we make our plans, the focus then becomes how we live and how we approach our doing. This includes trying to work and live with grace, awareness and good intentions; leaving ourselves open for growth, open to change our direction; not freezing future plans, not thinking that things will occur as we intended. The future may surprise us. Trying to be flexible and flowing, leaving ourselves open for the possibility of inner growth.

With our direction established, we try again to come back to the present, instead of going too far into the future and continually pushing away the present.

Continue to make the effort to come to all of the sits, all of the walks, to help strengthen the mind.

We try to open ourselves to the moment, whatever it contains. The moment can teach us, but only if we are open to it and do not push it away. When we see the mind resisting, pushing away, try to let go and soften around it.

An image I like to use when I find myself resisting is that of a gently flowing stream: trying to make the mind like water, softly flowing into, over and around everything; the water never sticking, but continually flowing onward.

We can try to be in the present here. Then, when the future becomes the present, we probably will be able to live it more fully also. If we push away the present now, will we really be able to live fully those moments of the future that we want, when the future arrives? If we strengthen our minds now, we will be better able to deal with difficult situations later. Try to let go of doubt, worry and fear.

Slowly, gently, we try to recondition the mind to stop reaching out, to stop reaching out for mind-created images—those self-images we project into the future, those self-images we reach back for from the past.

We also may learn not to compare these self-images with the process of body and mind arising in the present. If we hang onto these images and they do not correspond to the actuality of the moment, then they may come tumbling down around us and we may be left feeling shattered and unworthy.

If we hang onto the negative self-images, then we freeze ourselves again and this may only give the opportunity for grief, fear, worry and self-hatred to arise. This overshadows our potential for inner transformation, and may not allow us to flow into the subtle, inner changes that are occurring.

Instead, we can try to open, watch, learn and flow into the moment with non-resistance and non-clinging. Perhaps this way you will be able to live your life more fully. And in whatever we are doing, whether alone or with others, we will have awareness and good intentions.

We can try to live more at Peace with ourselves, with others, with life; learning and letting go; coming into harmony with things as they are.

On this day, many people also have the attitude that the retreat is almost over and they have learned enough. In many ways, however, the past days have been laying foundations. These foundations are necessary before you can begin another very important process in the practice—the process of reflective, analytical investigation. You needed to build a sufficient level of concentration and the quality of objective awareness so that you could observe the mind/body process.

These helped you to come to basic levels of understanding the Law of Cause and Effect of the Mind: that is, basic levels of knowing experientially what thought processes result in inner stress and suffering, and what thought processes result in inner peace. From this level of understanding, and also having more calm and stability in the mind, we can focus more deeply on the Investigation into Truth Factor of Enlightenment, shifting the focus away from the Concentration and Tranquility Factors of Enlightenment.

This can be compared to a film. In the beginning scenes we get to know a few characters quite well and we may think... "These are the stars of the film." That is, until a very important scene when the real star is introduced. We may then realize that the other characters are supporting players. We also realize that in order to have a full story we need all the characters in the film and not just the star.

An essential part of developing the Investigation into Truth Factor of Enlightenment is learning to use the thought processes to help come to a deeper realization of Truth. In Pali, this process is called "Yonisomanasikara." This part of the practice is often missed by many in the retreat due to attitudes such as; "Well the retreat is almost over, I've learned enough;" or "Well we've spent so many days developing the other techniques, this new one must just be an afterthought and not as important;" or "I don't need to bring up energy to do this, I'll coast on the calm that is already here." These people will miss the valuable opportunity to understand this essential part of the practice.

So I encourage you not to fall into these attitudes, missing your opportunity. Instead, try to practice this new technique in the next days. If you practice, you will learn how to develop the ability to think wisely. This can help you to deeply transform past unbeneficial thought patterns which are the cause for the arising of many of the hindrances.

**As we start this morning's sit, I am going to lead you through a shortened version of the reflections that Steve talked about last night.** This is so you may see how you can use these reflections as a start or an end to your sitting. I will be saying short statements and then there will be periods of quiet. During the periods of quiet either expand on this statement or observe how you react to it. After I finish the guided part I would like you to expand the reflections for the rest of the period so you can have more practice in contemplation without it needing to be guided.

With reflective meditation we try to keep our thoughts centered on the topic we are reflecting upon. Reflective meditation is not just thinking and letting the mind go anywhere. We make the effort to keep the mind on the topic.

Sometimes, while reflecting, the mind may start to wander off to other things because the reflection may stimulate memories, fears or worries. Just as with concentration on the breathing we try to note when this has happened, when the mind has wandered away from the main reflection. When you realize this you can note, "wandering," "thinking," "remembering," etc. and then return to the reflection.

Or if strong hindrances arise such as worry, fear, doubt, restlessness, then you can try to note these and investigate. This is a very valuable opportunity to investigate the fears, worries that have been stimulated by the reflection, helping us to see more clearly our attachments, denials, our hidden aversions, fears and worries.

We can try to apply the methods of investigation at this time, investigating into the energies as they manifest in the body and learning to let go. Developing deeper insight into ourselves. When we let go we can return the thoughts to the original reflection or go onto the next reflection.

We continue to expand our Understanding. This helps to let go of opinions and views based in ignorance and helps to strengthen the factor of Right View in the mind.

Please settle yourself into the posture and observe your breathing for a short while.

*****

May I try to remember how fortunate I am to have some teachings to help lead me out of difficulties, when there are so many people who are confused and do not know how to bring Peace to themselves.

*****

How fortunate I am to have health, when there are so many people who are sick and dying.

*****

How fortunate I am to have relative wealth and freedom, when there are so many who lack the basic necessities of life.

*****

How fortunate I am to have good friends, when there are so many who are alone and isolated.

*****

May I remember how precious this opportunity is and that these conditions are impermanent, that they will pass away.

*****

May I try to remember that death is definitely coming and that I do not know when. It could be today, tomorrow, next week, next month, next year or in 40 years, I do not know when.

*****

And at the time of death, I will have to depend on the strength of my own mind.

*****

The only thing that seems to have any real meaning is how much that I have developed the mind toward Compassion, Lovingkindness, Wisdom and Equanimity. So that I may have a balanced peaceful mind at the time of death and in my life now.

*****

May I try to remember the Law of Cause and Effect, the Law of Kamma; that if I wish for inner Peace then I have to sow the seeds for Peace in the present moment.

*****

Through Compassion to myself and to others, may I try to be mindful of my actions, speech and thoughts; so that the results of these will be beneficial to myself and to others.

*****

May I try to remember that in this life there is the existence of opposites; pleasure and pain. Dukkha, unsatisfactoriness exists. There is aging, sickness, continual parting from loved ones and death.

*****

May I try to develop the Peace coming from letting go and nongrasping—trying to develop Wisdom and Equanimity. There is the opportunity for the ending of the Dukkha of attachment, through cultivating the mind.

*****

May I try to remember "to care and not to care"—trying to always have an open caring mind, trying to have Compassion for all beings. Yet at the same time may I understand that the world is as it is. All beings must walk the path to Peace within themselves.

*****

May I always try to offer a helping hand, but also to realize that at times some will not understand or even want to be helped.

*****

May I understand that I can help best by balancing Compassion with Equanimity through the cultivation of Wisdom within myself.

*****

May all beings be able to find the path to inner Peace, walk the path, each according to their own ability and understanding, directing the mind towards the ending of Dukkha and towards Peace of Mind.

*****

Please continue to expand these reflections with your own thoughts.

*****

(end of period)

So far the special mindfulness activities that we have asked you to pay extra attention to have been fairly basic physical actions. In English we could use the word "gross" activities. There was going in and coming out of doorways; washing dishes; putting on and taking off your shoes; coming up and going down the stairs; the action of rising and the action of lowering of your body. And then yesterday, the action of scooping water and pouring it.

Today's special mindfulness activity is more "subtle." We would like you to pay extra attention to tasting your food. If it tastes pleasant, then to know that it tastes pleasant. If it tastes unpleasant, then to know that it tastes unpleasant.

Often when we are tasting our food, we may taste the first bite and then "off" goes the mind, thinking about how much we like the food or how much we do not like the food. The mind will go to the past, thinking about other foods that we had, comparing them to what we are eating in the present. Or it may go to the future, thinking about what we will eat later.

In our reaction to tastes, we may cause extra mental difficulty for ourselves. Often creating excessive desire or excessive aversion. Thus unbalancing the mind, pulling us farther away from Peace.

This is the benefit of the food reflections; they help us to keep a peaceful, calm mind while eating. If we have awareness of the food reflection, we remember that the food is mainly to keep us alive and healthy, we remember how fortunate we are, and we remember the difficulties in getting the food to us. We learn to be grateful and content, because we realize the suffering of other beings in the food chain and realize our interrelationship with others. This contentment does not depend on whether the food tastes pleasant or unpleasant.

It may also help if you try to chew your food well. By being aware of chewing, you will be very close to tasting. As well, it will help if you rest your spoon or fork on your plate while you are chewing. Often it is easy to get carried away with wanting the next mouthful, and instead of tasting our present mouthful, we are busy scooping up the next one.

So try to pay extra attention to tasting of your food. Try to be right there with the actual taste. No matter whether your food is pleasant or unpleasant, try to find the Peace that can exist right there with the tasting of your food.

# EVENING DAY EIGHT

# EFFORT AND BALANCE

Tonight I would like to speak about Effort and the importance of Balance in our practice.

There are many qualities needed to develop the mind. One particular quality the Buddha mentioned a great deal in the scriptures is Effort.

If we reflect a little, it is quite easy to see that effort is needed in any endeavor, both in worldly pursuits and in Mental Development. To be skilled athletes we have to apply effort to practice, practice, practice. After we do this, we may make our particular skill look effortless.

Watching skilled gymnasts, tennis players, swimmers, etc., they have found a grace and rhythm that looks natural and easy for them. Yet, this skill, this effortless grace, came about through their effort to practice, practice, practice. They gradually became familiar with all the fine details of their sport, made many mistakes, yet, they tried to learn from their mistakes.

They tried to perfect their skills when their ability was increasing, and did not allow themselves to become lazy so that their skill did not disappear. It also depended on them making the effort to be mindful and concentrated in the present moment, and to work with the actuality of things as they are.

With the path of Meditation and Mental Development, the same things apply. We try to practice, practice, practice. That is why we call it a "practice." We need effort to practice and continually learn from the difficulties and problems arising, in order to increase our Understanding.

Some people realize that they need effort to develop meditation. However, they may not understand clearly that effort has to be directed in the right way and be a balanced effort, Right Effort.

In order to know if our effort is correct, it is helpful to be familiar with the Noble Eightfold Path. When I talked about the Foundations of Mindfulness, the Satipatthana Sutta, I mentioned the Four Noble Truths: that Dukkha, unsatisfactoriness, exists; that the cause of Dukkha is ignorance, unwise reaction and craving; that the cessation of Dukkha comes from giving up ignorance, unwise reaction and craving; and that there is a path leading to the end of Dukkha—the Noble Eightfold Path.

In the scriptures, the Noble Eightfold Path is the path explained by the Buddha for training the mind, directing it toward the end of Dukkha. The eight factors are: Right View or Understanding; Right Intention or Thought; Right Speech; Right Action; Right Livelihood; Right Effort; Right Mindfulness; and Right Concentration.

If we are to have a balanced effort, it is important to know what is meant by Right Effort. Effort may be misdirected; it may be based on wrong intention or motivation, or on wrong understanding or view. So our effort may be taking us in the wrong direction.

Contained within Right Effort are the Four Great Efforts. These are: the effort to *prevent*, the effort to *abandon*, the effort to *develop*, and the effort to *maintain and strengthen*.

What does it mean, *the effort to prevent?* It is the effort to prevent unbeneficial qualities, those that harm ourselves and others, from arising or increasing.

If our intention is based on the alleviation of Dukkha, unsatisfactoriness, in ourselves and in others—the Compassionate Motivation—then the effort to prevent will be based on Right Intention, the second factor of the Noble Eightfold Path.

There then will be a constant seeking of ways to alleviate and cure Dukkha, trying to build a vigilance, alertness and awareness of ourselves in order to prevent unbeneficial qualities from arising or increasing.

Right Effort, the effort to prevent, also needs to be balanced with Right View or Understanding. Basically, this is understanding the

Law of Cause and Effect, the Law of Conditioning. All that arises in the mind comes from causes and conditioning.

All of our experiences and contacts in life create impressions within the mind. Some may be shallow, others very deep. These contacts and experiences influence our reactions. Our reactions influence how we view life, and they help to develop our views and opinions, which again influence our reactions to life.

What we expose the mind to and "feed" into the mind becomes very important in the path of Mental Development. I am talking here about our choices, our choices to live and act in certain ways.

Some things we have no choice over. In these instances, we try to prevent unbeneficial things from arising, through Awareness, Compassion, Wisdom and Equanimity. The effort to prevent helps us to develop Right Action, another factor of the Noble Eightfold Path.

An analogy that may help you understand what I mean about being careful with what we expose the mind to is that of growing a tree. A tree begins as a seed. It sprouts and starts to grow. Throughout its life, it is affected by and depends on its environment and the forces of Nature, such as rain, wind, shelter and the nutrients in the soil.

When it is a young seedling, we must be careful to give it special care, realizing its tenderness. Strong winds, pounding sun, pelting rain, insects can easily destroy it. So, often, we keep it in a pot in the nursery in order to create the right conditions for its growth. We give it the right balance of shelter, shade, water, protection.

In the same way, you are like seedlings, seedlings in Mental Development. You are trying to grow into strong, healthy plants. The mind needs right care.

We can realize that our conditioning can be towards beneficial qualities or unbeneficial qualities. Beneficial qualities increase our well-being and the well-being of others. They help to direct the mind toward the alleviation of Dukkha in ourselves and others. Unbeneficial conditioning tends to go in the opposite direction.

Through Compassion to ourselves, we try not to expose the mind to excessive situations about which we have a choice. This is so we may be able to find a balance in our living. Otherwise, we may have to struggle against a strong flow of conditioning, often having to use a great deal of force and willpower to resist temptation. This can make the path much more difficult than it could be.

For example, think of people who wish to go on a diet. It is a better choice to go for a walk in the park, taking a packed lunch, rather than going to the bakery shop to look at all of the wonderful cakes and delicacies that they are not supposed to eat. The first choice gives the dieters exercise and the ability to keep to their resolution, which, in turn, gives them the confidence to continue. The other choice exposes them to a battle of willpower. And if they give in and eat the cakes, then a lot of guilt and self-criticism can arise, in addition to a loss in their confidence. So then they may decide that it is just too difficult and give up.

After the dieters have strengthened the conditioning toward good eating and carefulness, they may be able to walk into the bakery shop and be unaffected by the temptations.

In order to know which situations make it difficult to react in a balanced, skillful way, we have to increase our Awareness of how we live, how we think and the results of our living and thinking as they affect our own minds and the lives of others.

In the Western world, moral restraint is not very much "in fashion." A lot of people feel that it interferes with their freedom and spontaneity; they feel that a good life comes from being able to indulge themselves and do anything they want to do.

Reflecting on the nature of Freedom...is it really Freedom to be swept away with all of the energies that arise in the mind? Is this true Freedom?

Indulging all of the waves of desire strengthens desire and a seeking outward for Peace. And when desires are not fulfilled, what happens? Aversion and grief may arise. This actually takes us further from true Freedom—freedom from Dukkha, and the Freedom and Peace that lie within. With the letting go of the hindrances and of selfishness, we start to touch true Freedom.

To indulge our selfishness also denies our interrelationship with others and with the planet. It denies that our actions will bring some results. It is like thinking that if one throws a stone into a lake, it will not create ripples.

True Compassion to ourselves and others is to begin to investigate into our lifestyle, habits and ways of doing things. It is beginning to take responsibility for our actions and our part in creating either suffering or harmony in ourselves and in our relationships with others.

Try to be careful to see the difference between investigating in order to simply increase our self-hatred and negative self-image, compared to the willingness to open to the often unpleasant feeling of being honest with ourselves. Self-hatred increases our Dukkha, freezes us, and does not allow us to increase our Understanding.

The unpleasant feelings of moral shame or remorse coming from honesty are a step in the letting go of selfishness and the increase of Compassionate Understanding. This may give us the strength and incentive to transform ourselves and to develop the Understanding of how unbeneficial things may not arise in the future.

Using investigation and honesty, having the willingness to change and to let go of selfishness, these are making the effort to prevent.

Right Living is a basic foundation of Meditation and Mental Development. It also is showing Compassion to ourselves and to others when we investigate and try to make our living more balanced and skillful. Then everything becomes included in Awareness. There is nothing outside of our practice.

So our effort to prevent covers our action, our speech, our livelihood. This effort to be compassionately aware helps to develop the Noble Eightfold Path.

We wish to encourage a style of living that conditions the mind toward calming, non-aggression, non-grasping, clear awareness and letting go—for the benefit of ourselves and for the benefit of others.

One thing that can aid in our efforts to prevent is to try to seek out good friends. In the scriptures, when the Buddha spoke about the things that aid in Mental Development, that prevent hindrances from arising, and help in letting them go, He mentions noble friendship and suitable conversation as being *extremely* helpful.

This is because we are extremely influenced by our friends. If we have a friend or friends possessing and/or interested in cultivating Compassion, Lovingkindness, Awareness and Wisdom, who live in a way that helps the growth of these fine qualities, then we are extremely fortunate. These people may inspire us and encourage us to do the same, and we will not have the feeling of being weird or strange for doing so.

If we only spend time with people who have no interest in this and who may believe that there is no value in it, then we will have to depend solely on our own energy. Often this can increase our feeling of isolation and lead us into doing unskillful actions through a sense of wishing to "belong." Peer group pressure is a very strong influence for most of us.

Many of you may be just starting meditation practice. You may have started to feel Compassion and Lovingkindness towards more people. And you may feel inspired to help, especially those people who seem to be having a lot of problems. But it is important to also realize that you have to understand your own mind sufficiently and have a firm foundation of new conditioning towards evenness of mind, Equanimity and Wisdom, to help balance the Compassion and Lovingkindness that you feel, in order to help in the best way.

Please remember the dieters who have strengthened their ability towards balance in eating, can later walk into the bakery shop and have enough resolve to only buy what is necessary. They are then able to maintain their health and well-being. Similarly, later we may be able to be with difficult people more often and not be so affected by their negative personality traits. We may be able to not react to them in unwise ways, which increase aversion and negativity within ourselves.

When Compassion and Wisdom are strong enough, are more balanced, we may not react unwisely to their personality. Instead we may feel Compassion for the Dukkha that these people are caught in, which often manifests and is the cause of their negativities.

We may then feel a stability and balance within ourselves so that we are less influenced by their negativities. We may also feel OK with our own decisions on the path we wish to take; even if it is criticized or we are derided for our choice of living.

Many people in the helping professions have realized that they need periods of solitude or retreat from others' problems. This is in order to renew and refresh their inner strength. To find a balance between going inward, and opening to and helping others.

If they can find this balance, then they can continue to help and encourage others to develop beneficial qualities, rather than wearing out their energy, and becoming influenced by others' unbeneficial qualities.

Solitude can refresh us and so can being with good friends who possess positive qualities of Compassion, Awareness and Wisdom. We then can have conversations that are inspiring, probing and soothing to the heart.

This is a broad view of the effort to prevent based on Right Living.

Coming down to a more moment-to-moment level regarding the effort to prevent: If we understand the Law of Cause and Effect, that all of our actions and reactions condition our mind and bring forth results in the future, then we can practice as follows. Whenever strong impulses to act in a certain way arise in the mind, we can ask ourselves some questions.

"What is my real motivation, real reason for wanting to do this?

"Is it based in Compassion for myself and others?

"Is it beneficial? Or is it unbeneficial? Can this action increase Dukkha for myself or for others? Now or in the future?

"Do I really want to flow with it and go in that direction?"

Understanding that we are helping to create our future with our present choices, conditioning the mind in some way, we can try to balance these strong energies with Wise Reflection, Awareness and Compassion, trying to purify our intentions. This is bringing forth the effort to prevent unbeneficial things from arising.

We gradually can develop the ability to gently resist impulsive action, learn to investigate and learn to let go, if we see that the action may increase unwise desire, aversion, agitation and therefore our Dukkha.

Reflection on the Truth, the Laws of Nature and the other reflections we mentioned earlier helps in preventing unbeneficial qualities from arising, abandoning those that have already arisen, developing beneficial qualities, and maintaining these—thus all of the Four Great Efforts.

The effort to reflect gives us a friend, putting into the mind powerful thoughts, based on reality. It helps to deflate the power of old conditioning, and to balance unwise conditioning by strengthening the factor of Right View within the mind.

Another practice that is very important and helps in the effort to prevent is "guarding" or "watching over" the sense doors.

From all of our sense contacts arise a feeling, Vedana, that if not seen clearly can be the start of unwise reaction, causing a long chain of thoughts and problems.

By a certain amount of sense contact control, we can narrow down the diversity of our contacts. Also, by trying to increase awareness of our sense contacts, we give ourselves the opportunity to be less influenced by external conditions and then we have more awareness and choice over how we react.

We encourage you to practice sense control within this retreat. Try to direct your attention down rather than gazing all around, seeking sights which distract you and can excite either aversion or longing.

When eating, we encourage the use of Wise Reflection and Mindfulness. And we help by having set times to eat, not throughout the day. We try to keep the place quiet and you keep to silence. This limits the amount of outward conversation and contact with others. These are some of the contacts that we have a choice over in reducing the outward going energy.

With the other contacts that occur try to be mindful, using investigation and Wisdom. Try to note the contact between the senses and their objects; the actual contact, the arising of feeling and the passing away of feeling.

When you are "out of retreat" you may not be able to practice this in such an intense way, because you probably will not have retreat conditions to support you. But even done in a little way, it may help us to prevent the tension and tiredness that comes from continual sense excitement.

For example, if we are in Bangkok, we often experience a sense "bombardment." There is an excess of excitement of the senses. Sights, smells, sounds may crowd in on us and it may be difficult to keep calm and "collected." Often what may happen is that we end up with a headache.

There are opportunities to narrow down the field of our awareness. If we know where we are going, while walking along the sidewalk, instead of gazing all around, we can direct our attention to our footsteps and the sidewalk in front of us—*walking meditation.* Actually this is almost essential for our safety on the sidewalks in Bangkok, there always seem to be dangerous obstacles to avoid!

I would like to share with you part of a letter that a meditator sent to me. This person had participated in two retreats here:

"It's great to break into walking meditation in the middle of noisy... Bangkok streets when your head, eyes, ears, feet ache, you have no patience left, and within minutes, feel calm and contented again."

Instead of the tightness of aversion toward the loud noises, the mingling of odors, you can try to put awareness and mental noting on keen alert: "hearing, hearing"; "arising, arising"; "passing, passing"; "smelling, smelling"; "eyes watering, eyes watering"; "sweating, sweating"; until swishhhhhh...you are sucked into the eye of the cyclone...where everything is swirling around you and you are in the calm center. What an opportunity! When everything is rather pleasant, it's easy to just drift with the pleasant feeling. You may forget about your inner potential. Then when difficult situations and sensations arise you may not know how to help yourself. Try experimenting with guarding the sense doors out of retreat, and see what benefits it can bring to you.

As the effort to prevent covers so much of our life, you can see that it is a very important effort.

The next effort is *the effort to abandon.* We touched on this a little in discussing the effort to prevent. Prevention involves Wise Reflection and Awareness of our actions and lifestyle. The willingness to change, the effort to change, also brings forth the effort to abandon or let go.

In particular, the effort to abandon refers to being in situations, seeing unbeneficial things arising, understanding that they are unbeneficial, and bringing forth the effort to let go.

In Meditation practice, the effort to let go is extremely important. This is because letting go is the letting go of attachment and involvement. Attachment and involvement continues the energies of these unbeneficial things and thus our Dukkha. The force of conditioning is powerful and these things will continue to arise in the mind.

We make the effort to become aware of anger, jealousy, worry, restlessness, doubt, etc. that has arisen. We make the effort to watch and investigate in order to develop the understanding of their energies, their characteristics, and through Compassion we make the effort to let go of attachment.

Without this effort to let go, we may become involved and attached to unbeneficial things that arise in the mind. This involvement can strengthen the unbeneficial things that have arisen, and it sows the seeds for their continual arising in the future.

Through Compassion to ourselves, we make the effort to step back and observe the energy of these mental objects as they manifest in the body, or use skillful reflections to help us let go of attachment.

With the effort to abandon, try to balance it with Right Understanding—understanding the law of Cause and Effect, the Law of Conditioning.

Try not to investigate with a lot of aggression and idealism in the mind. This could bring up a lot of judgment and self-hatred. We may think we are just terrible if we are only trying to let go with our intellectual understanding of right or wrong; or because these things do not correspond with the self-image we would like to have or because we feel inadequate.

If we understand that the seeds of these mental states already have been sown by past habitual thinking and actions, we will learn to have Patience and work with them, not against them, when they arise.

We cannot transform these energies with anger. We only can transform them with Wisdom and Compassion. We are then letting go through Insight into the Nature of Things.

This has a much deeper effect than if we try to let go of these energies with willpower or if we just suppress them, because we are not then feeding the energies with anger, another unbeneficial state of mind that creates more Dukkha.

A moment of pure Awareness is *objective*. It is a simple seeing of what is present. There is no condemning in the mind. It is just clear acknowledgment, honesty, and a wish to see the Nature of Things in order to develop Wisdom.

An analogy that may help is if you think about wanting to clean a shirt that has become very dirty. With this example, you may understand more clearly how emotional reactions, such as anger and disappointment, are not of much benefit.

A wise way to clean a shirt is to look at the stains. "OK, this is blood, this is chocolate, this is grease. What is the best method for removing blood?" And we clean that spot. "Chocolate? Grease?" And we apply the best remedy for each.

You do not get angry at the shirt, thinking, "It shouldn't be dirty!" That does not clean it. You just go about cleaning it in the best possible way. Some stains need more time than others—a lot of soaking, special solutions. Others are removed easily.

We can work with what is present, what we are at that moment. We cannot work with what we think we should be. One is the actuality of the moment. The other is unreal, an illusion, insubstantial, wishful thinking.

When we make the effort to step back and observe the energy of these mental objects without involvement, we also are practicing *the effort to develop*. The effort to let go and the effort to develop are deeply connected and dependent on each other.

Without the effort to develop beneficial qualities of Awareness, Understanding, Patience and Equanimity, it is difficult to let go. Letting go depends on having some of these qualities. And without the effort to let go of unbeneficial qualities, it is difficult to continue to develop and strengthen these beneficial qualities.

As you have probably seen by now, developing these qualities depends a lot on letting go of the many things that hinder them from arising.

With the effort to develop, try to be careful not to let Idealism creep into the practice. We have talked about Idealism before, how it is a burden to carry around, how it is future-oriented.

We try not to practice with the ideal of Equanimity and impose it on the mind, all the time with an ideal of how we "should" be equanimous. This may not actually be developing Equanimity at all. Instead this often just develops aversion, suppression, self-hatred and doubt.

Developing Equanimity depends a great deal on Right View and on the growth of Compassionate Understanding. This depends on our ability to investigate the characteristics of whatever is arising. It is the Wisdom of seeing impermanence clearly and deeply. It is understanding that grasping and clinging to impermanent conditions only increases our Dukkha, our stress, suffering and unsatisfactoriness.

This Wisdom starts to balance the power of ignorance and confusion in the mind and we learn how to have Equanimity bit by bit. With developing Equanimity and other beneficial qualities, we try to develop a sensitivity and awareness on a moment-to-moment basis. We become aware when these beneficial qualities are present. We try to see what factors caused their arising, and, using our past experience and understanding, we work toward bringing these qualities to fruition again.

With the effort to develop, it is helpful to have it linked with Right View in a second way. Understanding the Law of Cause and Effect will help to balance our efforts with Patience. All that arises comes from causes and conditions. We cannot expect instant Peace. We have to "sow" the causes for Peace to arise.

A farmer who wants to make a living out of growing fruit has to patiently plant the trees, care for them and allow the time for the trees to grow and fruit. The farmer cannot expect the crop just by wanting the crop.

I was talking with a meditator friend one day, and we were laughing about the lack of balance we often had at the beginning of our practice. My friend related this story.

"I was just beginning my second retreat in a meditation center in the West. I had a lot of expectations for this retreat and I made a vow to work very hard, never giving in to laziness. But in the back of my mind was the hope, 'Well, if I work very hard, perhaps I'll get an experience or enlightenment.'

"So I worked very hard, never giving in to laziness, doing more than I was scheduled to do. In the middle of the retreat, I became quite frustrated. Nothing was happening; no calm, no bright lights, let alone enlightenment.

"I reflected, 'What is the reason for this?' And thought, 'Well, perhaps I need to bring up some more effort. I know, I will sit and walk all night!'

"I made a vow to sit and walk all night. So I sat with desire, walked with desire, sat with desire, walked with desire. The other meditators slowly started to leave the hall. 'I am not leaving. I have the strength. I have the determination. I am going to sit and walk all night.'

"So I sat with desire, walked with desire, sat with desire, walked with desire. Nothing was happening. I looked around in the hall; everybody else had gone to sleep. A bit of loneliness started to arise, which I quickly pushed away. 'No attachments for me. I am going to become enlightened. I have the determination, I have the effort, I have the energy.'

"So I sat with, 'I am sitting,' walked with, 'I am walking,' sat with, 'I am sitting," walked with, 'I am walking.' Nothing was happening. I started to feel a bit down. It was 2 a.m. already. There were only two more hours to the wake-up bell. 'What if I don't become enlightened? Hey—that's doubt, doubt. No, I have the faith, I have the determination. I am sitting and walking all night. Perhaps I need to do some standing meditation. That brings up the effort and energy. That's what I will do.'

"So I stood outside amid the shadows of the trees, increasing my concentration—and my desire. Occasionally I opened my eyes and peeked: 'Am I still here? Yes, no empty space, just trees. Perhaps I need a new meditation object; this is not working. I know, perhaps if I use the power of my concentration and stare at the trees, perhaps I will be able to penetrate into their void nature and dissolve the trees.'

"I stared at the trees, and stared and stared, increasing my concentration. And I stared and stared. The trees stayed solid and unchanging! So I increased my concentration and stared at the trees. My eyes started to ache, tears started to roll down my cheeks. I closed my eyes again.

"By this time the unpleasant sensations had started to arise in the body. 'Pain, that is a good meditation object. I will concentrate on the pain.' So I started to concentrate on the pain. And the sensations increased, And I increased my concentration, and the sensations increased, and I increased my concentration, until suddenly...a soft sound pierced the silence.

"'What is that? Is that a heavenly sound? It is coming!' And then the realization came—but it was not what I was after. 'That is not a heavenly sound; that is the wake-up bell! I sat and walked all night and I am still not enlightened.' I went weak in the knees and collapsed. I was so exhausted that I had to sleep the rest of the day."

This is a true story. This meditator had a powerful amount of energy, but it was not balanced with Right Understanding. It is a gradual awakening. Try to learn to have Patience and not reach out for the results of the practice. It is a subtle transformation.

If the effort is based in Right View and Right Intention, then no effort is wasted. This understanding can be very encouraging for those who sometimes feel that they are "not getting anywhere." If the effort is based in Right View and Right Intention, then no effort is wasted.

It is helpful to have the effort to develop balanced with Right View in a third way.

Many people misunderstand the goal and the process of Vipassana, or Insight, Meditation. They think that the goal is to get concentrated, to get calm and to experience bliss. If they are not able to get calm and bliss, then they feel frustrated and a failure. Although calm and bliss may arise from time to time as a fruit of meditation, it is not the aim of Vipassana Meditation. The goal of Vipassana Meditation is the purification of the Mind through the development of Wisdom.

We ask you to try to become aware of whatever is happening in the body and the mind. Try not to push away any experience. Investigate and try to see the arising and passing away of each experience. We can develop the ability to have balance in any experience.

So when there is the unconcentrated state of mind, we know that there is the unconcentrated state of mind. It passes away when we are able to concentrate for a short while. When thoughts arise, Awareness knows it and when the mind is concentrated on the breath, Awareness knows it.

Whenever there arises a contact with the senses, we try to see the arising of the contact and the passing away of the contact. We are contemplating the impermanent, impersonal, conditioned nature of all that arises and the cause of Dukkha.

If calm does arise, we know calm arises, and we also know when it passes. We try not to bring up grief when it passes. We are trying to develop a non-attached Awareness and a Peace that does not depend simply on pleasant experience.

The mind tries to watch from a state of balance, looking deeply, observing everything that arises and passes away. We are looking deeply to discover who and what we are and the nature of experience. Only through constant observation can we come to understand the nature of the body and mind and life.

The goal of Vipassana Meditation is the purification of the mind through the development of Wisdom. If we can understand the Laws of Nature, of the body, of the mind, then we can come into non-grasping harmony with all of life. Instead of trying to resist it. Resisting it will not change the truth. It will only increase our Dukkha.

Can wishing for the sun not to rise stop it from rising? Can wishing for the sun not to set stop it from setting? If we do not understand on a deep experiential level, then there is no real deep opportunity for the letting go, and for the solid, deep Peace of Equanimity based in Wisdom to arise.

So we try to balance our efforts with Right View or Understanding, by realizing that our object is to develop Wisdom, and we try not to direct our energies and hopes only to obtaining calm and/or concentration.

If we only practice for concentration, it is a bit like people who see that they need sharp axes to clear some land in order to plant an orchard.

They start to sharpen their axes, getting so involved with sharpening the axes and wanting super-sharp axes, that they just sit and sharpen and sharpen and sharpen, admiring the metal and the sharpness, and then forgetting about the land they have to clear. They never get around to *using* the axes.

So try to remember that the object is to develop Wisdom. Try not to direct your energies and hopes only to obtaining calm and/or concentration.

As well, try not to judge your meditation only on the ability to get calm and/or concentrated. If calm does not arise, try not to worry and develop desire and frustration. Instead, try to develop an awareness of what is present at that moment. Developing Compassionate Understanding is trying to balance your efforts with Right Understanding.

The next effort is *the effort to maintain.* This effort can be seen first as directed toward our lifestyles. We may have become aware of how and why we do things, and perhaps we may have changed our lifestyle to some degree in order to prevent unbeneficial things from arising.

After we do this, we may find that it increases the power of the beneficial factors of mind and therefore our well-being. So we make the effort to maintain this new style of living.

Because we may not be accustomed to new ways of doing things and they have not yet become strong habits, the old habitual ways of doing things are still strong drives in our mind. So we try to bring forth effort to continue, to persevere in our efforts.

For example, we may have seen that meditation brings forth beneficial qualities of mind. In order to keep developing the mind, we make the effort to maintain the practice—by meditating every day, by reflecting on Truth, by trying to be mindful.

Again this effort is connected to the other efforts because we have to bring up the effort to let go of the many things which encourage the mind to give up, and slip back into the easier way of following old habitual thinking and ways of doing things.

The effort to maintain is extremely important when you leave a retreat and try to bring the practice into your daily life. Many people leave a retreat having experienced some degree of increased Awareness and Compassionate Understanding. They may have seen some of their Dukkha fade away by the letting go process, and the increase of beneficial qualities of mind.

Some of these people, however, expect that this will enable them to "sail through" their problems; they have done the work and now they can relax, take it easy. Although you may not be able to meditate all day outside a retreat, some effort to be mindful, to do formal meditation is extremely important to keep the mind developing and healthy.

If you do not try to bring the practice into your everyday life, expecting the retreat to solve all of your problems for the future, then you will be a bit like the following type of people.

These people want to travel a long distance by car. At the beginning of the journey, the car gets filled up with gas, the water and oil levels are checked, air is put in the tires. Then the trip begins.

Enough fuel and momentum are present to keep the car going for some time. However, the fuel, water, oil and tires are not checked regularly. The car is working fine, so the driver just relaxes, settles back.

Eventually, the car runs out of gas, the water and oil levels drop, or the air in the tires escapes. The car breaks down. The driver gets out and gets all upset at the car: "Why did it have to break down?! We're only halfway there!" But it was really the driver's fault. A car cannot run without proper care.

Similarly, your mind cannot develop without proper care. The mind cannot concentrate or be mindful without practice. It cannot bring forth Compassion and Lovingkindness unless you continue to make the effort to let go of anger and aversion in your everyday life.

Our minds cannot find Peace and Happiness if we do not maintain our efforts to develop the beneficial qualities of Awareness, Equanimity and Understanding, which help to heal the mind.

The effort to maintain is like taking care of the car: putting in the fuel, keeping the water level up, checking the tires. And it is similar to feeding the body. Just as we feed the body with nourishing food to keep it healthy, we try to continue to feed the mind with nourishing thoughts and practice meditation to keep it peaceful and healthy.

With this effort, it is helpful to approach ourselves and the practice with a loving, caring attitude. Having worked hard to see the arising of beneficial qualities by the effort to let go, we try to have Compassion and Kindness towards ourselves and care for the mind by the effort to maintain.

To maintain the presence of balancing beneficial qualities that increase our well-being, we try to care about the practice, bringing loving care to our actions, our speech, our thoughts, our steps, our breath. Trying to make everything important. We try to continue to give the mind nourishment through Wise Reflection, helping to add beneficial conditioning to balance unbeneficial conditioning and ignorance.

Effort is extremely important in our practice. Without effort, we cannot develop the mind or find deep inner Peace. In order not to increase your difficulties, try to balance your efforts with Right View or Understanding and with Right Intention. Effort balanced in this way will bring the best benefit.

Please remember the analogy of the effort needed as being similar to tuning a stringed instrument. If one tunes the strings too tight or too loose, then the instrument will not bring forth beautiful music.

The "too tight" often comes from the energy of wanting to achieve, reaching out with desire for the fruits of our practice. We can learn to balance this tendency with Wise Reflection on the Law of Cause and Effect and by investigating into the unsatisfactoriness that arises from the achievement mind. We gradually can learn to let go and develop the patience to continually sow the seeds of Peace in the present moment.

The "too loose" is not enough effort. It is letting the mind wander and drop into laziness and dullness. It is not caring enough. We can try to balance this tendency by reflecting on both the preciousness of our opportunity, and that we do not know when this opportunity will end. This is trying to increase our Compassion for ourselves and others.

A lot of people talk about wanting more Peace on the Earth. To really manifest this wish, it is up to each one of you to develop your potential to the highest level you are capable of doing, to use your precious opportunity. This is so others may be able to see what they

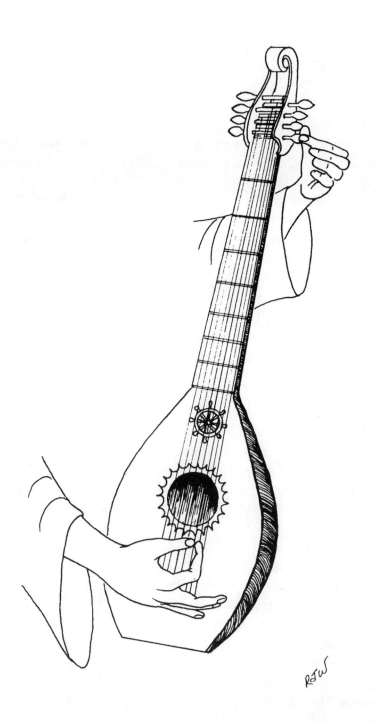

are capable of being as well.

The world needs every one of you... There is so much suffering in this world... Do not become complacent... Develop that energy factor within and touch your inner potential... The human potential is so great... It is vast ...

When we first began teaching, often we were afraid to ask more of the people who came to meditate here. Yet when we started to be less hesitant and ask more, we saw people were capable of bringing it forth. We realized we had to bring up our own efforts and to continue to ask more and more of each one of you, to appeal to the potential in each one of you, because *so much* is needed and there are *so few* people willing to help in this way.

Please do not drift, becoming content with lower levels of Wisdom and Compassion. Do not close your heart. Develop your Wisdom and your Compassion as much as you can, so you can be of more benefit to yourself and all living beings.

Haven't we had enough of people indulging themselves, using up the resources of the Earth, harming others for personal gain coming from greed and ignorance? Please give something back to the world. Become courageous. Develop your mind. *Perhaps if only one person responds to these words, it will have been worth our efforts.*

**When Effort is balanced with Right Understanding and Right Intention, the Compassionate Motivation, then we will learn to live more skillfully in order to *prevent* unbeneficial qualities from arising.**

We will learn what needs to be *abandoned*, and we can try to let go. We will know what factors of mind increase our well-being and the well-being of others. And through Compassion and Lovingkindness to ourselves and others, we try to make the effort to *develop* these beneficial factors and qualities.

After we see these beneficial qualities arising, we try to see clearly their healing energy in the mind, the fading away of Dukkha and the deepening of our Understanding of ourselves and others.

This Compassionate Understanding will strengthen our efforts to *maintain* the practice and to continue to maintain the causes for the deepening of Wisdom and Peace.

## MID-MORNING DAY NINE

# HAVE YOU GROWN?

Occasionally there are a few people who continue to have difficulty with Compassion/Lovingkindness meditation. Especially in regard to having Compassion and Lovingkindness toward so-called "bad" people in the world, in particular those who create extreme difficulties and problems for so many others.

In this regard, I would like to mention three different instances related to myself. Two of them are true stories; one is imaginary. And yet, although imaginary for me, situations like this are happening in many places around the world.

As I relate these three instances, try to be aware if you can see how to separate the people from their actions. That is, we can have aversion toward actions which are harmful, but we still can have Compassion toward the people.

The first instance: Suppose I come into the meditation hall and I immediately start kicking the people in the front row, hitting them, yelling and screaming. How would you feel?

Normally, most of you would have a feeling of shock and bewilderment, as to: "What's happening to Steve? What is going wrong with Steve? There is something wrong." And many of you would try to stop me from what I am doing because you know that these actions are unhealthy and can cause a lot of trouble for me and for others.

In this particular case, you probably would have Compassion for me, knowing there is something wrong inside. And yet, you would have aversion toward my actions. This is one example of being able to separate the person from the actions, having aversion toward the actions but having Compassion toward the person.

Another instance happened here some time ago. One evening before a talk, I noticed a Thai man hanging around the monastery. I had a little chat with him and I could not understand much of what he was saying. Since my Thai is not 100 percent, I did not worry so much about it, but I told him to go and talk to the monks.

About half an hour later, the head monk, Phra Jarun, came up to me and said, "Did you see that Thai fellow that was hanging around the Wat?" I said, "Yes." And he said, "Be careful with that man. He is not well. He may do something wrong." In the Thai language, he said, "Mai mee sati," which means, "He does not have any mindfulness."

The next day at just about the same time in the evening, Phra Jarun came up to me and he said, "Do you remember that man that was here in the monastery last night?" I said, "Yes." He said, "This afternoon they arrested him down at the beach. He was stealing from the bungalows. He is not well."

Now try to consider Phra Jarun's reaction and how he described this man, compared with what many other people would think. If people saw someone hanging around where they were staying, a typical attitude would be, "Oh, that person is up to no good. They are a bad person." And yet, Phra Jarun said, "He is not well. He may do something wrong."

Then the next day, when one finds out that he has been arrested for stealing, a very common attitude might be, "Yeah, I told you so. He is an evil person; he is bad. He should be locked up." And yet Phra Jarun's reaction was, "He is not well. Be careful with this man."

This is another example of being able to separate the person from the actions. We can have aversion to the actions, but we do not have to have aversion to the person. We can have Compassion toward that person who is not well.

The third instance came in the form of a letter we received from a woman who is over 70 years old, a friend of our family and had known me when I was a child. My mother had sent her one of our books. She felt that the teachings in the book related very closely to how she has practiced and tried to develop in her own way.

Although not a "Buddhist meditator," she is very religious and felt that the book was a very nice example of many things she understood. She wanted to express this thankfulness and appreciation, and encourage us in our efforts.

In the letter, she related a reflection that she uses whenever she sees the face of a criminal on the TV or in a newspaper or magazine. She uses this reflection: "Looking at the faces of criminals in the media, I often think, `That person was once an infant, later a child. What was lacking? Who was not aware of the needs, the small things worrying the little one? Who was not there when the child yearned for love?'"

What went wrong in their childhood? Can we separate the person from the actions? Having aversion toward the actions that are unwise or unkind, and yet having Compassion toward the person.

I would now like to repeat some of the things that I said in the very first talk of the retreat. You may remember some of this and some you may not remember. Much of this we have restated many times during the retreat. What may be of value here as I repeat these things, is for you to be aware whether there has been any change in your attitude or understanding concerning these things. That is, the attitude or understanding that you have *now* compared to the attitude or understanding that you had on the *first day* of the retreat.

**"Compassion is a basis of Mental Development and Meditation practice.** Without seeing difficulties and having Compassion towards the difficulties, then there may exist no desire to solve the difficulties and possibly no desire to practice Mental Development and Meditation."

"We think certain ways due to our past conditioning. We react certain ways due to our past conditioning. Some of our reactions are wise, some are not wise. Some are proper, some are not proper. Some arise with Compassion and Love, some with anger and hatred. Some lead to Peace and Happiness, others to problems and difficulties.

All of us would like to have more Peace and Happiness. All of us would like to have fewer problems and difficulties. Developing Mindfulness of our thoughts, our speech, our actions and our reactions is a major step in the process of mental development. This is not easy. It takes time. As we have been conditioned to be who we are over many, many years, we cannot change things overnight. We have to respect that our habits and thought patterns have become strong over so many years and that it takes time to change. Patience is needed. Compassion is needed. Perseverance is needed. Equanimity is needed. Different beneficial mental qualities need to be developed and strengthened.

Keep in mind that practicing and developing Meditation is much like learning something new in everyday life."

"Some will learn quickly. Some will learn slowly. If there is Perseverance, Patience and Endurance, continual trying, learning and practicing, then Meditation can be developed."

"It is very important to keep an *open* mind. Some of what we say might be very clear and most of you will understand what is meant. There also may be parts that are not very clear and some of you might not understand. That is OK. Try not to worry about it. There will be a lot of information given during these 10 days and it may not be possible to understand everything. Take whatever you do understand and try your best to work with that. Leave whatever you do not understand for now. It might be of help at a later date.

There are many different aspects of Mental Development and it is basically impossible to work on all of them at the same time. Due to our different personalities and conditioning, each of us will tend to work on different aspects of the practice at different times."

"... with Compassion, Lovingkindness and Mindfulness, we can develop the Understanding necessary to gradually change our conditioning little-by-little, bit-by-bit. Mental Development is a gradual process.

Our habits and tendencies have energies that are very strong at times, and to try to stop these energies often can create more difficulties. Instead of trying to get rid of any unbeneficial habit or tendency all at once, we can use the energy present and gently bend the direction of this energy. With Compassionate Understanding of why we are doing, saying or thinking things in certain ways, we can bend unwise energies into wise energies."

"Much of Mental Development is to learn who and what we are. In understanding who and what we are, we will learn how to accept ourselves and accept others, how to forgive ourselves and forgive others, how to have Compassion and Lovingkindness toward ourselves and toward others. We will learn about our interrelationships with others and with the environment. We will learn how we have been conditioned. We will learn about our qualities that are beneficial and about our qualities that are unbeneficial. As we understand these things, we will be better able to apply remedies and solutions to any problem that we encounter.

This is basic: If we want to change our thoughts, habits or patterns of living in beneficial ways, we first must start to understand ourselves."

"It is important to try to work with basic practices and with smaller problems before working with larger ones. We frequently cause extra difficulties for ourselves because we want to accomplish something that is beyond our limits. There is often a big difference between what we *can* do and what we think we *should* be able to do. This is a difference between Reality and Idealism.

The reality of a situation is what we can work with, objectively seeing who and what we are and starting from there. Too many people want to start with who and what they think they are or think they should be, having some ideal about themselves or about their capabilities. Frequently this causes aversion, pain, grief, despair and frustration. When we think we should be a certain way, but in reality we are not, then a lot of self-hatred and doubt can arise."

"Problems and difficulties can be lessened if we start with who and what we are, learn some techniques and methods of *how* to do things, and try to apply these techniques and methods to ourselves."

These words that I just repeated from the first night's talk...can you see any change in your attitude or understanding concerning these things?

You may have strong Concentration or maybe not.

You may have strong Mindfulness or maybe not.

But more important than these...has your Compassionate Understanding grown?

Many people know that we teach how to develop Concentration, and some people think that developing Concentration is most important. It is true that we teach how to develop Concentration, but we do not think that the development of Concentration is most important.

Many people know that we teach how to develop Mindfulness, and some people think that the development of Mindfulness is most important. It is true that we teach how to develop Mindfulness, but we do not think that the development of Mindfulness is most important.

Many people know that we teach how to develop Compassionate Understanding, trying to open the heart and purify the mind from selfishness, greed, aversion and ignorance, and some people think this is most important.

It is true that we teach how to develop Compassionate Understanding, trying to open the heart and purify the mind from selfishness, greed, aversion and ignorance. And it is true that we think this development of Compassionate Understanding, trying to open the heart and purify the mind from selfishness, greed, aversion and ignorance, is most important.

Too often, some meditation practices tend to encourage a closing of the Heart, not always understanding Compassion and Lovingkindness and their relationship to the practice. And often confusing Equanimity with indifference, not caring.

As you continue with your Meditation/Mental Development practice, try to keep your Heart open with Compassionate Understanding.

Trying, watching, learning, bit-by-bit, bit-by-bit.

As we start this sitting meditation, I would like to lead you through the Five Reflections briefly. So please settle yourself and take a few moments watching your breathing, relaxing into the posture.

Just before beginning I would like to mention a few words on the importance of Wise Reflection. Learning how to think wisely, training our mind to think wisely. There are basically three things we can do with our mind. We can think wisely, we can think unwisely or we can learn to let go of thoughts. It is thinking unwisely that creates so much of our mental Dukkha.

Thinking wisely and learning how to let go of thought will help us end mental Dukkha. Sometimes it is as if there is a little battle going on in the mind, which many of you may have seen already, between Wisdom and Ignorance. When our Wisdom is strong then our Ignorance is weak. When our Ignorance is strong then our Wisdom is weak. Almost like a seesaw, with Wisdom on one side and Ignorance on the other.

So in this practice, on one side we can learn to let go. On another side we learn to develop. Trying to have a balanced practice. That is what we are trying to do here, teach a *balanced* practice. In order to develop a balanced practice, we must learn how to think wisely, we must train our mind to think wisely.

The first two factors of the Noble Eightfold Path are Right Understanding and Right Intention. We must have some degree of Right Understanding and Right Intention in order to guide the six other factors of the Noble Eightfold Path. Learning to think wisely is so important. As the Buddha is quoted from the Sabbasava Sutta: "For a person who reflects wisely, anxieties and troubles which have not yet arisen do not arise. And in addition those anxieties and troubles which have already arisen disappear."

*****

Please first reflect on many of the different ways that you are fortunate. Consider the beneficial, fortunate aspects of your life; health, money, education, freedoms, the opportunity to learn meditation, develop Compassionate Understanding, or whatever else it may be.

*****

Now please reflect on Death and Impermanence. That everything seems to have its own birth, existence and death. That death is a natural event for all of us and that we do not know when we will die. Possibly consider how you would like to die; with agitation and fear in your mind or with Peace and Contentment in your mind.

*****

Next please consider actions and results of actions, or the Law of Kamma, or Law of Cause and Effect. Consider that by improving your actions, speech and thoughts in beneficial ways, you will be providing yourself with the best conditions for a better life both now and in the future.

*****

Now please reflect upon Dukkha or unsatisfactoriness. That it is a basic part of our existence. That we will continually from time-to-time experience things that are unpleasant, unsatisfactory, Dukkha. Just natural. However, we can work to alleviate the extra Dukkha that we often cause for ourselves in our reactions.

*****

Lastly consider the relationship between Compassion and Equanimity. To care, to always have Compassionate Caring but to be balanced and strengthened by Equanimity. To try to understand when not to care and yet always with Compassionate Understanding.

*****

Please continue to expand one or all of these reflections for the rest of the period.

*****

(end of period)
This morning we do not have a new activity for you to work with strong mindfulness, extra attention. I would like to talk more about the one that we gave you yesterday. Trying to be aware of tasting. Trying to be right there and aware of tasting your food.

This is quite a bit different to the six other activities that we gave you on the other mornings of the retreat. The other six are basic physical actions that you have to do which normally do not arouse much liking or disliking... At least, we do not think so ...

Umm, we have not noticed any of you kinda playing with the doors because you like it so much ...

We have not noticed any of you washing the dishes 5 or 6 times just to get the practice ...

Nobody has been coming into the hall, sitting down, standing up, sitting down, standing ...

They are just things that we have to do. So, it is just physical, we just do it. We do not love it, we do not hate it. Just what we do.

*But* when it comes to eating...and tasting our food...this is usually a bit different. We taste something pleasant, and we *like* it. We taste something unpleasant, and we *do not like* it.

So what comes in here is some more reactions to the basic process. And these reactions of liking and disliking can often lead to types of emotional states which bring about the Five Hindrances!

If we like it too much—sense desire, we want, we want. If we do not like it—aversion, we hate, we do not want. If we like it too much, then a lot of restlessness and worry can come about because we start thinking, "This is really good. I'd like to have some more. I wonder if there is going to be enough?" And we start looking to see if there is more:

"Oh no! Someone else is getting it!"

So the different hindrances can come about very easily, when we are tasting or immediately after the taste of our food.

Try to be mindful right there with your tasting. If it is pleasant, fine, it is pleasant and then we continue eating and the next taste might be pleasant and the next. And we are right there with pleasant food. Without creating a mind "spin" thinking and thinking about the food and not even tasting any of it.

If it is unpleasant, OK, it is unpleasant, but we have used our food reflection and we know that it is to keep us alive, to keep going and we are content.

So the pleasantness does not send us off on an emotional state of greed and sense desire. And the unpleasantness does not send us off into hating and being upset at the cooks and so on.

And we are more at Peace. We can be right there in that moment. We can be experiencing eating and tasting and be right there.

So try to pay extra attention again to your eating. Try to be very involved in your chewing, try to chew mindfully; that brings you very close to your tasting. It will also help if you put your spoon down and rest it on the side of your plate. Often we are in a hurry to scoop up the next mouthful and while doing so we fail to taste our food, because the mind is thinking about the next bit of food, not the one that we are chewing.

Try to be right there with the tasting. Watch and see if you can keep wise reactions to it. And not cause extra problems for yourself.

# SYMPATHETIC JOY

I would like to talk about another beneficial quality of mind that is so helpful for us in our practice. This quality is called Sympathetic Joy.

Just as Compassion feels with the Dukkha, the Unsatisfactoriness, experienced by ourselves and others, and seeks to alleviate it, Sympathetic Joy feels with our own and others' growth, good qualities, happiness and successes in life.

Compassion helps to break down the sense of separateness by dissolving those bubbles in which we isolate ourselves. Sympathetic Joy also starts to dissolve our isolation by helping us to take joy with our own and others' good qualities. It allows us to find more Joy and Contentment.

Sympathetic Joy also acts as a balancing quality for Compassion. This is because there is the realization that there is a way out of Dukkha. We can share in the Contentment, Relief and Joy that we and others can experience in walking the path and seeing the fading away of Dukkha.

It is very helpful to reflect on our own growth. Look back, remember. Remember those moments of Understanding. Look at how you view life and your difficulties and problems now, compared to how you used to view life and your Dukkha. Try to open to the transformation. It is OK to open to it, to see the subtle, gradual growth within ourselves.

Often we miss these growths, because they are so subtle or because we are not able to step back enough, frequently being "drowned" in negativities, unworthiness or self-pity.

If you remember, look back, it also will help to give you energy and inspiration to continue with the practice. It will help to banish doubt and give you confidence. It can help renew your motivation and your confidence in the teachings that are leading you out of Dukkha, your problems and difficulties.

It will help to give you more Strength and Patience—Patience with the difficulties arising in the practice and Patience with yourself.

Sometimes during the practice of Insight Meditation, the mind can get very tired from constant observation. The energy can get depleted in the mind and agitation may arise. It takes a lot of energy to observe, investigate and reflect in such a fine way. Also, sometimes what we see may be a bit overwhelming.

If you find the mind getting too agitated, exhausted, "strung-out" or overwhelmed, this often means that the mind is off-balance in some way. There may not be enough calm, energy or concentration to give strength to Awareness and Investigation.

Switching the meditation subject to Sympathetic Joy has proven very helpful for many people at this time because it is a confidence-inspiring object. It helps calm the mind and bring forth Joy and Concentration.

In the scriptures, the Buddha says to Ananda, his attendant, "Herein followers dwell contemplating the body…contemplating feelings…contemplating states of mind…contemplating mind objects…ardent, clearly comprehending and mindful, having put aside covetousness and grief concerning the world.

"While they thus dwell practicing, there arises in them, with body…feelings…states of mind…or mind objects as object, some bodily excitation, physical discomfort or mental sluggishness, or their mind wanders to external things, those followers, Ananda, should direct their thoughts to any confidence-inspiring object.

"As they direct their thoughts to an inspiring object, delight will arise in them. When they are thus delighted, rapture will arise. When they experience rapture, inner tranquility will appear. They who are tranquil will feel joy. Being joyful, their mind is concentrated.

"They then reflect, 'The aim on which I set my mind is now fulfilled. Let me now withdraw my mind (from the inspiring object).' So they do, without starting or continuing the thought process. And they are aware of being free from reflection and considering, inwardly mindful and joyful.

"This, Ananda, is directed meditation."[1]

Reflecting on and taking Joy in the teachings and your inner potential will help gladden your mind, giving you a refuge, a sense of security. In this way, we can protect the mind from "burn-out" by seeing and applying methods that are needed to balance the mind.

Trying to take Joy with others' good qualities or successes in life also will help to lessen envy, jealousy, competition and feelings of either inferiority or superiority in your relationships with others.

When we see others benefiting in life, receiving something we would like, or possessing and developing strengths and beneficial qualities that we admire, rather than bringing up envy, jealousy, unworthiness or comparative judgments, we can try to view life through their eyes and share in their joy and happiness.

At that moment, these are beings who are not overcome by Dukkha. They may be finding Peace and refuge in their strengths, helping others with these strengths, or developing their beneficial qualities so they may, at some time, be able to help others. They also may be simply experiencing a happiness, lightness and peace from good fortune—however impermanent it may be or we consider it to be. Whichever way, there are beings who need Compassion less.

A question many people ask us is, "You don't get paid—what are you doing this for? What do you get out of this?"

In answering this question, one may see the close connection that can exist between Sympathetic Joy and the qualities of Compassion, Lovingkindness and Generosity arising in Compassionate Action.

The development of Generosity is often the manifestation in action of the Compassion and Lovingkindness that one feels for others. As Compassion and Lovingkindness grow, it becomes increasingly important for many people to express these feelings in some Compassionate Action.

Often there is the wish to give. There are many forms of giving and we often find that in giving we also are receiving. One may find that giving continues to aid in the letting go process, the letting go of the separate self by reducing selfishness.

Our well-being may increase because giving can aid us in lessening the feeling of separateness, helping us to feel more the interrelationship between ourselves and others.

We also may feel an energy arising within us as a result of giving. Touching the sources of energy within ourselves, we may seek less to renew ourselves from outside. We may see the source of Energy, Peace and Well-Being as lying within, a result of our wise responses to others and to experience.

One source of this energy can be the arising of Joy. In our case, it is Sympathetic Joy. The Joy of watching people grow, finding a strength they did not know they possessed within themselves. We watch people growing in their understanding of the power of the mind and of the teachings to show them the way out of Dukkha.

We watch people realizing that it is by transforming themselves that they walk the path to Inner Peace. We watch people letting go of the feeling of searching and finding only an emptiness in their life, replacing it with the understanding that there is a path to inner contentment and the fading away of Dukkha. We watch people going from dependence on external things to dependence on their own inner strengths and Wisdom.

When Compassion and Lovingkind wishes are fulfilled in some way, these wishes can be transformed into the positive beneficial energy of Sympathetic Joy. The power of Joy, Sympathetic Joy, Joy with others' growth and one's own growth as well, is so very powerful. It recharges the energy within, helping to give more incentive to continue walking the path and trying to help others walk the path also.

In the scriptures, when the Buddha spoke about Compassion, Lovingkindness, Equanimity and Sympathetic Joy, he called them the Brahma Viharas. The Pali word "Brahma" means God or Divine Being. "Vihara" means abode or home. So in English, they often are referred to as Divine Abodes.

Why did the Buddha refer to these states of mind as Brahma Viharas? He called them this because when we feel them deeply enough, he said that we are living as if we were Divine Beings or

Gods—finding an abode, a home, a security in these beneficial states of mind, these healing states of mind.

**I would now like to lead you through a guided Sympathetic Joy meditation.** Please settle yourself in the posture if you have not already done so and concentrate on your breathing for a short while.

*****

Bring your attention to yourself. Try to remember the moments during this retreat where you suddenly understood something, glimpsed your inner strength or gained insight, were able to open, come into the moment in a non-resisting, non-clinging way and see the fading away of Dukkha at that time.

*****

Try to take Joy and Contentment with the good qualities that helped these moments to arise. At the same time try to take Joy and Contentment in your efforts now, to understand, to open, to continue. Try to allow the healing energy of Joy to arise for yourself.

*****

In times of discouragement, may I be able to remember my good qualities. Take Joy with them, in the gradual awakening and my inner potential. Feeling Joy in the teachings, may it give me a refuge, giving me confidence and energy to continue.

*****

Now focus your attention on the person sitting next to you. Reflect about this person's efforts; their patience, endurance, sometimes going through difficulties during this retreat, perhaps at times being able to flow into the moment, gain Insight or Understanding, or let go of their Dukkha and finding a Joy and Contentment within.

*****

Try to allow the healing energy of Sympathetic Joy to arise for this person.

\*\*\*\*\*

In times of discouragement, may this meditator be able to remember their good qualities. Take Joy with them, in the gradual awakening and their inner potential. Feeling Joy in the teachings, may it give them a refuge, giving them confidence and energy to continue.

\*\*\*\*\*

Focus your attention on the other meditators in the room. Reflect about their efforts.

\*\*\*\*\*

Try to allow the healing energy of Sympathetic Joy to arise for them.

\*\*\*\*\*

In times of discouragement, may these meditators be able to remember their good qualities. Take Joy with them, in the gradual awakening and their inner potential. Feeling Joy in the teachings, may it give them a refuge, giving them confidence and energy to continue.

\*\*\*\*\*

Now focus your attention on your parents or special relatives. Try to remember a time in their life when they were able to face and overcome a difficult time, overcome a challenge in their life, or, when they were able to help others. Try to take Joy in the arising of their beneficial qualities at that time.

\*\*\*\*\*

Try to allow the healing energy of Sympathetic Joy to arise for them.

\*\*\*\*\*

In times of discouragement, may my parents or special relatives be able to remember their good qualities. Take Joy with them and reach for the strength, their inner potential. May it give them a refuge, giving them confidence and energy to overcome their challenges and develop their beneficial qualities.

*****

Now focus your attention on some of your teachers or people who have taught you valuable things in your life. Reflect on some of their beneficial qualities, and in their efforts to develop these beneficial qualities. Try to take Joy in their efforts.

*****

Try to allow the healing energy of Sympathetic Joy to arise for them. Taking Joy with their growth, sharing with it.

*****

In times of discouragement, may my teachers or people who have taught me valuable things in life be able to remember their good qualities. Take Joy with them, in the gradual awakening and their inner potential. Feeling Joy in the teachings, may it give them a refuge, giving them confidence and energy to continue.

*****

Now expand your awareness to the nuns and monks and others in this monastery. Reflect on their Generosity, allowing us to use their home, helping to look after us so that we may experience the Buddha's teaching within ourselves.

*****

Allow the healing energy of Sympathetic Joy to arise for them.

*****

In times of discouragement, may all who live here be able to remember their good qualities. Take Joy with them, in the gradual awakening and their inner potential. Feeling Joy in the teachings, may it give them a refuge, giving them confidence and energy to continue.

*****

Now reflect on your home country. Bring to mind many of the positive characteristics of the people of your own country; the protection of freedoms of belief, travel, speech, protection of their citizens from the few with greed for power, etc. Also reflect on the many people within your country dedicated to improving the education and welfare of others, those who help the poor, the sick, the oppressed, in their own and in other countries. Those who are searching for their inner potential and Wisdom.

*****

Allow yourself to see the beneficial characteristics of your own country, the people of your own country. Try to take Sympathetic Joy in their qualities.

*****

May those in my own country dedicated to Truth, Freedom and Goodness be able to remember their good qualities when their mind gets discouraged. Take Joy with them and reach for the strength, their inner potential. May it give them a refuge, giving them confidence and energy to continue.

*****

Now expand your awareness and think about, reflect on, or visualize some different people of the world dedicated to growth. Those people who are developing within themselves the higher qualities of Peace, Compassionate Action, Lovingkindness, Generosity.

*****

People who are walking the path of Mental Development, each in their own way.

*****

Each of them expressing the potential of living beings.

*****

Some people willing to give their life for it.

*****

Other people giving their energies tirelessly for the benefit of others.

*****

While other people are working on themselves to find Wisdom within to be able to share with others. They are bringing forth effort within themselves to reach for that inner potential, and to demonstrate to others that each of us has that inner potential.

*****

Allow Sympathetic Joy to arise for them all. Joy for all beings' potential and the expression in action of their growth and beneficial qualities.

*****

In times of discouragement, may these people be able to remember their good qualities. Take Joy with them, in the gradual awakening and their inner potential. Feeling Joy in the inner teachings, the inner Truth. May it give them a refuge, giving them confidence and energy to continue.

*****

At this time please expand the meditation in this way, considering the many people in the world who are expressing beneficial qualities by their actions. Try to feel Sympathetic Joy with them.

*****

Please end the meditation by bringing your attention back to yourself. Reflect on your beneficial qualities and your efforts to develop these beneficial qualities.

*****

Allow Sympathetic Joy to arise for yourself.

*****

In times of discouragement, may I be able to remember my good qualities. Take Joy with them, in the gradual awakening and my inner potential. Feeling Joy in the teachings, may it give me a refuge, giving me confidence and energy to continue.

*****

---

[1]An adapted translation of Sutta #10 in "The Samyutta Nikaya, Satipatthana Samyutta," of the Theravadin Buddhist Scriptures. Readers may want to explore *The Heart of Buddhist Meditation*, by Nyanaponika Thera (York Beach, ME: Samuel Weiser, 1965), p. 153, or *Samyutta Nikaya: an Anthology*, part III, by M. O'C. Walshe (Kandy, Sri Lanka, Buddhist Publication Society,1985), p. 75.

# TALKING AND LISTENING

This afternoon we will be having a bit of a change in the usual schedule. After about 190 hours of a fairly intensive meditation retreat with silence, we are going to relax the silence for a few hours until 6:15. Then we will go back into silence until the retreat ends.

Rosemary and I have come to know each one of you in various ways. And each of you have come to know us a little also. But there is another very important relationship going on here.

That is between yourself and the other meditators. A type of "bond" has been formed between many of you even though you may not know very much about each other.

Since many of you will leave the Wat soon after the retreat is over, we would like to give you the opportunity to get to know each other and possibly form some new friendships.

Before we allow you to start speaking to each other, we would like to give you one more mindfulness activity.

Try to pay extra attention to both your speech and your listening. Try to be aware of the energy and motivation behind your speech. Do you just want to talk, talk, talk...telling someone what you want to talk about, without any concern or interest in the other person's background? That is, are you just talking *at* the other person or are you talking *with* the other person?

Try to be aware, in particular, if you are allowing any aversions to come out in your speech. Try to be mindful of what you say. Is it beneficial or is it not beneficial? Is it being affected by a mental state of aversion and anger or is it being affected by Compassion and Lovingkindness?

Try to guard against any of your aversions affecting your speech so that you do not disturb the peacefulness of yourself or others.

And, when you are listening, try to be right there, try to listen as best you can. Listening is a very important part of our life, but many people do not know how to listen very well. So often when people are listening, they're not really there, but are thinking about what the other person is saying, or thinking about something totally different, or thinking about what they want to say as soon as the other person stops talking.

In a similar way to watching your own speech, try to be aware of the energy and motivation behind the other people's speech. Is their speech coming from a mental state of aversion and anger or is it coming from a state of Compassion and Lovingkindness? Is it beneficial or is it not beneficial? Are they only talking at you or are they talking with you?

If you realize that the other person's speech is coming from a mental state of aversion and anger, try to have Compassion for the obvious difficulties that this other person must be having.

Our relationships with others are so very much influenced by our talking and listening. So much so that there are actually some words and phrases that are almost like magic in that they can help us to have much more pleasant relationships. Our words can be a manifestation of our Compassion and Lovingkindness, and their powers can be very great.

Some of you have read about different powers that can come from using certain words and we have not yet talked about this aspect of the practice. So at this time before you start talking with each other, I would like to give you three very powerful phrases that you can use when you are talking with others.

The powers that these three phrases have are quite vast and can help us throughout our life. And if you use them frequently, you will see for yourself the powers that they have.

Their powers include the ability to help make new friendships, to help continue and strengthen old friendships, and to help renew friendships that have difficulties.

These three phrases have been passed down by wise people for thousands of years, and I would like to pass them onto you at this time. It is even possible that you have heard about them already and perhaps know about their powers.

These three powerful phrases are: "Please... Thank you... I'm sorry."

(You were expecting, perhaps, some Tibetan mantras?!)

They can be like magic in our relationships with others... "Please... Thank you... I'm sorry."

So when you start talking with others, try as best you can to have a two-way conversation, a sharing experience coming from a place of Compassionate Understanding. Try not to let aversions affect your speech and affect the peacefulness and contentment that you or the others may feel. And try to make use of these three magical phrases: "Please... Thank you... I'm sorry."

# EVENING DAY NINE

# DOUBT AND OPENNESS

At 3:30 this afternoon, we had a bit of a change in our normal schedule. After about 190 hours of a fairly intensive Meditation Retreat we relaxed for nearly three hours and got to know each other a bit. Talking, listening; some talk about the retreat, some talk about the past and some talk about the future. Some of you possibly talking a lot and some of you possibly talking a little. Perhaps there were a few of you who did not want to talk at all. After many hours of much silence and looking inward, most of you had a few hours of talking and going outward with others.

Then an hour ago we went back into silence. Sitting meditation, walking meditation, maybe some standing meditation. If you compare your meditation in the last hour with yesterday or earlier today, was there any difference??? If your mind is anything like my mind, then you may agree that there was indeed a difference!!

After such a long period of silence and then a few hours of talking, going back into silence often brings with it much of the talking and excitement of those few hours. During much of your last hour of meditation, you may have realized that your mind was frequently thinking of what was talked about during those three hours. And for the few of you who may not have done much talking, it is probable that your meditation also had some differences to before. But these differences would not have been of the same nature to those meditators who did much talking.

For some of you there may have arisen mental states such as disappointment, aversion, doubt, restlessness, worry. Some of you may be feeling happy, joyful, peaceful. We are all different personalities and our reactions during this retreat will differ from person to person. The ending of a retreat as well as this change of schedule often brings with it various emotional reactions.

Many times during this retreat Rosemary and I have talked about Impermanence. Everything around us having its own arising, existing and passing away. Our bodies, our thoughts, our emotions all having their own arising, existing and passing away. This retreat had its arising, it is now still existing, but soon it will pass away.

How we *react* to whatever experience we encounter will determine whether we create more problems, more difficulties, more Dukkha for ourselves and others, or whether we create more Peace, more Happiness, more Contentment for ourselves and others. How we react to any experience.

The Mindfulness techniques, the Reflection techniques, the Compassion/Lovingkindness techniques; all that we have been discussing here have been used by many, many people for thousands of years to help themselves and others to develop more Peace and Contentment, true Happiness.

During the last hour of meditation, some of you may have felt that you could not concentrate as well as before the talking started. With so much stimulus and excitement, your mind may have been very restless and wandering thoughts may have been at a higher level than before.

We have never stated that the object of this overall practice is to stay concentrated on something like the breathing. Nor have we ever stated that we can judge our Meditation/Mental Development ability on how long we stay concentrated on the breath.

Developing strong concentration has its benefits, but what we have been stressing throughout this retreat is the developing of Compassionate Understanding and Wisdom. Then using this Compassionate Understanding and Wisdom to lessen unbeneficial qualities and to strengthen beneficial qualities, in order to lessen our difficulties and problems, and to increase our Peace and Happiness.

Whatever reactions you may be experiencing here as the retreat ends can be valuable learning opportunities. Seeing the increase of wandering thoughts that may be arising is another opportunity to gain Understanding and Wisdom.

Every experience can be used. We do not have to throw any away or "lock them in a closet." If we reject any experience, then we may miss a rare chance for deep growth.

Concentration has its own conditions which help to bring it about. Having quiet and peaceful environments are helpful conditions for building concentration. Having noise and excitement often decreases concentration ability.

However, if a meditator has strong concentration, this by itself does *not* mean this meditator has strong Understanding and Wisdom. It just does not work this way.

Understanding and Wisdom can be developed anywhere, anytime. Quiet or noisy, cold or hot, rainy or sunny. Understanding and Wisdom can be developed anywhere, anytime.

The Five Hindrances are called hindrances because they normally hinder a meditator's ability to develop strong concentration. But in Vipassana type meditation practices, these same Five Hindrances can be used as a source of valuable aid to our growth of Compassion, Lovingkindness, Patience, Endurance, Equanimity, Joy, Peace and Contentment.

No matter what arises, whatever the experiences are that we encounter in life, we can benefit from them all.

We can use Compassion and Mindfulness to view all of life, watch things come and go, get to know and understand how and why we react in certain ways, learn more about who and what we really are, learn more about who and what everyone and everything else really is, learn what all of life really is and not just what we think life is, understand about conditioning and the results of conditioning.

So tomorrow the retreat ends and within some period of time, short or long, all of you will probably leave the Wat and continue on your journeys. We sincerely hope that you will continue to work on Mental Development, using these techniques and/or other beneficial techniques. Continuing on this path of Mental Development towards Peace and Happiness, no matter which beneficial techniques you use. Helping yourself and helping others.

Whether you use these techniques or others, there is some very good advice in the scriptures said to be given by the Buddha 2,500 years ago. This advice concerns whether or not we should believe and practice various religious and meditation teachings that we may encounter. And, in general, it refers to any and all teaching, advice or information of any type that we receive from others, as to whether we should believe it or not.

This teaching is called the Kalama Sutta. Sutta basically means discourse or teaching, and Kalama refers to the name of the people to whom the Buddha was speaking. This is not an exact translation but the Kalama Sutta goes something like this.

At one time, the Buddha had come to stay near the village of the Kalama people. At that time, it was a custom of the Kalamas that whenever any famous meditation or religious teacher visited their village, many people of the village would welcome the famous teacher and ask for instruction or advice.

As many of the Kalamas had heard about the Buddha, that he was a famous, wise and respected teacher, they came out of their village to greet him. After greeting him, they spoke as follows:

"Sir, certain meditation and religious teachers come to our village. As to their own teaching, they illustrate it and explain it in full. But as to the teachings of others, they abuse it, revile it and pull it to pieces.

"Moreover, sir, yet other teachers when coming to our village do the same thing. When we listen to them, we have doubt and uncertainty as to which of these famous teachers is speaking the truth and which is speaking falsely."

The Buddha replied, "Yes, Kalamas, you may well doubt; you may well be uncertain. In a doubtful matter, uncertainty does arise." He then pointed out ten different instances which simply by themselves are not good enough reasons to believe what we read or are told by others.

The ten are as follows: A person does not have to believe just because there is a tradition; an unbroken succession of teachers; report and hearsay; the authority of scriptures and books; speculative theories; points of view and inference; reflections on reasons; acceptance of a statement as true because it agrees with a theory in which one already believes; reliability or fame of a person; or, lastly, just because our teacher says, "This is so, this is so."

For these ten reasons, by themselves, one does not simply have to believe.

The Buddha then continued, "But, Kalamas, when you know for yourself that such teachings are unskillful, such teachings are blamable, such teachings are rejected by wise people, and if followed and performed, such teachings will lead to harm and ill, then it is good not to follow and perform such teachings."

Then the Buddha discussed with the Kalamas what can happen when people develop too much greed, aversion or ignorance. And they all agreed that this type of person may perform many unbeneficial actions such as killing, stealing, etc. They also agreed that such unbeneficial actions would be unskillful, blamable and rejected by wise people, and that such actions normally would result in loss and sorrow, difficulties and problems.

The Buddha repeated the ten instances which simply by themselves are not good enough reasons to believe what we are told by others. When we know for ourselves that such teachings and actions are unbeneficial and encourage too much greed, aversion and ignorance, then it is good not to follow and perform such teachings and actions.

He then spoke nearly exactly the same way, but instead of talking about unbeneficial actions, greed, aversion and ignorance, he spoke about beneficial actions, non-greed, non-aversion and Wisdom. The Kalamas agreed with him that such teachings and actions would produce benefit and happiness.

"Kalamas, when you know for yourself that such teachings are skillful, such teachings are praised, such teachings are approved and encouraged by wise people, and if followed and performed, such teachings will lead to benefit and happiness, then it is good to follow and perform such teachings."

The Buddha then followed this advice by encouraging the Kalamas to develop Compassion, Lovingkindness, Equanimity and Sympathetic Joy. He assured them that if this advice was followed and if they strongly developed these four beneficial states of mind, then they would definitely produce the conditions for benefit and happiness in the future.[1]

This Kalama Sutta gives us some advice so that we do not have to believe things just because our teacher tells us, or just because a person is well-respected and famous, or just because it is written in some books, or just because it is an old tradition or for any other such reasons.

How often in our lives have we been told to believe certain things and yet we did not always agree with what others were telling us? Many times in our lives, we have been told to believe this, to believe that.

Here we are being told that it is OK not to believe and perform certain teachings if we see, if we feel that they would produce unbeneficial results. But we are encouraged to believe and perform certain teachings if we see, if we feel that they would produce beneficial results.

As I said earlier, this advice applies to everything that we do in life, and in particular, it applies to our relationships with meditation and religious teachers and teachings. This includes Buddhist teachers and the Buddhist teaching.

When you know for yourself that certain teachings are unbeneficial, then it is wise to turn away from them. When you know for yourself that certain teachings are beneficial, then it is wise to follow them.

There are some meditators who do not feel comfortable with this advice considering the phrase "when you know for yourself." After all, if we are not perfect yet, then we know that there is much that we do not know; and that probably there are things that we think we know, which are not correct. So how can we always believe or trust ourselves?

Well...we can only be as wise as we are at each moment and a good little saying to keep in mind is: "When in doubt, don't. Consider the task, and ask."

We try our best. If we are continually trying to develop Compassionate Understanding, trying to avoid actions, speech and thoughts that lead to harm and ill, trying to develop actions, speech and thoughts that lead to benefit and happiness, then we must be head-ing in the right direction.

We may make some wrong decisions from time to time but if our Motivation is centered in Compassion and if we keep a guiding force of Moral Shame, then each time that we make a mistake, we try to use Mindfulness to understand the situation better. And, if we can, we try to correct the mistake we made, to apologize if we can, to forgive if we can, accepting the results of our actions.

We do not have to develop self-hatred, but we accept our responsibilities and we try our best to help the situation. If we cannot undo the difficulties that we have caused, then we try to understand how this will not happen again in the future.

The advice here is; "When you know for yourself that such teachings are skillful, such teachings are praised, such teachings are approved and encouraged by wise people, and if followed and performed, such teachings will lead to benefit and happiness, then it is good to follow and perform such teachings."

And, "When you know for yourself that such teachings are unskillful, such teachings are blamable, such teachings are rejected by wise people, and if followed and performed, such teachings will lead to harm and ill, then it is good not to follow and perform such teachings."

This puts a responsibility onto each of us to continually examine and try to understand what is skillful, what is unskillful, what is praised, approved and encouraged by wise people, what is blamable and rejected by wise people, what is benefit and happiness, and what is harm and ill.

We have to make decisions that apply to ourselves for where we are now, as best we can. It is not considered healthy to try to put ideals, concepts, views and opinions about some Ultimate Reality, Voidness, Oneness, God, Enlightenment, etc., onto ourselves at this time. Indeed, when some people start to believe that they need to go beyond such things as "good" and "bad" right now, this can be very dangerous.

Skillful is skillful, unskillful is unskillful, beneficial is beneficial, unbeneficial is unbeneficial, as we know them at this time, this moment. Tomorrow we may see things in a different way. We try the best we can with the Compassionate Intention of wishing to lessen difficulties and problems, harm and ill.

When you can see for yourself that certain teachings are unbeneficial then it is wise to turn away from them. When you can see for yourself that certain teachings are beneficial, then it is wise to follow them.

Some years ago, there was a religious leader from the U.S. named Jim Jones. He had a following of many hundred people and they all moved to a small country in South America and set up a type of community. Evidently he had done some illegal activities and was being investigated by the United States Government.

For some insane reason, he and hundreds and hundreds of his followers committed what appeared to be a mass suicide. Incredible. Seemingly unbelievable, but it happened only a short time ago.

Had these other people, his followers, known, understood and used the advice of the Kalama Sutta, then this could never have happened. This is an extreme case, but unfortunately, there are insane people in the world and some of them do become religious and meditation teachers. When each of us has future contact with teachers and teachings, the Kalama Sutta advice can be very helpful.

Keep in mind, though, we are not saying that we must doubt every teacher and teachings. We must try to be *open* and discover what it is that the teacher is trying to teach.

Is it helpful or harmful? If it is helpful, then we do not have to doubt. If it is harmful, then we may well have doubt. In other words, if something is beneficial to oneself and to others, then that is good and it can be used. If something is unbeneficial to oneself and to others, then that is not good and it need not be used.

Within all the different techniques of Mental Development, there are many different teachers stressing many different aspects. An analogy to keep in mind when meeting methods that are different to what we already practice is this:

Suppose all the people of a village near a mountain wished to get to the top of the mountain. Some went up the north side, some went up the south side, some the east and some the west. Some went straight up and others took side tracks. But all of them met at the top of the mountain. Then they returned to their village.

Now, suppose you go to that village and you want to climb the mountain. You go around the village asking the people how to get to the top of the mountain. All of the villagers tell you a different way to go...and yet, every answer would be a correct way to get to the top of the mountain.

Many different teachers. Many different techniques. Many different aspects of the practice.

It's very important to try not to have a fixed image of what you think a teacher should be. There are some people who become so closed in their views and opinions that they think they know what a teacher should do, how the teacher should act, walk, dress, talk. If you do have some strong fixed image of what you think a teacher should be, this will block you from learning from a person who does not fit that fixed image.

In one of our early retreats, before it became well known who the teachers are here, after registration, I took a new meditator to the dormitory. This person was very excited, turned to me and said, "Where do the Western monks live?"

I replied, "There are no Western monks here."

Watching the response to my words, I could see there was obvious surprise and a feeling of disappointment. The new meditator then brightened up again and asked, "Oh, I guess the Thai monks teach the retreats. Do they speak good English?"

I answered, "No, the monks here do not speak very much English and they do not teach the retreats."

This seemed to disturb the person again. Then, slightly more subdued, the meditator said, "Oh, the head nun who speaks English, does she teach the retreats?"

I replied, "No, none of the nuns teach the retreats."

This person now seemed quite bewildered and turned a bit pale. The new meditator looked at the dormitory, then looked back at me, and said, "Well... well...who does teach the retreats?!"

I answered, of course, "Me and Rosemary."

The meditator stood there staring at me, a little bit shocked, and said, "Oh...this will be interesting!"

Fixed images...fixed images...try not to have a fixed image of what you think a teacher should be. This can block your own growth, causing you to become upset and stopping you from being open and learning from someone who does not fit some fixed image.

If we like a teacher and their teachings, then there is basically no problem. But what if we do not like the teacher or their teachings? Perhaps there is just something about the personality of the teacher that we do not like. But can we be open to see whether the teachings are OK or not? Can we try not to let our reactions to a personality get in the way of our own learning and growing?

Sometimes the vocabulary that a teacher uses may not be perfect to explain the teachings, yet perhaps a slight change in vocabulary may be all that is needed to aid in understanding and benefiting from the same teachings.

An example of this is found in the difference between the word "should" and the word "try." I could say, "You should be mindful; it will help you and others. You should be compassionate; it will help you and others. You should do this, you should do that."

Or I could say, "Try to be mindful; it will help you and others. Try to be compassionate; it will help you and others. Try to do this, try to do that."

There is a difference here, and it can affect many people in different ways.

This aspect is extremely important if we meet with teachers who do not speak our native language. The manner in which their teachings is being translated into our language could have mistakes. So it is very important to be aware of difficulties arising.

In one retreat, I was having an interview with a non-native English speaker, and after talking about the basic meditation practice, the person said to me, "Can you answer a question about the exercises?"

I said, "Well, I know basically what Rosemary's teaching and perhaps I can. Go ahead and ask."

Then came the question, "What does Rosemary mean when she says, 'Relaxing the brain?'"

I said, "'Relaxing the brain?'"

"Yes, what does Rosemary mean when she says, 'Relaxing the brain?'"

Well, I thought I knew all of Rosemary's exercises but this one took me by surprise. I had to think pretty fast. Then it came to me: "Are you sure she wasn't saying, `Relaxing the breath?'" And, of course, she was.

It's very important to make allowances for these sort of problems, the best we can. And, it's very important to know the difference between your brain and your breath.

Some teachers may understand their teachings very well but they may have difficulty in compassionately expressing what they understand. Some teachers may be "great" teachers but they just are not quite "right" for us. This is an important point. When we say that they are not quite right for us, what do we mean?

The English word "right" has various meanings. One meaning could be "right" as in correct and true. Another meaning could be "right" as in appropriate and beneficial. Some things are both correct and true, and appropriate and beneficial. Yet sometimes that which is correct and true may not be appropriate and beneficial. And sometimes that which is appropriate and beneficial may not be correct and true.

A very clear example of when something can be correct and true but not appropriate and beneficial, is if a University Mathematics Professor wants to teach Algebra and Calculus to a six-year old who is in the first grade, and who cannot yet add or subtract. Normally a University Mathematics Professor will know to teach Algebra and Calculus correctly and truly...but is it appropriate and beneficial for a six-year old in the first grade who cannot yet add and subtract?

I am sure most people would agree that this is neither appropriate nor beneficial. Instead this would normally produce much confusion and difficulty for the child. Possibly causing the child to become upset, frustrated and angry; with many self-doubts as well as doubts about mathematics and doubts about the teacher.

And, certainly if the professor only tries to teach these advanced subjects to a child who is not ready, who is *not* prepared with the *basic preliminaries,* then there will be very little, if any, ability for the child to understand such teachings.

This is an obvious case when something can be correct and true but it is neither appropriate nor beneficial.

An example of when something is appropriate and beneficial and yet not correct and true is illustrated by the following little story:

Once there were some children playing happily in the front room of a house when a fire occurred in the back rooms. An elderly person who lives across the street sees the fire and the children playing in the front room. Unable physically to go and save the children, the older person calls to the children, "Children, run out the front door! The house is on fire!"

However the children are having too much fun and they do not even know what it means for a house to be on fire. So they do not care about leaving the house.

The elderly person then calls out, "Children, come out the front door! I have some candies and cakes for you!" Then the children run out as fast as they can to get the candies and cakes. But when they get to the elderly person, there are no candies and cakes.

The elderly person then points to the house and the children now realize what it means for a house to be on fire. And they also realize that yes, indeed, the old person lied to them, but yes, indeed, the old person saved their life!

This is an obvious example of when something can be appropriate and beneficial and yet not be correct and true.

There are quite a lot of meditation teachers who may know for themselves that a particular thing is correct and true. Or they may feel confident that what they have read or have been taught is correct and true. And they often try to teach this information to anyone, without ever considering whether or not the information is appropriate and beneficial.

Unfortunately, this can cause much difficulty and many problems for their students and may slow down or even stop the students' development of Compassionate Understanding and Wisdom. And, sadly, sometimes this way of teaching may even turn people away from practicing Mental Development.

If something is both correct and true, and appropriate and beneficial, that is best. But if not, then when we say "not quite right," it is very important that this "right" refers to *appropriate and beneficial.*

If you do not agree with all of the teaching, then just take whatever you do like, and leave the rest. Try not to reject the rest. There is a difference between "leaving" the rest and "rejecting" the rest. If we just leave the rest without rejecting it, then we are allowing for the possibility that perhaps the rest will be of value in the future. This shows, again, the importance of staying open.

All of us have changed our views and opinions about some things in life. Some of what we thought 5 or 10 years ago may no longer be what we think now. And we understand many things now that 5 or 10 years ago, we would not have even believed.

It is also very important to understand and very important to keep in mind that book knowledge and knowledge gained only through thinking—trying to figure things out with our thought process—does not always compare to knowledge gained through experience.

Many teachers and students, and many of the people writing and reading books about Meditation and Buddhism, have not always done the practice and gained the experience necessary to actually know and understand how to use or apply the intellectual knowledge that they have.

Often these people feel that to do the basic practices of Mental Development is just not good enough for them. Sometimes they feel that they know all about those little things, and that the basic practices are not as important as the ideas, concepts and views about the end results that they believe in. That, somehow, they are "beyond" all of the basic practices.

This is rather like someone who studies all about building houses, learns all about the fine details of floors, walls, roofs and so on, knows all about the best materials for this part of the house and that part. But this person does not yet know how to use a hammer, saw, screwdriver, etc., and does not yet know the basic practices of simple construction.

I was once working on a road construction job with men who had not even gone to High School. But after 20-30 years of working on roads, their experiential understanding was very deep. They had to put some very large pipes under the road for water to flow during heavy rains. A young road engineer came from the head office, fresh out of University and filled with book knowledge.

The engineer took a look around, saw that the area was fairly flat and was not quite sure which way the pipes should slope for proper drainage. Because when pipes are put under a road they must tilt so that the water flows downhill. Mountains were over to the left about 15 miles away and the ocean was to the right about 30 miles away. Of course all engineers know that rivers flow towards the ocean, so the decision was made to put the pipes tilted so that the left side was higher than the right side.

One old man on the construction job said, "No, no, the water here runs from the right to the left." But unfortunately, much of our society thinks that certificates and titles are more important than experience and the young engineer did not know any better. So the old man's words were not accepted.

Soon after they had put in the pipes, heavy rains came and the pipes did not work properly. They had to be removed and put in as the old man had said.

It is very important to understand and very important to keep in mind that book knowledge and knowledge gained through only think-ing—trying to figure things out with our thought process—does not always compare to knowledge gained through experience.

Some of the teachers whom you meet may only have book knowl-edge and thinking knowledge, while others, hopefully, will have ex-periential knowledge. As well, try not to let your own book and think-ing knowledge get in the way of being open to learning from some-one who has experiential knowledge, even though what they teach may seem just too simple, too basic.

Staying open, allowing for change. Allowing for our thoughts, views and opinions to change. Allowing for growth.

One thing to expect when you go visiting other different Medi-tation and religious centers and different teachers, is that normally they will expect you to practice the methods that they are teaching while you are at their center.

Some meditators become upset with this requirement. The thoughts may come; "Well...there are many ways up to the top of the mountain, Right?! What is wrong with these people?! Why won't they let me do what I want?! They must think their way is the only way!! Pretty narrow minded eh?! They can't be very wise!! They must be going up the *wrong* mountain!!"

Well, maybe sometimes this is true. And maybe sometimes it is the meditator who is trying to go up the wrong mountain. But often there are other considerations that are important.

When you want to learn to play the piano do you go to a violin teacher? When you want to play tennis do you go to a swimming coach? It seems rather obvious, doesn't it?

Playing piano and violin are both ways to make music. But they are different from each other and they are taught differently. Playing tennis and swimming are both ways to exercise. But they are different from each other and they are taught differently. In Meditation and Mental Development there are also many methods that are different from each other and taught differently, and they cannot always go together.

The person who climbed the mountain from the north may have crossed deserts on the way and become skilled and expert in crossing deserts. The person who climbed the mountain from the south may have crossed rivers and lakes on the way and become skilled and expert in crossing water. They may not know anything about the other way of travel and may not be able to help those who wish to go the other way. But they are expert on the journey that they traveled.

If you try to practice techniques that are different to those presented by the teacher, then it is best to talk about it, see if it is OK and fits in with what is being taught. If the teacher feels that it should not be done at their center, then it is best not to. Or, if you do, then please accept responsibility for your actions. This is important because if you get into any difficulty with doing your own practice when advised not to, then you may not be able to receive any help if needed. In this case, it would not be proper to try to claim that it was the teacher's fault.

And as to claiming that any of your difficulties you have in your practice are the fault of the teachers, please be very careful about this, because it may just be that you are not practicing properly. And if you don't practice the techniques in the right way and then you have difficulties, well, it's not right to say it's the teacher's fault.

We teach many different techniques, including the formal postures of sitting, walking, standing, with lying down briefly explained during the stretching exercises. There's the breathing awareness, body awareness, awareness of sensations, observation of the hindrances, Compassion/Lovingkindness meditation, Sympathetic Joy meditation and the different Reflections: How Fortunate You Are, Death and Impermanence, Actions and Results of Actions, Dukkha or unsatisfactoriness, the Relationship between Compassion and Equanimity, and more.

We have encouraged you to use each one of these, to practice them formally and informally, such as grabbing doors, washing dishes, etc. and to incorporate them into your life. We are giving you tools to use for *all* of your life, different tools for different purposes. Some will help to lessen your greed or your ignorance. Some will help to develop your Compassion, your Equanimity, Patience, Love, etc. We are trying to teach a *balanced* practice.

We feel that all these techniques are important for you to use. Liking one technique more than another is quite natural. But if you want to get the benefits that this practice can produce, then it's very important to use all the techniques that we have been explaining. If you do only a small part of this practice, then you cannot expect to get the benefits that we talk about.

This would be rather like people who want to build a very special house. These people realize that they have to know how to use all the different tools necessary for building. It's a very special, very complicated house they would like to build and they have never actually done any building before. They realize that they have to go to a school and learn how to use different tools before they can actually build their house.

So they go to this special school that teaches building techniques and they show the teachers a picture of the house they want to build. They ask, "Can you help us, teach us what to do? We've never built anything in our lives. We don't know any tools at all. Can you teach us so we can build this type of house?"

The teachers look at the house—it's very special, very complicated—and they do have a special program that will teach all the different tools that these people will need. They say, yes, they've actually built houses very similar to this one.

So these people join this special course, and start to learn about using all the different tools. The first tool that they use is the hammer. And, gee, do they like using the hammer. They've never used a hammer before in their life, and they've never seen anything like it— if you hit a nail just right, it will go right into the wood. Disappear! It's really amazing!

And then they discovered how you can take two pieces of wood, nail them together and they become kind of one piece and, wow, they really liked the hammer. They practiced a lot with the hammer.

Then they were taught how to use the saw. Well, they didn't like the saw as much as the hammer. The saw was messy, it made lots of dust, and every once in a while you had to sharpen the little teeth on the saw and you even had to set them just right. It was kind of complicated, not as simple as the hammer. The hammer was just so easy and simple—well, they liked the hammer much more. They really enjoyed practicing with the hammer.

They were then taught how to drill holes and, well, they still liked the hammer a bit better. The drill wasn't as messy as the saw and it only made a little dust. But if they didn't drill just right, they could break the drill bits, and bits were expensive, much more expensive than nails. To bend a nail is not a big deal, but breaking a drill bit...well, they liked the hammer better than the drill.

Then they were taught about the screwdriver. Gee, this was very complicated—there were lots of different sizes of screwdrivers. And even the ends of the screwdrivers—some were flat and some were like an "X." Then there were all these different kinds of screws. Pretty hard to understand—some went into wood, some went into metal, some went in and some went out. It was really complicated to learn how to use the screwdriver and screws. And, well, the hammer and nails were *so simple and easy.* They really loved the hammer much better than the screwdrivers.

They were taught the rest of the tools, and yet with each tool that they learned, they kept comparing it to the hammer. The hammer was just so simple. They liked the hammer better than all the other tools.

When the course was over, and they had practiced using all the different tools, the teachers explained that when they went home, they should buy all the tools for themselves. Then practice a lot with small things like boxes and bookcases before they tried building this special house. The teachers also gave them a complete list of all the wood, metal, doors, windows, etc. that they would need plus detailed diagrams of how to build the house.

These people were just so happy and excited that they had learned how to use all these different tools. They thanked the teachers so much. They thought the teachers and the school were just wonderful. When they got home, they went to the store and, well, the first tool they wanted to buy was the hammer because they loved the hammer so much. So they bought a hammer, lots of nails and lots of little pieces of wood, then went home and started practicing with the hammer.

Gee, it was fun; they hit the nail just right and, "whoosh," it went right into the wood. They put two pieces of wood together to make one. They were so excited.

And then they discovered that with a lot of little pieces of wood that were just the right size, they actually could put together a box—with only a hammer and nails. They didn't need any of the other tools at all.

So they practiced a lot with these little boxes; it was just so much fun, and they didn't need all that other stuff. The hammer and nails were so simple and nice.

They made lots of little boxes and they realized that a box, "Well, it's kind of like a house, isn't it? You know, it's just real small but it's kind of like a room...we're so good at building boxes, now we're ready to build a house. We've got our hammer and we'll be able to build our house."

Yet during all this time, they had forgotten about the saw, the drill, and all the other tools. They couldn't remember anything about them because they were so wrapped up in this hammer.

They still had the list from their teachers of all the supplies they would need for building the house. They ordered the wood, the metal, the windows, the doors and everything else they needed. They also ordered a lot of nails, and even a spare hammer, just in case the handle broke.

When all the materials came, they started trying to build their house. Yet, it didn't take very long to realize that it was impossible to build this very complicated house with only a hammer and nails.

They started getting quite upset. They couldn't remember anything else they had been taught, except the hammer. They started thinking that the teachers were very stupid; all they were taught was a hammer, and they couldn't build this fancy house with only a hammer. So they started blaming the teachers and the center, saying that the center was a terrible place to learn how to build.

This story, of course, seems nearly impossible in normal life, especially if someone really did want to build a house. Only people who did not have normal mental abilities would act in this way.

Yet although this is so rare in normal life with this type of thing, it's amazing how many meditators do a 10-day retreat with us, then leave and only practice a little bit, only one or two of the methods that we teach, somehow thinking they can develop the results of Meditation and Mental Development that we are talking about, by only using one or two or a very small number of all the techniques that we are explaining. This is as foolish as a person trying to build a special, complicated house with only a hammer.

We know many students have left here and continued practicing all of the methods we teach. They have been able to find deeper Peace and Happiness in their lives and have received benefits from their continued work. They find their meditation practice developing and growing in many fine ways.

We also know many students have left here and have not continued practicing all of the methods we teach. Many get stuck thinking that awareness of the breathing and basic mindfulness are all they need. They often discover that they do not find deeper Peace and Happiness in their lives and instead just get more frustrated and upset, especially concerned with their meditation practice. Many of them start thinking that what Rosemary and I are teaching is not right for them, and some may even quit meditating entirely.

Although only a very few people would try to build a special, complicated house with only a hammer, it is amazing and sad that large numbers of people try to do a Meditation/Mental Development practice with only one or two or a very small number of methods and techniques.

Try not to cause extra problems for yourself. If you wish to get the same benefits from this Meditation/Mental Development practice that Rosemary and I have, then it's very important that you use all these different methods and techniques that we are teaching. If you do not use all these techniques or use them improperly, and then have difficulties, it would not be right to think, it is the teacher's fault.

If we watch a teacher whose manner and teaching appears to be good, kind and wise, then indeed, we can try to adapt those teachings to our own life. But if we watch a teacher whose manner and teaching appears not to be good or kind or wise, then we can use that experience also but in a different way. We may not want to stay very long around such a teacher, but during whatever contact that we do have, we can learn.

From good teachers we often learn what *to do*. From teachers who are not good, we can learn what *not to do*. If we do not like a certain quality in another person, we then can take an honest look at ourselves and see whether we have similar qualities. If we do, then it is possible for us to work more openly toward trying to change this quality within ourselves, because we already have made the acknowledgment that we feel this quality is not very good. We can apply this not just when dealing with teachers but also in dealing with everyone and every experience that we meet in life.

Using our Understanding and Wisdom to try to see what is beneficial and skillful, and what is unbeneficial and unskillful.

We can also use our contact with teachers who are not very good to further our growth of Compassion and Lovingkindness. In the same way that we reflected upon our difficult people during the guided Compassion/Lovingkindness meditation, we can reflect upon this person.

As well, there is an important extra thought to add to reflecting upon a person who is a teacher. That is to consider how many of their students might be affected in unbeneficial ways. Especially with Mental Development, we are dealing with our minds. If improper methods are taught, there could be many unbeneficial results.

Often when doubt about some instruction or teaching arises, some people are hesitant or embarrassed to ask questions. Many times when we were children, as well as later in life, we have doubted certain matters and asked questions about them.

Unfortunately, for many of us there have been occasions of being answered in very unkind ways. Sometimes we were laughed at. Sometimes we were yelled at. Sometimes we were told that we were stupid and dumb. Frequently the hurt and embarrassment we felt at that time conditioned us in such a way that we stopped voicing our doubts and stopped asking questions.

Early in the retreat, Rosemary spoke about the Five Hindrances. Doubt is the fifth. Within these teachings, among the ways to solve doubt is the encouragement to ask questions, to talk to more people about the doubt, read more concerning the doubt, debate with people about the doubt, and look to our own experience as advised in the Kalama Sutta. Then when we know for ourselves, the doubt will fade away.

Doubt has been called the most important hindrance because it has the ability to destroy one's practice. As well, it has the ability to destroy relationships that one has with teachers and other meditators.

If one does not try to solve one's doubt, often doubt will change into aversion. Doubt about oneself can change into self-hatred. Doubt about the practice can change into hating the practice. Doubt about the teacher can change into hating the teacher.

The "immature Yogi mind" that I talked about a few days ago frequently comes from doubt. Even if teachers are very good there may be times when we doubt their ability or their style of teaching and yet we do not try to solve the doubt by talking to the teachers, asking questions, and being open to their answers. Instead, on occasion, we may think;

"Well...I haven't seen that happen before." And then we may think; "Well...no one else does that, and it's not in any books I've read. I think it might be *wrong!*" And then the thought becomes stronger and we develop the view and opinion; "Yes, it *is* wrong!" And then the thoughts; "Obviously the teachers are stupid, they don't know what they are doing!" And perhaps we continue to build aversion without ever trying to find an answer to the doubt.

Then we may find another meditator with the same doubt, and this makes us even more confident in our view and opinion so we feel that we do not even have to ask the teachers, that we know better. We may feel that the teachers are hypocrites teaching one thing but doing something else. Yet all the time we never went and talked to the teachers about our doubts. Instead keeping them inside and turning into aversion so that finally we refuse to even listen to the teachers and start rejecting any advice that they give us.

This can cripple, even destroy one's practice and certainly will destroy the relationship that one has with one's teachers. One stops learning at this point because one is no longer open. Doubt has become too strong and turned into aversion.

It is important to try to guard against this happening. On the first night of the retreat I mentioned a little saying: You can please some of the people all of the time. And you can please all of the people some of the time. But you cannot please all of the people all of the time.

No teacher can please all of the people all of the time. Even the Buddha could not. People tried to kill him and abuse him in many ways through dislike and jealousy.

Rosemary and I cannot please all of you all of the time. And yet, we encouraged you to ask questions about anything you do not understand. Many times, people run away from what they do not like. But often what we do not like is simply what we do not understand.

In order to relieve yourself of much difficulty and the possible slowing down, or even stopping, of your development of Compassionate Understanding and Wisdom, please take advantage of the opportunities to ask questions about your doubts. You do not have to hold your doubts inside and turn them into aversion.

Nearly all of the teachers within this tradition of Theravadin Buddhism receive no pay for their teachings. It is free. Many of their students understand this and help support their teachers with their basic living conditions. But when they teach, they teach for free, often working many hours a day, giving their time freely, offering their help freely, expecting nothing in return.

Take advantage of such a *wonderful* gift. When you have doubts, go to your teachers and ask questions. If one teacher cannot answer your questions, then go to another. You do not have to hold your doubts inside, turning into aversion.

About one hour ago, I was talking about the probability that there were differences between your last hour of meditation and your meditations prior to the talking period. Some people find that when they see this change, doubts about their own ability to meditate can arise. And when the retreat ends, most of you will probably not continue trying to do so many hours of meditation every day.

Many times trying to keep a meditation practice going in everyday life is much harder than here at a retreat. Often discouragement can arise and with it can come doubt. The ability to concentrate may not be as good.

Try to keep in mind that certain conditions produce certain results. Try to keep in mind also that strong concentration does not always mean strong Understanding and Wisdom.

We do advise you very strongly that you at least try to keep doing some formal sitting, standing or walking meditation. We advise doing formal practice after you wake up in the morning and before you go to sleep, as much as possible. If you miss some sessions or a few days, then just start again, keep trying.

Try to use Mindfulness throughout the day. Try to use Compassion and Lovingkindness, try to use the Reflections whenever they can help. Perhaps special Mindfulness activities.

Some of you may have noticed that many of the special Mindfulness activities we gave you were actions you do when going to the bathroom:

If you ever start finding that the Hindrances are arising very strongly at work or at home, with friends or others, then perhaps you could "excuse" yourself and go to the bathroom. Normally no one gets too upset if someone else has to go to the bathroom. And others do not usually worry if you are gone 3 minutes, 5 minutes, 7 minutes.

Take the time "out"...walk to the bathroom...grab the door... open the door...walk through...close the door...sit down...all alone...a meditation room!!!!! watch your breath...watch your mind...watch your body ...

Try to recharge your energies right there in the bathroom.

Try to use any and all techniques you know to help develop your mind in beneficial ways, helping you to solve your difficulties and problems, helping you to gain more Peace and Happiness.

Every effort that you make to try to increase beneficial mental qualities; every effort that you make to try to decrease unbeneficial mental qualities; every effort that you make in these directions is going to aid you and others to have more Peace and Happiness.

Even if you are sitting in meditation and the mind is wandering everywhere and never goes to something like the breathing. Even if you are sitting in meditation and you fall asleep.

Just the *effort to sit with good intention* is a beneficial action which will produce some beneficial results.

Try, always trying. Every effort that you make in this direction will help, no effort will be wasted.

Difficult situations, weaker concentration, doubt, etc., these may arise from time to time but as we have said often during this retreat, every experience can be used for the growth of Compassionate Understanding and Wisdom. You may wish to change the causes and conditions that bring about certain things, but whatever you do experience can be used for growth.

As each of you go back to the everyday normal life, you can take with you the tools of Mindfulness, Compassion, Lovingkindness, Patience, Acceptance, Endurance, Letting go, Equanimity, Sympathetic Joy, Effort, Understanding, and more. Hopefully with these tools you will find deeper Peace and Contentment compared to 10 days ago. And perhaps be able to help others find deeper Peace and Contentment.

Please remember that silence is back in effect until the retreat ends. If your meditation periods seem to be affected with many wandering thoughts, try to treat it with Mindfulness and Compassionate Understanding.

Nothing needs to be a problem. Everything can be a challenge.

---

[1]A much shortened modification of one of the most well known teachings of Theravadin Buddhism, which is Sutta #65 in "The Anguttara Nikaya, Tika Nipata, Mahavagga," of the Theravadin Buddhist Scriptures. Readers may want to explore *A Criterion of True Religion: Lord Buddha's Discourse to the Kalama People,* translated by Bhikkhu Khantipalo (Bangkok: Mahamakut Rajavidyalaya Press, 1986); or *Kalama Sutta: The Buddha's Charter of Free Inquiry,* translated by Soma Thera (Kandy, Sri Lanka: Buddhist Publication Society, 1981.)

# RESPECT, GRATITUDE, GENEROSITY AND JOY

Please take a few moments here to reflect upon, to think about just what these ten days have meant for you and what they may mean for the rest of your life.

*****

I would now like to talk a little about a relationship in our Mental Development practice concerning Respect, Gratitude or Thankfulness, Generosity and Joy. This is a very important relationship which if understood will be of much value to each of you.

Respect; Respect for others. Respect for what is good and of value. Respect for beneficial qualities. Respect for beneficial teachings. Respect for those who have helped you. Respect for others who are worthy of respect.

Unfortunately, many societies around the world, and many people around the world, do not respect what deserves to be respected. It is quite obvious that much of the world respects money and power more than human goodness and purity.

Respect for those who have helped you: this is a very important quality that is needed by all who wish to develop in beneficial ways. How often have you forgotten what others have done for you? How often have you taken for granted your relationships with others? How often have you actually shown your respect for those who have helped you?

Frequently whenever we return back to the West we find it almost incredible to believe some of the stories about teachers in high schools and the near total disrespect in which they were held by many students and parents. Stories of students abusing verbally and physically their teachers and not being punished or disciplined afterward. Other times when students were disciplined for such actions and later the teachers were sued in court.

Why is this happening? Lack of respect can be a main reason. The contrast to just 30 years ago in the West is quite outstanding.

Respect, a very important quality which is needed by all who wish to develop in beneficial ways.

Many Western societies stress equality of human beings—and yet we are *not* all equal in every aspect. And often this thought of equality denies respect that is well deserved.

There is a saying, "Familiarity breeds contempt." I would think probably all of us have at one time or another fallen into this: taking others for granted; not showing our respect to those who deserve our respect; forgetting what others have done for us.

When this happens, a person is not thankful. There is no Gratitude. Gratitude, Thankfulness, is another very important quality that is needed by all who wish to develop in beneficial ways.

Gratitude and Respect are so closely related that it is hard at times to tell whether one comes before the other or whether they arise together.

Developing Gratitude includes being thankful to others when they have helped us in some way; being thankful to our teachers, being thankful to the teachings, being thankful to those who have fed us and taken care of us.

Gratitude, being Thankful, having respect and showing this in our actions. These are things not often taught or explained in many of the societies that we come from.

A bit of advice: Do not miss an opportunity to show your Gratitude and Respect. If you do, then this may be a cause for regret in the future. And regret of this kind is often a cause for self-hatred.

We have talked quite a bit about self-hatred and about having Compassion to help alleviate self-hatred. Out of Compassion for yourself, do not miss an opportunity to show your Gratitude and Respect. Help yourself to avoid regret and self-hatred.

We also have talked about Moral Shame. The development of Moral Shame helps us to strengthen our understanding of Gratitude and Respect. With developing understanding of when we have done unskillful actions, we try not to take others for granted. We try not to develop contempt coming from familiarity. We try to remember those who have helped us and we try to be thankful for their help.

As we develop our Gratitude, our Thankfulness, toward others, we often find that we wish to repay those who have helped us in some way or we wish to help others in a similar way, knowing how valuable this help was for us.

This Gratitude that we feel toward those whom we respect can be manifested in helping, in being generous. Generosity—this is another very important quality that is needed by all who wish to develop in beneficial ways. Generosity can be the manifestation of our Gratitude, our Thankfulness. It also can be a way that we manifest the Compassion and Lovingkindness that we feel.

Without the generosity of others, you would not be here doing this retreat. The monks and nuns have been generous in opening their monastery for you, taking care of so many of the necessities of running this retreat. The teachers show their generosity by giving so much time and energy for you. There is the generosity of the Thai people and other western meditators who have donated so much money, time and effort for the benefit of all of you.

Since we have been here much building has occurred just for all of you to benefit; new dormitories, new toilets, larger kitchen, dining hall, office, tables, benches and more. Much money has been donated freely to buy many of the things you have used here; mosquito nets, blankets, pillows, sitting mats and more.

Why have others been so generous with their time, money and material things?

Because they have deep Respect and Gratitude toward these teachings on Mental Development. They also have Compassion and Lovingkindness toward others such as all of you. And they wish to help so that you and many more will have the opportunity of learning these teachings that are so valuable.

It has been the Respect, Gratitude and Generosity of millions of people for over 2,500 years that has enabled us to learn about these teachings, these teachings that have been passed on down from the days of the Buddha.

Millions of people who have felt that they were given something of value from these teachings developed a deep Respect toward them and toward the teachers who helped them. As well, they developed a feeling of Gratitude toward these teachings and the teachers.

From this Respect and Gratitude, together with their Compassion and Lovingkindness, they developed their Generosity and gave in return, either back to those who had helped them or to others in ways similar to how they had been helped.

Yet by being generous, they did not only give. Because in giving, we can find that we receive as well—receiving a type of Joy, a type of Sympathetic Joy. We know that what we are doing is helping others. We know that what we are doing is helping ourselves, also. Sympathetic Joy is another very important quality that is needed by all who wish to develop in beneficial ways.

The monks and nuns here have much Sympathetic Joy with all of you as they watch your hard efforts during this retreat. They know that by giving you this opportunity to learn these teachings that all of you will benefit in some way. And they are sharing in this Joy. With the growth of Generosity we can grow in Sympathetic Joy.

With this Joy comes more Contentment and Energy; as well, a deeper Appreciation and Respect for these teachings that are so helpful. With the deepening of Appreciation and Respect, then again our Gratitude will deepen. And continually in these ways, these four beneficial qualities—Respect, Gratitude, Generosity and Joy—will develop a relationship that will be of valuable help in our Mental Development.

Often the teachings of Mental Development taught within Buddhism are referred to with the Sanskrit or Pali words "Dharma" or "Dhamma," which also can mean the Truth.

There is a saying in the scriptures, "The gift of Dhamma is greater than all others." Perhaps you feel the same, that the Gift of Dhamma, the Gift of these teachings that can help all of us, is greater than all other gifts. Perhaps you have developed a feeling of Respect and Gratitude toward those who have helped you to receive this gift.

And perhaps out of this Respect, Gratitude and your Compassion and Lovingkindness, you may feel that you would like to repay those who have helped you or to help in some manner so that others may benefit as well.

The most important thing that you can do to help in these ways is to continue on with your Mental Development practice. Continue growing, learning. Continue trying to understand life; to understand where there is Dukkha, unsatisfactoriness; to understand where Dukkha comes from; to understand how it goes away; and most importantly, to understand how Dukkha, unsatisfactoriness, can be avoided in the future.

This is most important, but there is also another level, the level of physical necessities. In order for these retreats to continue, in order for Mae Chee Ah Mohn to continue improving facilities here, in order to replace old blankets, broken laundry buckets, pay electricity bills, to name just a few expenses, the Wat needs money.

The money that you paid before the retreat covers only food related expenses. That is all. Payment for everything else is by donations only. The Wat has no other income. Only donations. Nearly all monasteries and meditation centers here in Thailand exist only on the donations from the people who use the center.

We would like you to consider this deeply. Others have given so that you can be helped. Can you give something so that more can be helped? Can you be generous in any way? Large or small, money, work, material items, anything? Any and all donations to help this Wat, to help others, will be greatly appreciated.

Perhaps you can consider how much you would have spent in 10 days of traveling. Perhaps you can consider how much you would have spent staying 10 days at the beach. Maybe considering how much you would have spent in just one day of having what you consider "a good fun time." How does one day of fun and normal happy times compare to your 10 days here??

Just a few questions that may be helpful for you to consider when you think about whether or not you wish to give the Wat a donation or how much you can afford to give.

This is an opportunity to help others, to help yourself, to express your Appreciation, Respect and Gratitude, to express your Compassion and Lovingkindness. Generosity is a foundation of the practice. With strong Generosity, our practice will be strong. With weak Generosity, our practice will be weak.

Sitting on a pillow or mat, walking back and forth, standing still, you can do the formal practice—that's one thing. And you can have all your dreams about Enlightenment, Voidness, Non-self, God and other such things if you wish. But if you cannot develop more human goodness in your normal, everyday life, then something is not working right.

In the scriptures, the Buddha once was asked about Generosity and the results of giving. He said something similar to this: "If you knew what I know about generosity and the results of giving, you would not let a single day go by without giving something to someone."

Take advantage of the wonderful opportunity to give, to be generous, to express your Respect, Gratitude and Appreciation for what you have been given, to express your Compassion and Lovingkindness to others. And have Compassion for yourself, helping to avoid unnecessary future regret and self-hatred.

This is a time when you can easily be of help.

As well, you can have some Joy, Sympathetic Joy, knowing that what you are doing is going to help others, knowing that what you are doing is going to help yourself.

And we can all share in this Joy.

# COMPASSION AND LOVINGKINDNESS MEDITATION

# GOING BACK

Today is the last day of the retreat. Congratulations, you made it!

In this period, we will have a guided meditation, then there will be a short break, and then a talk before the end of the retreat. The guided meditation will be on Compassion and Lovingkindness.

Some people may be visual people. That is, they can use visualization of people and situations to help them reach the Compassion and Lovingkindness within. Other people find that the reflection process is more dominant, helping them to reach the Compassion and Lovingkindness within. Either way, it is important to focus on the Dukkha of the subjects so that we can develop Compassionate Understanding of them. Then Lovingkindness, a wish for their peace of mind, is a natural arising.

In the beginning, many people may find it difficult to get any feeling generated. If this happens to you, please try not to worry. This is a meditation exercise to try to develop the feeling. Just keep trying throughout the meditation to practice as instructed. Perhaps later you will be able to adapt the meditation to people and circumstances which you can relate to easier.

Please settle yourself into the posture and concentrate on your breathing for a short while.

*****

Focus your attention on yourself. Try to remember some of your difficulties, some of the painful conditioning that you may have seen acutely during this retreat. It may have made it difficult for you to keep your balance. And it may still be causing difficulties for you. Perhaps confusion, self-doubt, some aversion that you still feel toward yourself or others.

*****

Try to allow the caring, spacious energy of Compassion to arise toward yourself, followed by the wish of Lovingkindness, the wish to find peace of mind.

*****

May I be able to let go of anger, fear, worry and ignorance. May I also have patience, courage, wisdom and determination to meet and overcome difficulties and problems, challenges in life.

May I find peace of mind.

*****

Now, think of or picture in front of you your parents or another special relative. Try to understand some of the difficulties that they may have had or may be experiencing now. Maybe confusion, lack of mental calm, fear of aging.

*****

Try to allow the caring, spacious energy of Compassion to arise toward your parents or special relative, followed by the wish of Lovingkindness, the wish that they may find peace of mind.

*****

May my parents or special relatives be able to let go of anger, fear, worry and ignorance. May they also have patience, courage, wisdom and determination to meet and overcome difficulties and problems, challenges in life.

May they find peace of mind.

*****

Now direct your attention to the other meditators in the room, perhaps bring their faces to mind. Those meditators who have been struggling like yourself to develop Compassionate Understanding. Try to identify with some of their difficulties. During these days you may have experienced much of the same. Perhaps they still feel impatience, aversion, and cannot let go of some of their unwise reactions.

*****

Try to allow the caring, spacious energy of Compassion to arise for these meditators, followed by the wish of Lovingkindness, the wish for their peace of mind.

*****

May the other meditators be able to let go of anger, fear, worry and ignorance. May they also have patience, courage, wisdom and determination to meet and overcome difficulties and problems, challenges in life.

May they find peace of mind.

*****

Continue to expand your vision/thoughts to all on this island, those who are not yet free of difficulties, still under the power of negative conditioning, still making mistakes.

*****

Try to allow the caring, spacious energy of Compassion to arise for them, followed by the wish of Lovingkindness, the wish for peace for them.

*****

May all of the people who live on this island be able to let go of anger, fear, worry and ignorance. May they also have patience, courage, wisdom and determination to meet and overcome difficulties and problems, challenges in life.

May they find peace of mind.

*****

Continue to expand your vision/thoughts to all in Thailand, young, old, male, female, rich and poor. They are living each day, waking up, going through their daily life, going to sleep; all wanting happiness and to be free of Dukkha. But they are not yet free of difficulties.

*****

Try to allow the caring, spacious energy of Compassion to arise for them, followed by the wish of Lovingkindness, the wish for peace for them.

*****

May all those who live in Thailand be able to let go of anger, fear, worry and ignorance. May they also have patience, courage, wisdom and determination to meet and overcome difficulties and problems, challenges in life.

May they find peace of mind.

*****

Now direct your attention to your home country, to those people who are closer in conditioning to you. Reflect on some of the conditioning which may make it hard for them to experience contentment and which tends to increase their agitation and stress. Those beings who have some difficulties and have ignorance of how to bring peace to themselves.

*****

Try to allow the caring, spacious energy of Compassion to arise for them, followed by the wish of Lovingkindness, the wish for peace for them.

*****

May all those who live in my country be able to let go of anger, fear, worry and ignorance. May they also have patience, courage, wisdom and determination to meet and overcome difficulties and problems, challenges in life.

May they find peace of mind.

*****

Now direct your attention to one or more of the troubled countries of the world. One with famine or where there is fighting, killing, maiming and destruction, either from aggression or defense of their country from aggression, political suppression, religious intolerance or similar reasons. Try to feel with the pain of these people, those involved in or victims of the struggle. Each day they may wake up to pain, fear, loss, grief.

*****

Try to allow the caring, spacious energy of Compassion to arise for them, followed by the wish of Lovingkindness, the wish for peace for them.

*****

May those in the world who are living in these strife filled countries be free of the will to fight or the need to fight. May they see that we are all relatives in birth, aging and death. May they be able to let go of hatred, anger, fear, worry and ignorance. May they also have patience, courage, wisdom and determination to meet and overcome difficulties and problems, extreme challenges in life.

May they find peace of mind.

*****

Continue to expand your vision/thoughts until you are viewing all of the world. You are looking down at the Earth, the fragile Earth. Try to think of or picture some of the vast multitude of living beings in the world before you. People of all races, ages, animals and insects, large and small, on land, in sea, in the air. Most of them are engaged in the struggle to survive; being born, living, some being oppressed or killed by others. But most of them want life and freedom from Dukkha.

*****

Allow the caring spacious energy of Compassion to arise for all of these living beings. Try to break down some of the barriers that we have between ourselves and them. Follow it by the wish of Lovingkindness; that all beings could free themselves from Dukkha and find peace of mind.

*****

May all living beings be able to let go of anger, fear, worry and ignorance. May they also have patience, courage, wisdom and determination to meet and overcome difficulties and problems, challenges in life.

May they find peace of mind.

*****

Keeping the vision of these many living beings before you, visualize yourself in the middle of them all. You are another living being, not separated in some isolated bubble, but connected with life, with its challenges, with its Dukkha, and wanting Peace and Happiness.

*****

Try to continue feeling Compassion for all these living beings, including yourself.

*****

Allow the vision of the other living beings to fade away leaving only the vision of yourself and the world.

*****

Try to continue feeling Compassion for yourself.

*****

Let the vision of yourself slowly fade and feel yourself sitting here in this room.

*****

Allow Compassion to continue to flow for yourself, followed by the wish of Lovingkindness, the wish for total peace of mind.

*****

Having seen that I am not yet free of Dukkha, may I try to let go of the pain of anger, fear, worry and ignorance. With patience, courage, wisdom and determination may I be mindful of my thoughts, speech and actions so that I can manifest and strengthen this Compassion for myself and for all living beings. So that I will come closer to peace and be able to help others come closer to peace.

*****
*****

(end of meditation)

You have done more than just wish yourself Compassion and Lovingkindness. During this time spent here, you have 'actually worked towards fulfilling your wish.

You may not think that you have done or progressed very much, but consider this; a big forest appears to be made up of very big trees, but each tree began as a very small seed. Take this moment to feel some Joy—Joy that you have sprouted some seeds or continued to grow some that you have already sprouted. Feel some Joy that you have progressed somewhat in your development of a forest of Peace and Balance.

You have all been working hard. It has been a real joy for Steve and myself to watch you in your efforts to develop Mindfulness and

Compassionate Understanding.

By looking inward, we may start to understand our own minds a little better and this may enable us to understand others more easily. This can help us to slowly break down some of those barriers and feelings of separateness that we create.

So here, maybe you have come to a feeling of communion with each other. We have been sharing these days with each other, supporting each other with this "group" energy.

Sometimes in the retreat, you may have experienced great difficulty, other times you may have experienced ease. We hope that you have gained a little in understanding your mind and that you can see a way to bring more Peace and Understanding into your life, and into the life of others.

Many of you have possibly wished for this time to come, especially when you were experiencing difficulties. Others may be somewhat fearful of losing the Peace or Concentration they may have obtained. But we have been trying to stress that Meditation and Mental Development is all of your life, and giving you some methods to work with.

You have experimented with these methods here, and now you will have the opportunity to experiment with them out there. You will not have retreat conditions to support you but you can try to fall back on Mindfulness and Compassionate Understanding to aid you.

In order to help you in the transition that you may experience when you return to your life "out there," I would like to talk a little about some of the difficulties that many meditators experience "going back" and also some possible solutions.

One thing that you may notice is the "overload of the senses." Here we have restricted the diversity of your contacts, the noise, conversation, the speed of life. When you come out of retreat and return to normal life, your awareness may still be greatly heightened and sensitive. There has been an opening occurring. Many varied contacts may come charging in and it may give you a sense of being disorientated.

This is normal. Try to flow with the changes with non-resistance. Try to think of the mind as that gently flowing stream; it is now

going over rougher territory, more obstacles.

However, also try to bring up some wise consideration. See if a lot of your outward activity really needs to be done, or if it is an avoidance of something, possibly an avoidance of bringing forth the effort to continue your practice. Try to learn when silence and stepping back from activity are needed in order to recharge the energies within and find more balance in your living.

We each have a choice between the "slow" and the "fast lane" in life. Try to balance the outward energy with inward seeking.

Another point is to try to be prepared for your own inner changes. You may not feel comfortable with your previous aims, opinions and self-images. Be willing to let them go.

With old friends, you may have a conflict arising. They may expect the "old" you. Perhaps you used to be talkative, the "life of the party." It is possible now that you may feel more inclined towards silence. You may not wish to talk about certain topics.

Allow yourself to embrace these changes, and try not to be too concerned with what other people may think of you or be worried about their expectations of you. It is ok to be considered a quiet person.

You can reflect within on what is most valuable in your life. What others think of you cannot bring you inner Peace, but what you think of yourself, how you react, and how you open with Compassion and Lovingkindness can bring you inner Peace.

At the other extreme, try not to be so absorbed in yourself and your own activities that you do not open to others with Compassion and Lovingkindness. They may need an ear to hear their fear.

Also try to recognize the grief that often arises from change. The loss of a certain image or identity can cause a feeling of loss of security. Even losing that "unworthy," negative image which may have caused you so much pain, can give you a feeling of lack of security. Everything may not seem so neat and cozy as you may have once felt things were.

As you grow in understanding, there now is a *challenge* in life. With this growth comes extra responsibility, the responsibility for our own peace and happiness lying *within* yourself.

Maybe this is different to the ease that you once felt in putting the responsibility onto others, the blame onto life and just drifting through life.

Sometimes there may be a battle between the new Understanding and the deeply conditioned old ways of viewing things. This is normal. Try to help the growth and strength of the new Understanding with Wise Reflection.

Reflecting on the Truth is very beneficial at these times. Reflection on the Truth, the Dhamma, gradually may enable the emotions to accept what we know deep inside to be true.

We can think about anything. Thinking leads to action. It would be helpful to think in beneficial ways rather than unbeneficial ways.

The path to inner Peace and Wisdom sometimes is not very comfortable because it is a purification process.

Sometimes if you find yourself really off-balance, doubtful, stressed, it may be helpful to write it down. You may see more clearly by writing what thoughts are unbeneficial, erroneous and are creating the difficulty. Confide in yourself if you do not have a spiritual friend. Investigate with the understanding and the wise consideration that you do possess. If you do know of a good friend, then perhaps go talk with them, or you can try to meet and be with others who are interested in Mental Development.

Another consideration is to beware of Idealism, both Idealism toward yourself and Idealism directed toward others and the world in general.

Concerning Idealism towards yourself; while in retreat you may have been able to let go of many hindrances, developed heightened Awareness and Understanding. This was aided by guidance, retreat conditions, and group support.

When these extra supports are not there, when you are in a busy life, and when you see imperfect reactions to life arising, then a lot of doubt may arise, especially about your ability to practice.

Try to reflect on conditioning and conditions at this time. Encourage yourself to try again. Try to have Compassion and Patience with yourself. Start again. Learn to forgive yourself.

You may have to adjust your expectations. Try not to aim too high and create so many ideals so that you find it impossible to live up to them—always looking at the top of the mountain and never considering where you really are.

Try to work with who and what you are *now*. Try to live more in the present moment, developing Understanding in the present moment, and sowing seeds for the arising of Insight and Balance. The present moment is all that we have.

Treat the practice like nurturing a small plant. Apply water—Compassionate Intention. Put on fertilizer—Wise Reflection. See that insects do not invade—Mindfulness/Awareness. Have a tender, caring attitude. Try to take joy in the gradual growth of the plant. The power of joy gives one energy to continue.

Try to become more content with a broader, more normal paced Mindfulness and a watching of mind states as they arise and pass away. We have to try to adapt the practice to life's situations. A story that may help to illustrate what I mean about adapting the practice to life's situations concerns a meditator friend:

This friend was living in a meditation center in the West and found that money was running low. There was then a need to find a job. My friend had been working quite hard to develop Mindfulness in the center, and wished to continue the effort in the new job. The job was opening and closing the gates of a vehicular ferry at a river crossing.

It was a simple enough job, a repetitive task which could help in the Mindfulness development. So my friend tried to be careful, aware of all the movements from the beginning to the end, and sometimes became quite absorbed.

It was a bit of a shock a few days later, when the boss called my friend in and said, "You're fired!" The reason... "Just too slow!!" Rather than doing things at a normal speed, my friend had slowed down excessively to aid the Mindfulness.

You can save yourself a lot of grief if you try to see the over-view—your responsibilities not only to yourself but also to others and to the practical necessities of life. Be willing to change the focus of your practice and try to get used to the different levels of Awareness. It is all Mindfulness. Try not to judge one better than the other.

Seeing what is *appropriate* links Mindfulness to Wisdom-in-Action.

In Vipassana practice, we try to be mindful of all mental states coming and going; the concentrated, the unconcentrated, broad awareness, focused awareness, slow movements, fast movements. We try to flow with each, not resist the moment, or become attached to the focused. If we become attached grief may arise when it passes, and lack of contentment with anything else.

Concerning Idealism towards the world and others; here at Wat Kow Tahm, we are trying to develop beneficial mental qualities, trying to work with our reactions. All of us having some interest in Mental Development. This makes it easier for us to get along with each other.

But "out there"…well…there are bound to be many people who are not in the slightest bit interested. People who act in many ways that are far from beneficial to themselves or to others. The world is also far from "perfect."

Idealism tends to wish to make others and the world conform to what we think they should be. But there have been many people in this world who have tried to force their ideals upon others. Idealism quickly can transform into resistance, aversion, hatred and even violence.

The world and people are as they are. This is not to say that we do not try to improve ourselves or the conditions of the world. It means that we try to learn what we can change and what we cannot change.

Try to see whether you simply are lost in the "Reactionary Mind," and are indulging in this conditioning. Investigate to see whether you are attached to your selfish viewpoints and opinions, or whether you really *are* motivated by Compassion in your wish to change things.

Sometimes the "Reactionary Mind" is just a cover-up for a mind that likes to indulge in negativities; a mind that enjoys seeing only the negative sides of people, places, institutions, causes, and often blinds itself to the positive qualities that lie within everyone and everything. It may be seeing only a partial view, not the whole.

Try to see the positive sides as well. Investigate the motivations behind people, trying to see through their eyes, and the motivations and purposes of certain places, institutions and causes. Are these motivations based in Compassion or other positive intentions?

Try to see whether your reaction may be misplaced. Try to recognize the idealism that turns to aversion and hatred, creating so much resistance, tension and stress within you.

If you see that you are just indulging in the "Reactionary Mind," try to redirect that strong energy inward, to the *inner* revolution—to the liberation of the mind from *greed, hatred and ignorance.*

The harm you see outside begins within the mind. If you wish to reduce the suffering in the world, begin by reducing your own. If you wish to see more Compassion and Love in the world, begin by increasing them within yourself. Then the energy you bring to your causes will be based more in Compassion than in aversion.

Try to flow more with people and the world, having Compassion for their inadequacies. This may also soften your attitude toward yourself, your expectations of yourself, and, help to ease the meditative development.

Non-resistance to the moment, acceptance of the Laws of Nature, of Life as it is, is so important to our Peace of Mind. It cannot be overstated.

There's a little story that a meditator shared with us in one of our retreats. This retreat was quite a difficult one. I had been quite sick just prior to the retreat and did not have a lot of energy. There was a bit of concern over whether I would be able to teach the retreat. But there was a long waiting list and people arriving wanting to do the retreat who were not even on the waiting list. We did not want to disappoint anyone so we decided to go ahead.

On the second day, I collapsed and became very ill again. Steve had to look after me a lot of the time. The interviews had to be cancelled... Can you imagine, "No Interviews"!! Steve gave questions/answers in the hall to make up for it. Luckily we had an experienced meditator there who took over leading sittings and played tapes of our talks when Steve was unable to come to the hall. And another person led the exercises.

If this was not enough, there was a fever circling the island and, one by one, half of the retreatants became sick. For many, it was a retreat in learning to deal with unpleasant sensations and unfulfilled expectations.

When Steve was working with some of the meditators, encouraging and trying to guide them in their reactions, he was continually impressed by one meditator who, despite being quite ill, always seemed to be in good spirits, coping very well with the experience.

After a while, he commented on it and the meditator related a story which is of great value to remember when encountering unpleasant experiences. The story goes like this:

Once there was a farmer who had a stallion workhorse. It was strong and worked hard, helping the farmer with the plowing and transporting of goods, etc. One day, the farmer found that the stallion had disappeared. Upon hearing this, the farmer's neighbors said, "Oh, what bad luck, what bad luck!"

The farmer simply shrugged his shoulders and replied, "Good luck, bad luck, who knows?"

Two weeks later, the horse still had not returned. The neighbors continued to say, "Oh, what bad luck, what bad luck!"

The farmer again shrugged his shoulders and said, "Good luck, bad luck, who knows?"

The next day, the stallion returned, bringing with him seven wild mares. The farmer's neighbors exclaimed, "Oh, what good luck, what good luck!"

The farmer simply said, "Good luck, bad luck, who knows?"

Then the farmer's son was trying to train the new wild horses, and he fell off one, breaking both of his legs. The neighbors exclaimed, "Oh, what bad luck, oh what bad luck!"

The farmer simply said, "Good luck, bad luck, who knows?" Shortly after, the army general of the province came around drafting all able-bodied men to go fight an unpopular war in a distant province. The farmer's son was not drafted. Good luck, bad luck, who knows?

The simple phrase, "Good luck, bad luck, who knows?" can be quite powerful in blowing away negative reactions and helping us to approach each experience, especially seemingly unpleasant ones, with a more non-resisting attitude.

Also, looking back on our lives, we often can see that some experiences that were unpleasant contained within them valuable learning opportunities, or were the beginning of a new direction in our life, leading toward deeper Understanding.

No experience need be thrown away. We can try to learn and grow from them all. Good luck, bad luck, who knows?

What some people consider to be good luck—such as being wealthy, comfortable, having continuous pleasant times—other people may consider to be bad luck, if it prevents those people from understanding life and finding the path to inner peace.

Perhaps you can remember this little story when you return to your normal life, and find yourself confronted with imperfect conditions, and possibly reacting with grief or aversion to the arising of experiences. It may help you to flow through the experience a little easier. It could allow you to see the overview, the broad picture. "Good luck, bad luck, who knows?"

Concerning keeping your practice going, through Compassion to yourself, make the effort to do some formal meditation morning and evening. This will help you to begin and end your day in a more peaceful and balanced way.

In the beginning this may seem difficult. The mind may find one hundred or more excuses why you cannot do it. Try to remember the importance of Mental Development and Peace of Mind compared to the many frivolous activities that we normally consider so important. You may want to use the first two reflections at this time; reflect on how precious your opportunity is, How Fortunate You Are, and Death and Impermanence. You just do not know when this opportunity will end!

Especially helpful is to remember not to seek instant results, instant calm from each meditation period. Just *trying* can bring good results.

Sometimes we feel like nothing is happening, we are not getting anywhere. But we are often missing the subtle inner growth that is occurring. The gradual awakening. One day you may be open enough to see the changes and the results of the practice.

It is helpful to reflect back a little on how you used to view life, yourself, your problems. Sometimes, perhaps, your problems seemed insurmountable, impossible; there may have seemed no way out.

But at least now you may know how to investigate, perhaps with a little more detachment, and you may know where to look for the causes and then apply remedies. Any growth in Understanding is so valuable.

In your daily practice, try not to let a "bad" sit create negative feelings toward meditation and freeze the experience into a static, unchanging "I can't." Today is a new day; this moment is a new moment. Maybe you will be able to be a little more present, more non-resisting and more relaxed.

I remember, often after a busy hectic day, approaching the meditation mat thinking, "I'm just too exhausted tonight. I'll just fall asleep. Why don't I just go to bed." or "My mind is just so wound-up, I won't be able to concentrate, maybe I'll just have a nice cup of hot herbal tea instead."

But I would try to sit anyway. Sometimes the tiredness evaporated as soon as I sat down. I often saw that being tired sometimes meant that there would be less resistance in the mind and that the meditation would go well. Or other times I found that the thoughts started to wind-down the longer that I sat.

Sometimes there was just the familiar feeling of "just sitting"; taking time-out from the quick pace of life, "just sitting." I was trying to be there, just trying. Or, I was simply learning a lot from seeing resistance slowly dissolve, even if it took the whole sit to do so.

Try to make the morning and evening meditation sessions something that you would not consider missing, like cleaning your teeth or taking a bath, so that taking care of the mind becomes as important as you consider taking care of the body.

Reflect a little... What causes more harm in the world—body odor or the untrained mind?

If you find that your practice is deteriorating, slacking-off, and that you find yourself missing your daily sessions, try to just start again. Forgive yourself and drop the past. Try not to bring up self-judgment or hatred. Just start again.

Try also to realize that the practice is not just the formal sitting, standing, walking sessions. Try to use Mindfulness throughout the day. You could try to encourage the growth of Mindfulness by "special Mindfulness activities"—washing the dishes, putting on and taking off your shoes, opening doors, sweeping, eating, etc.—as we have tried to encourage you to do here. Make a conscious effort to do these simple things with as much awareness as you can, to be with the process of doing rather than just to obtain the results.

Try not to become too attached to narrow, one-method type practices. Learn to adapt. See what results arise from certain ways of doing things, both in formal meditation practice and in your daily life.

Try to see what is appropriate for that moment. Measure what you do from the viewpoint of whether it nurtures the "awakening mind" and points in the direction of the alleviation of Dukkha.

When you find yourself in a state of confusion, try to investigate the cause. What mental state is clouding the mind? What hindrance? Investigate. Try to base it on the Compassionate Intention, to alleviate your difficulties. Try not to go in with a lot of judgment, idealism, doubt or the intention of proving how terrible you are, which only builds self-aversion. Try to remember the analogy of washing the shirt. Getting angry at the shirt will not help to clean it.

Remember, too, that no matter where you are in the world, there will always be the body—sitting, standing, lying down, walking, the body rising, the body lowering, the feet touching the ground. Ground yourself in the body and the moment to cut through the "spinning" in the mind.

Concerning the methods that we have given you to practice during this retreat—briefly repeating them may help you to remember.

With developing the mind in a busy, hectic life, perhaps isolated from others who are doing the same, it is important to try to use any or all of the techniques that we know to help us. Try not to get stuck into a common attitude of many new meditators that the ability to concentrate on the breath and do sitting meditation is all there is to the practice.

Try to concentrate on what you *can* do, and not get too carried away with what you cannot do.

So how do we practice? We can try to watch the breath, the body and the mind. We can try to watch impermanence in experience, in ourselves, in life. Often our practice will be a broader-based Mindfulness than in retreat, but it still is so beneficial.

Watching the rise and fall of experiences, watching impermanence, helps us to develop deeper Understanding. This Understanding allows us to develop more acceptance and Equanimity, with less clinging and resistance.

Try to continue to watch your reactions. It is such a key place for the arising of either contentment or pain. Try to watch your reactions to places, people, stimuli. See how you react, see how and why difficulties and stress arise. Learn how to be honest with yourself. Try to be able to recognize when your reactions are unbeneficial.

Look inward rather than outward. Take responsibility for your Peace or lack of Peace, for your actions, your speech, your thoughts. Try to learn how to let go of the stress arising from unbeneficial things by letting go of unwise reactions, with Compassion for your Dukkha.

Sometimes it is a painful process to admit to ourselves that we may be wrong, and let go of habitual responses. But if we investigate and understand the results of these unwise responses, then this Understanding may aid us in emotionally accepting the Truth.

We really do not have to protect an image of ourselves that leads to pain. Actually, to let go of our self-images shows great strength, not weakness.

The balancing calm of Compassion/Lovingkindness meditation and a Compassionate way of approaching life can aid us in the letting-go process as well. Developing Compassion and Lovingkindness can help us to develop deeper acceptance of ourselves, others and all situations that arise for us.

There also is Sympathetic Joy meditation. This can help reduce jealousy and competition. It can give you extra Energy, Joy and Contentment in the practice, helping to renew your motivation and to banish doubt.

Concerning Reflection; thought plays a major role in Mental Development. Reflections such as the Preciousness of our Opportunity and How Fortunate We Are; Death and Impermanence; the Law of Cause and Effect; Dukkha, unsatisfactoriness; Caring and

Not Caring, the Relationship between Compassion and Equanimity—these are very powerful and can help to deflate the greatest fears and worries.

We cannot just "blank" the mind in a busy life. We have to think and perform various functions. Thinking leads to action; intention precedes all action. We can allow ourselves to get "side-tracked" into thought patterns that result in inner turmoil and pain, or we can use thought wisely to help de-condition the mind away from unwise patterns and strengthen the factor of Right View in the mind.

Out of retreat, Wise Reflection, directed thought, becomes increasingly more important. Often you are separated from others who practice, from perfect conditions and from people who are able to guide you. Thought can become a balancing spiritual friend. You have to counsel yourself, encourage yourself, when you walk the path alone. Sometimes it seems so difficult with so many forces going in the opposite direction.

The more we reflect on Truth, the Dhamma, the path and the teachings, the more this wise reflection balances our old conditioning, our old views that may be based in ignorance.

The more that we direct thought in Reflection, the deeper it goes into the mind. And it can enable us to measure our life, our expectations and our reactions with the "yardstick" of Truth, the world as it really is.

Reflection may allow us to find the strength to say no, even if there is a bit of a struggle with our past conditioning, and with what we may feel like doing. This is because our inner Wisdom may see that this action could lead to more stress, Dukkha, for ourselves and for others.

Compassion linked with Wisdom is not always gentle, and is certainly not "wishy-washy." It is sometimes like a firm, strong, seemingly stern, kind parent. Yet just like the kind parent, it also is forgiving when we make mistakes, because Compassionate Understanding realizes the extent of Dukkha and the forces of the world.

What is past is past. We can admit we made a mistake, taking responsibility for our actions, speech and thoughts, helping to develop Compassionate Understanding. This Compassionate Understanding helps us to realize what actions are skillful, leading to peace, and what actions are unskillful, leading to more pain. In this way we develop the understanding of how to prevent Dukkha from arising in the future. We can try to forgive ourselves.

We can start again now. Hatred rarely solves anything, especially self-hatred.

Another bit of encouragement. Wherever you go, try to find some other meditators. The conditioning of the world is very strong. There are so few people interested in Mental Development.

Try, if you can, to stay as long as possible in the East. There is so much more encouragement for you on this path. The respect for meditation and the encouragement towards the path of Mental Development are so woven into the religions and people of the East.

It is easier for you to live a simple, basic existence, leaving aside, for now, thoughts of career, acquisition of material things. Living from a backpack, it is really hard to acquire unnecessary possessions.

This will help nurture and support the initial stages of opening on this path. You will not feel that you have to resist the overwhelming currents of materialism, conditioning and peer-group pressure. If you are returning to the West, or when you do so, try as best you can to nurture the new conditioning of simplicity, non-acquisition and walking the path of Mental Development.

You may find a bit of "culture shock" taking place if you have stayed very long in the East and especially in meditation centers. In the beginning you may clearly see the powerful drives towards acquisition, materialism, consumerism mixed, also, with fear of loss.

The current can become like a very strong river going downstream and you may feel like you are trying to swim upstream. Sometimes you may feel that you are not getting anywhere and instead that you are being swept back by the forces of the current.

In some people feelings of frustration may arise. You may feel a pushing away. Sometimes you may feel a defensive reaction. It is like putting up a shield to protect yourself, protecting the fragile bud of the Dhamma, the flower of Compassionate Understanding within.

In many, the reactionary mind arises. It is often connected to aversion yet it can also be connected to the penetrating sight of Wisdom and Compassion. Sometimes it is a very uncomfortable feeling.

Aversion has its own characteristics of stress and suffering as we have seen by investigating its energy within ourselves. It is also a powerful, strong energy. This energy we can try to bend and use, rather than trying to suppress it, which may cause extra stress within. We can use this energy to give us incentive and strength—the strength to be different and to reject the destructive forces of greed.

Yet we can also link this powerful energy to Compassion and Wisdom until we can transform it completely. Compassion and Wisdom rightly reject a path that does not acknowledge the interrelationship of all living beings on the planet. Compassionate Understanding rejects a path that does not acknowledge the destructive effects that greed has on the whole planet.

Compassion and Wisdom acknowledge that our actions have far-reaching effects on the cycle of life and on the other people of the world. Compassionate Understanding rejects exploitation, waste and indulgence, as it sees that these actions increase difficulties and suffering, causing the destruction of the environment and other living beings, and having a destructive effect on our minds.

Aversion transformed into Compassionate Understanding can give us the resolve and strength to try the best we can to stay open. Staying open and aware of the interrelationship of life means concentrating on seeing how important our actions are.

We can express Compassion by consuming less, trying to live a simple life, trying as best we can not to flow into the stream of exploitation and greed. This may not mean that we withdraw from all aspects of life, our livelihood, family, friends, etc., but it means we try to be strong enough, aware enough, to live as simply as we can.

Conserve rather than consume; save rather than spend. Cherish your free time by using it for meditation and inward seeking, rather than trying to fill it up with the media and endless activity that can dull the mind and close the mind off.

Meditation can recharge us so that we will have the strength and balance within in order to go out again and be confronted with the destructive characteristics of materialism. Meditation nurtures our awakening.

By saving, we may be able to retreat from responsibilities for a longer time; coming back to Southeast Asia or going to a meditation center in the West. Places where it may be possible to go inward within a protective supportive environment.

Try as best you can to separate people from their states of mind. That is, do not embrace the stress of greed, aversion, fear and worry, but see that many people within the culture are suffering from these...conditioned by the incessant forces of advertising and materialism, and unable to reject the loud volume of voices that say happiness lies on the path of wealth, wanting and gaining.

Try to remember that the voice of Dhamma is not very loud and that perhaps others may never have heard about viewing life in a different way. Try to view others and yourself with the open, sympathetic eyes of Compassion. Yet try to balance it with the strength of Wisdom, realizing that things are as they are—Dukkha is Dukkha. And you do not want to increase Dukkha in yourself or others.

This may not mean that you become active in a social change movement, although some do this, it may mean that you become more active within yourself, working on seeing the nature of conditioning: the greed, aversion, fear, worry within. Try not to exploit, try to protect the openness, the understanding of the interrelationship of life by living as best you can, with Awareness, Simplicity and Wise Intention.

Try to find friends who also wish to help in this way, and support each other. Support meditation centers, which create space and encouragement for meditation and inward seeking. This is doing more than simply shouting with aversion and reaction at the culture, and at others. Transform yourself, rather than being an "armchair reactionary" who may only be increasing the forces of aversion and confrontation in the world.

Take responsibility for yourself, reflect on the Earth and all living beings, carry them in your Heart. Try to open to the suffering and unsatisfactoriness, so the forces of Compassion can grow even more. This adds a *powerful* incentive to practice. Yet remember to protect this opening with the strength of Wisdom and Equanimity.

This can often mean drawing back, retreating, when you cannot allow the opening to become overwhelming. You can try not to expect the ideal within yourself. When you find you are being swept away with the current again, instead of bringing up self-hatred, you can try to have joy and relief that your Awareness has penetrated.

You then can try to start again, even if it means sitting with tension, a feeling of lack and resistance all throughout the body. You can try to open to the unsatisfactoriness—see the results, the powers of conditioning in this very body, in this very mind. And you can allow Compassion to arise for the Dukkha. Let it be. And in the letting be, there may be a letting go.

Begin again, healed a little by the willingness to open to the reality of the moment. Try to be with what is there, penetrating with Insight into the nature of the mind and body. See the truth of the Noble Truths within: the existence, the cause and perhaps the fading away of Dukkha.

In another way there may also be a tendency in some people to get swept away and lost in the pleasantness of comforts very quickly, the dulling of the mind. They may want to be entertained whenever a bit of boredom arises. They may turn off the mind to the possibility of making the effort to investigate, let go and reach for their inner potential. They turn off their inner voice.

They may feel that it is just too difficult to resist the enticement of sensual objects. The mind may go to sleep. The convenience may be too alluring, the objects too dazzling, the status too enticing. With pleasantness in abundance, it is easy for the budding flower of Compassionate Understanding to shrivel and die.

They may think that it is easier not to take responsibility for their actions, not to spare a thought for the planet and other living beings. It takes Effort and Awareness to live in an open, Compassionate way, to investigate boredom and desire rather than indulging them by dulling the mind and by rejecting the silence and inward seeking.

However, again, you do need to forgive yourself if you find you have allowed yourself to be swept away. You can reflect on the powerful forces of the world and habitual action, and yet realize that you do have the power within to change...now.

Reach for the Inner Potential.

Perhaps draw away from the forces for awhile. Try to find good friends to encourage you. Spend a weekend or more at a meditation center. Perhaps visit the East. This is so you may see the difference between living in a vital, open way—the Joy of exploring and learning—compared with the emptiness of living as if one were asleep.

There are meditation centers in most Western countries. Try to find them. Help support them.

Practicing meditation in normal life can be quite difficult. Sometimes it seems impossible. At those times, it is helpful to reflect on your meditation friends elsewhere in the world.

Let the faces, places come to your mind. Link up in thought with your meditation friends everywhere in the world. Reflect that at that moment they may be sitting down in meditation. You can join them.

Sit down. Feel good wishes of Compassion, Lovingkindness and Joy with their efforts in order to let go of the feelings of isolation and separateness.

As we all need frequent inspiration and recharging, it is also helpful to do at least one retreat each year to recharge your energies, and more if you are able.

It is sincerely hoped that all of you will continue to develop the qualities of Compassion, Lovingkindness, Sympathetic Joy, Equanimity, Mindfulness and Wisdom. By developing these qualities you may be able to come closer to understanding your mind, solve your Dukkha and find a Balance and Peace within. And, perhaps you may also be able to help others find a Balance and Peace within

...with Compassionate Understanding.